# CURRENT THINKING AND RESEARCH IN BRIEF THERAPY

An annual publication established by
The Milton H. Erickson Foundation

VOLUME 1

# CURRENT THINKING AND RESEARCH IN BRIEF THERAPY

*Solutions, Strategies, Narratives*

*Edited by*

William J. Matthews, Ph.D.

*and*

John H. Edgette, Psy.D.

Routledge
Taylor & Francis Group
LONDON AND NEW YORK

First published 1997 by Brunner/Mazel, Inc.

Published 2018 by Routledge
2 Park Square, Milton Park, Abingdon, Oxon OX14 4RN
52 Vanderbilt Avenue, New York, NY 10017

First issued in paperback 2018

*Routledge is an imprint of the Taylor & Francis Group, an informa business*



ISSN 1092-2067
ISBN 13: 978-1-138-88376-5 (pbk)
ISBN 13: 978-0-87630-819-6 (hbk)

For my little guy, Jake,
who seems to have Erickson-like perseverance.

J.H.E.

To my wife, Megan,
my son, William III, and my daughter, Devon,
who let me stay at the computer as long as was needed, and
to my music teacher, Bob Gullotti, who teaches the
importance of creativity and precision
in whatever you play.

W.J.M.

# *Contents*

# *About the Milton H. Erickson Foundation*

Dedicated to the promotion of the contributions of Milton H. Erickson, MD. to the health sciences and to articulating the ongoing impact of those contributions on the field, the Foundation sponsors a number of educational and professional activities. Whether hosting the internationally renowned Evolution of Psychotherapy Conferences, the popular Brief Therapy Conferences, or the historic International Congresses on Ericksonian Approaches to Hypnosis and Psychotherapy, the Foundation provides forums in which divergent voices join to discuss, to contrast, to further the field.

In addition to the conferences, The Erickson Foundation organizes seminars, training programs, and workshops throughout the world. The Foundation's library boasts a rich variety of media, including audiotapes, videotapes, and a wide range of publications. These materials, some of which are available directly through the Foundation, offer unique access to the innovation and intellectual breadth of the field of psychotherapy.

For the contemporary professional interested in honing his or her craft, the Foundation stands as a multilevel resource in technique, theory, and research. More than 60 Milton H. Erickson Institutes in the United States and abroad now offer clinical services and training, and the Foundation newsletter expands the information base even further.

As time goes on, the role of the Foundation evolves. The organization embraces an ever-greater international community in its efforts to continue to foster lively, respectful, and stimulating exchanges of ideas. At the threshold between Erickson's work and that which is Erickson-inspired, there are many important voices, people who, themselves, have made great contributions to the field. It is the Foundation's goal to inspire many more.

The Annual "title" is a project of the Milton H. Erickson Foundation. We are gratified by the efforts of its editors, William J. Matthews, Ph.D. and John Edgette, Psy.D., who have assembled a renowned group of authors for the first issue of this timely and invaluable resource.

The Board of Directors
The Milton H. Erickson Foundation, Inc.

# *The Editors*

**William J. Matthews, Ph.D.,** is a professor and director of the School Psychology Program in the School of Education at the University of Massachusetts at Amherst. He has published numerous research studies and articles on the theoretical and clinical aspects of hypnosis and brief therapy. He was a contributor to the recent *Handbook of Clinical Hypnosis* and *Handbook of Family Therapy, Volume II.* Dr. Matthews has been an invited faculty to the International Congress on Ericksonian Approaches to Hypnotherapy as well as serving as an advisory editor for the Ericksonian Monograph series. He has lectured both nationally and internationally on hypnosis and brief therapy.

**John H. Edgette, Psy.D.,** is codirector of the Milton H. Erickson Institute of Philadelphia and is a clinical psychologist with faculty appointments at the last five International Congresses on Erickson Approaches to Hypnosis and Psychotherapy. He is the coauthor of *The Handbook of Hypnotic Phenomena in Psychotherapy* and has numerous other publications including brief therapy with the agoraphobic and hypnosis with dangerously psychotic inpatients. Dr. Edgette is Vice President of Clinical Operations for Alpha Divorce Mediation Centers and an adjunct faculty member at the graduate school programs of Widener University and Immaculata College. He also maintains a full-time private practice.

# *The Contributors*

**Peter B. Bloom, M.D.** is Clinical Professor of Psychiatry, University of Pennsylvania School of Medicine; Senior Attending Psychiatrist, Institute of Pennsylvania, Philadelphia; Fellow, American Psychiatric Association; and Diplomate, the American Board of Psychiatry and Neurology and the American Board of Medical Hypnosis. Dr. Bloom is President of the International Society of Hypnosis, Vice President of the American Board of Medical Hypnosis, foreign member of the Swedish Hypnosis Society, and honorary member of the Australian, Hungarian, Italian, and Swedish Hypnosis Societies. He is Fellow and Approved Consultant of the American Society of Clinical Hypnosis; Fellow, Society of Clinical and Experimental Hypnosis, through which he was honored with The Shirley R. Scheck Award and The Bernard B. Raginsky Award (the Society's highest award). Dr. Bloom has published widely in the field of clinical hypnosis and medicine. He is also in private practice in Philadelphia and in Bryn Mawr, PA.

**Roger J. Booth, M.Sc., Ph.D.** is Senior Lecturer in Immunology, Department of Molecular Medicine and on the faculty of Medicine and Health Science. Both positions are held at the University of Auckland, Private Bag 92019, Auckland, New Zealand.

**Gary R. Elkins, Ph.D.** is an Associate Professor of Psychiatry and Behavioral Sciences, Texas A&M University, Health Sciences Center, and Senior Staff Psychologist at the Scott & White Clinic in Temple, Texas. He is President of The American Society of Clinical Hypnosis and has been awarded Diplomate status by the American Board of Psychological Hypnosis (ABPH) and the American Board of Professional Psychology (ABPP). Dr. Elkins is also an ASCH Approved Consultant in Clinical Hypnosis and is Co-Chair of the workshop program for the 14th International Congress of Hypnosis. He is coauthor of *Standards of Training in Clinical Hypnosis.*

**Jeffrey B. Feldman, Ph.D.** is Program Director of the Mid-Atlantic Center for Pain Medicine at Presbyterian-Orthopaedic Hospital in Charlotte. He was a founding member of the New York Milton H. Erickson Society (NYSEPH) where he served as Administrative Vice President from 1980 to 1989 and also as a faculty member in the hypnotherapy training program. Dr. Feldman has had an independent psychotherapy and consulting practice in New York City, has worked as Program Coordinator for the Chronic Pain Rehabilitation Program at the Charlotte Institute of Rehabilitation, and as Consulting Psychologist at Carolinas Medical Center.

**Stephen Gilligan, Ph.D.** is a licensed psychologist practicing in Encinitas, CA. Since 1975, he has been a highly regarded teacher and trainer in the field of Ericksonian psychotherapy. In addition to publishing many articles and chapters on hypnosis and psychotherapy, he has authored *Therapeutic Trances: The Cooperation Principle in Ericksonian Hypnotherapy* and coedited *Brief Therapy: Myths, Methods, and Metaphors*, and *Therapeutic Conversations.* His current book, *The Courage to Love: Principles and Practices of Self-Relations Psychotherapy* will be published shortly.

**Irving Kirsch, Ph.D.** is a Professor of Psychology at the University of Connecticut. He is former President of the American Psychological Association's Division of Psychological Hypnosis and the current North American Editor of *Contemporary Hypnosis,* Associate Editor of *Hypnosis International Monographs* and the *International Journal of Clinical and Experimental Hypnosis,* and an Advisory Editor of the *American Journal of Clinical Hypnosis.* Dr. Kirsch has written or edited six books and more than 100 journal articles and book chapters on placebo effects, hypnosis, psychotherapy, the history of psychology, and the philosophy of science.

**Daniel P. Kohen, M.D.** is the Director of the Behavioral Pediatrics Program, Division of General Pediatrics and Adolescent Health, Department of Pediatrics at the University of Minnesota Medical School. He is also Associate Professor of Pediatrics and Family Practice and Community Health at the University of Minnesota. In 1996, Dr. Kohen was reelected to a second two-year term as President of the American Board of Medical Hypnosis. In 1993, he was honored by the *American Journal of Clinical Hypnosis* with the Milton H. Erickson Award for Scientific Excellence in Writing in Hypnosis and in 1992 received a Special Award of Merit from the American Society of Clinical Hypnosis for outstanding teaching at ASCH meetings. Dr. Kohen has recently coauthored the 3rd edition of *Hypnosis and Hypnotherapy* with Karen Olness, M.D.

**Tannis M. Laidlaw, Ph.D., DipClinHyp, M.Sc., DipTchg, DipOT** is Research Manager for the Forensic Psychiatry Unit at the University of Auckland in New Zealand. She has had 12 years of psychiatric clinical experience in pediatric and mental health settings, has run a hospital department, and has taught at three educational levels. Dr. Laidlaw's research interests are in hypnosis, psychoneuroimmunology, mental health, forensics, and stress research, and she has published extensively in these areas.

**Stephen R. Lankton, M.S.W., DAHB** and **Carol H. Lankton, M.A.** currently teach and train internationally, covering therapy topics for clinical professionals and Knowledge Engineering and Interface Management Sciences for corporate clients. They have authored *Tales of Enchantment, The Answer Within: A Clinical Framework of Ericksonian Hypnotherapy, Enchantment and Intervention: Goal-Directed Metaphor and Practical Magic*, as well as editing a dozen other books and numerous chapters on therapy and corporate consulting topics. Stephen Lankton received the 1994 Milton H. Erickson Foundation's Lifetime Achievement Award for Outstanding Contributions to the Field of Psychotherapy. They are both known for creativity, humor, behavioral science acumen, and theoretical depth. Their broad background in therapy is well-grounded in various disciplines and therapy approaches. However, they are best known for their growth and creative goal-oriented models of brief therapy, hypnotherapy, and family therapy.

**Robert G. Large, M.B., Ch.B., DPM, Ph.D.** is Associate Professor of Psychiatry, Department of Psychiatry and Behavioral Science at the University of Auckland, New Zealand. He is also Consultant Psychiatrist to the Auckland Regional Pain Service, Auckland Hospital. Dr. Large is Past President of the New Zealand Society of Hypnosis.

**Michael J. Mahoney, Ph.D.** is the author of 15 books and numerous scientific articles and has served on the editorial boards of 12 scientific journals. He has helped to pioneer the "cognitive revolution" in psychology and is a continuing contributor to the growing interface between the cognitive and the clinical sciences. Honored as a fellow by both the American Psychological Association and the American Association for the Advancement of Science, he was chosen to be a Master Lecturer on Psychotherapy Process in 1981 and a G. Stanley Hall Lecturer in 1988. Dr. Mahoney has been honored with the 1984 Fulbright Award, the Faculty Scholar Medal from the Pennsylvania State University, and a 1985 Citation Classic from Science Citation Index in recognition of his book *Cognition and Behavior Modification.* Since 1978 he has worked with the U.S. Olympic Committee in the area of sport psychology.

**Kevin M. McConkey, Ph.D.** is Professor and Head, School of Psychology, University of New South Wales, Sydney, Australia. He is a Fellow of the Academy of the Social Sciences in Australia, the Australian Psychological Society, the American Psychological Association, the American Psychological Society, and the Society for Clinical and Experimental Hypnosis. Dr. McConkey is a Past President of the Australian Psychological Society and is Chair of the National Committee for Psychology, Australian Academy of Sciences.

**Myer Stratton Reed, Ph.D.** is a retired Professor of Sociology. He maintains a counseling practice in Roanoke, VA. He is a clinical member of the American Association of Marriage and Family Therapy and a member of the American Society of Clinical Hypnosis. Dr. Reed has worked hard to improve conditions for local gay students and citizens.

**Alan W. Scheflin, M.A., J.D., L.L.M.** is Professor of Law at Santa Clara University School of Law. He has authored or coauthored the following books: *Civil Obligations, The Mind Manipulators, Trance on Trial,* and (in 1997) *Memory, Trauma Treatment, and Law.* He is Forensic Editor of the *American Journal of Clinical Hypnosis* and Associate Editor of the *Cultic Studies Journal* and has published numerous articles in legal, psychological, psychiatric, and hypnosis journals. Dr. Scheflin has been the recipient of the American Psychiatric Association's Manfred S. Guttmacher Award and the American Society of Clinical Hypnosis' Irving I. Secter Award. He serves as an expert witness in court on suggestion, hypnosis, memory, social influence, and mind control and is a frequent speaker at conferences around the world.

**Francine Shapiro, Ph.D.,** is the originator and developer of EMDR and is a Senior Research Fellow at the Mental Research Institute in Palo Alto, CA. She is the author of two books about EMDR: *Eye Movement Desensitization and Reprocessing* and *EMDR* and has written over 30 articles and chapters. Dr. Shapiro has been a presenter at most major psychology conferences over the past 10 years and has served as advisor to three trauma journals. She was the recipient of the 1994 Distinguished Scientific Achievement in Psychology Award presented by the California Psychological Association.

# *Reviewers for Volume 1*

Stephen Jay Lynn, Ph.D., Department of Psychology,
SUNY-Binghamton

Peter Thorneycroft, Ph.D., Centre for Effective Therapy,
Melbourne, Australia

John Chaves, Ph.D., School of Dentistry,
Indiana University

Marc Kessler, Ph.D., Department of Psychology,
University of Vermont

Robert McNeilly, M.D., Centre for Effective Therapy,
Melbourne, Australia

Douglas Flemmons, Ph.D., School of Systemic Studies,
Nova University

Shelley Green, Ph.D., School of Systemic Studies,
Nova University

Jerry Gale, Ph.D., Department of Child and Family Development,
University of Georgia

Anne Levinger, Ed.D., School of Education,
University of Massachusetts

Tannis Laidlaw, Ph.D., Forensic Psychiatry Unit,
University of Auckland, New Zealand

Ronald Havens, Ph.D., Department of Psychology,
University of Southern Illinois

# *Acknowledgments*

We are grateful to the Milton H. Erickson Foundation and to Jeffrey Zeig for inviting us to become the editors of this series and for their support and encouragement in the process. Specifically, we would like to thank Roxanna Erickson-Klein for her enthusiasm and belief in us, particularly at the outset of this project when such support was most needed.

We would also like to thank the authors and reviewers for their scholarship and commitment to excellence, as well as our developmental editor at Brunner/Mazel, Suzi Tucker, for her professionalism, direction, and good humor. Most of all, we wish to acknowledge the editorship of Stephen Lankton, who laid the foundation for this series through the Ericksonian Monographs.

# *Introduction*

## ERICKSON AND BEYOND

The influence of Milton H. Erickson throughout the world is a given. Interest in his work, in his ideas, in his unusual clinical virtuosity continues to grow. Perhaps the true test of the intellectual stamina of his perspective lies in the strength and flexibility of its weave; in other words, as those of us who come after Erickson question, challenge, poke holes, patch and repattern, the essential fabric of his view still holds. So we stand, cloth in hand, at a crossroads in Ericksonian inspired therapy, indeed, a crossroads in psychotherapy.

Where do we go from here? The field is under a great deal of pressure from inside and out. The basic questions are still with us; this time, however, there is added urgency in the quest to find answers. Third-party payers demand accountability in terms of the effectiveness of various therapies. Does the therapy relieve client distress? Can relief be traced to a particular component of the therapy? What role does client expectancy play in recovery or recidivism? Accountability is a tall order, and some will bristle at the idea: Accountable to whom is a touchy issue. Nevertheless, the order is in, and ultimately, the answer is, of course, we are accountable to our clients. If we cannot state clearly what we do and what is or is not effective, the public loses confidence in the field, insurers see no basis for our treatment, and the biological model—with its concomitant drug therapy—looms ever larger as a seductive alternative.

*Current Thinking and Research in Brief Therapy* will provide access to a range of theoretical ideas, clinical cases, and empirically based research related to solution-focused, strategic, and narrative brief therapies. As an annual, we have the advantage of being able to enlist the contributions of an expanding group of "evolutionaries" and to follow some of the great debates among them. This book, and the succeeding volumes, is designed to give a continuing voice to the theoretical and empirical work of psychotherapy—and to the future builders of the field.

With *Current Thinking and Research in Brief Therapy,* we hope to promote an ongoing dialectic between the revolutionary inspiration and conservative skepticism that together fuel scientific progress. The intended result: an insightful, entertaining, and thought-provoking contribution to this truly viable field of ours.

William J. Matthews

John H. Edgette

# CURRENT THINKING AND RESEARCH IN BRIEF THERAPY

# 1

# Living in a Post-Ericksonian World

*Stephen Gilligan*

The deep parts of my life pour onward,
as if the river shores were opening out.
It seems that things are more like me now,
that I can see farther into paintings.
I feel closer to what language can't reach.

*Rainer Rilke, "Moving Forward"* (Rilke, 1981)

Before his death, Rabbi Zusya said, "In the coming world, they will not ask me: 'Why were you not more like Moses?' They will ask me, 'Why were you not more like Zusya?'"

*Martin Buber, in Tales of the Hasidism* (Buber, 1947)

For many years, I tried to be more like Milton Erickson. This chapter is about the more difficult challenge of trying to be more like Gilligan. It is based on 22 years of teaching, practicing, and writing about hypnotic psychotherapy. It indicates how my path has diverged from Ericksonian thinking. I hope it encourages others on their own paths.

What was really astonishing about Erickson was his willingness to be himself, to accept his "deviancies" from the norm. This courage translated directly, I believe, into compassion for and acceptance of others. To follow a similar path is remarkably challenging. But this is what we stand for as therapists.

In describing where this post-Ericksonian path has led me, I'll start by honoring a few core ideas from Erickson's legacy that still light my way. I'll then raise questions about how these ideas are put into practice. The main intent is to stimulate thinking, rather than to argue about truth.

## THE HEART OF ERICKSON'S LEGACY

Milton Erickson contributed several radical and enduring ideas to psychotherapy. These ideas are deceptively simple, slowly revealing their extraordinary value over years of practice. The first has to do with the uniqueness of each person. In these days of corporate domination of mental health, where diagnostic labels loom larger and therapy freezes into more standardized forms, the idea that each person is unlike anybody else is increasingly disregarded. One-size-fits-all methods proliferate, and an alternative model based on the fact that each case is unique is even seen as unethical in some quarters.

But in many ways, problems arise when individuals lose a sense of their own unique goodness and gifts. To me, Erickson emphasized that the therapist begins by sensing that goodness and those gifts, and that all effective technique arises from that relational connection. We in the Ericksonian community have been surprisingly silent about how to make and sustain this connection experientially—especially nonverbally. Without specific traditions from which to draw, seeing and sensing the unique consciousness that is each person may exist only as platitude or concept, not as practice or experience.

A second extraordinary idea offered by Erickson is that the therapist accepts and utilizes whatever the client presents, no matter how strange, unusual, or esthetically repugnant it might seem. This includes behaviors, experiences, cognitions, and idiosyncrasies. Since the potential value of a given aspect of a person's experience is often not immediately clear—indeed, with symptoms it seems to have a distinctly negative value—it is immensely challenging to consistently translate this simple idea into practice. It requires that before "doing," the therapist must find a way to "be with" a person's experience. This experiential relationship is, of course, central to the experience of trance, where a person can fully "be with" an experience without a fight (domination or control) or flight (dissociation, denial) response. Moving beyond the inner world of traditional hypnosis, Erickson applied this principle in a dynamic way to ongoing relationships with patients. He was like an aikido master, blending and harmonizing with whatever was presented, neutralizing the violence and reconciling the conflicts inherent in a symptomatic behavior.

This idea of acceptance and cooperation puts that of deliberately trying to change a person in a different light. It means that life is moving through the person, distinct in each moment, and, therefore, change is already in motion. Rather than imposing something on clients, the therapist senses and blends with their immediate processes. This is an active and dynamic responsiveness, not a passive and purposeless one. It is an art that requires enormous devotion and study. How does the therapist center his or her attention, be attentive yet flexible, expect nothing but be ready for anything, be soft yet effective?

A third key idea in Erickson's legacy involves therapy as a restoration of balance in a person's life. To me, one of Erickson's great talents was moving effortlessly between the interior worlds of experience and personal meaning and the exterior worlds of behavior and social community. In reading Rossi (Erickson & Rossi, 1979, 1981; Erickson, Rossi, & Rossi, 1977), one sees transcript after transcript in which patients are hypnotized and their inner worlds of experience are activated and transformed. One gets the impression that Erickson's primary interest was to activate inner resources and "spontaneous creativity" in others. But in reading Jay Haley (1967, 1973, 1985a, 1985b, 1985c), one finds more emphasis placed on how Erickson manipulated patients to behave differently in their outer worlds. Here one gets the impression that Erickson's primary interest was in directing behavioral changes.

Which version of Erickson is the "true" one?[1] The answer seems to be both: Erickson went both ways. Sometimes he focused on the outer world, sometimes on the inner, but at all times he seemed to recognize the importance of both. I believe this skill reflected an enormous appreciation of a principle of balance.[2] This balance might be between doing and not doing, between experience and behavior, between self and other—indeed, virtually any distinction to be made has its important complement. Erickson seemed to operate with what Jung (1916) called the transcendent function or what the Eastern traditions call the way between the opposites, where a course including, and often integrating, opposite or complementary values is navigated. This might translate into a hypnotic induction in which a person is encouraged both to withhold or resist *and* to let go and disclose. Or it might translate into a therapy where strategic directives to do something different in the social environment are interlaced with hypnotic trances for self-identity reorganization. Erickson was remarkable in his capacity to know when to use one approach and how to combine both approaches. None of us, it seems to me, has remotely approached this skill. A deeper understanding of the balance principle might be helpful in this regard.

A fourth idea central to Erickson's legacy is that life is to be expe-

---

[1]It should be noted that Haley studied with Erickson in the latter part of the 1950s into the early 1970s, when Erickson's health was much better than during the later 1970s when Rossi was a student and when age and illness were taking an increasing toll on Erickson. It may be that Erickson was a different type of therapist during these two eras, contributing to some of the differences in the two authors' versions of him. A counterpoint to this argument, however, can be found in Erickson and Rossi's (1989) publication of the February man case that occurred in 1945. Here, as in most other cases reported by Rossi, the primary emphasis is on hypnotic work. So while Erickson may have changed some, the differences between Haley and Rossi may reflect more of their own biases. That Erickson's work could support such differences is perhaps the most interesting point.

[2]A good example of this commitment to balance is found in Erickson's dedication in Erickson, Rossi, and Rossi (1977): "Dedicated to an ever progressing understanding of the total functioning of the individual person within the self separately and simultaneously in relation to fellow beings and the total environment."

rienced and enjoyed. For Erickson, therapy was not primarily about analyzing the past or teaching a new conceptual approach, but about helping people to enjoy the "here and now" of life. There was a preference for curiosity over control, acceptance over rejection, experience over intellectual understanding, and flow over fixity. Erickson was a beautiful example of living life on life's terms, and accepting and working with whatever life has to give.

## DEPARTURES FROM ERICKSONIAN TRADITIONS

Erickson and his students have detailed some of the many ways in which his simple yet generative ideas can be applied in therapy (Zeig, 1982, 1985a, 1985b, 1994). The appreciation of his work has led, inevitably, to some reified version of Ericksonian psychotherapy, which just as inevitably, seems more limited and less creative than the original version. Jung used to say, "I'm certainly glad I'm not a Jungian." Erickson no doubt would echo such sentiments, and I hope most of us would ultimately concur.

Letting go of defining one's self as an Ericksonian allows new understandings and approaches to emerge. In my own case, this process has raised questions about premises that seem to be implicit in the Ericksonian community. I raise these questions here with the intention of nurturing the "beginner's mind" so crucial to therapists. As in hypnosis, the holding of a question is usually far more important and productive than the seizing upon of any specific answer.

1. *What do we call these "other than conscious" presences?* A cornerstone of the Ericksonian approach is that an intelligence exists within a person that is beyond the normal egoic self. Erickson talked about this in terms of the unconscious mind, and demonstrated beautiful ways to work with it (Erickson & Rossi, 1981, 1989). In my own explorations, it has become increasingly clear that to singularly refer to this other-than-conscious process as the unconscious mind is too limiting and can be misleading. The possibility for reification is too great and the connotations of the term are too limited for therapeutic flexibility. Alternative references include "the inner self," one's center, heart, soul, or what Chogyam Trungpa (1988) has called the indestructible tender soft spot with which each of us is born.

We use such terms primarily for practical reasons. We approach therapy assuming that a client has become stuck in a narrow understanding of, or limited connection to, his or her potentiality. Identifying resources and activating them are seen as central to helping the client. The idea of the unconscious is used poetically, not literally, to access an intelligence greater than, and different from, what a person is doing. As a poetic term, it invites and evokes a different, more productive way of being. The term is not used in an intellectual exchange as much as it is utilized as an experiential-symbolic one intended to produce a felt sense of nonintellectual intelligence. In short, a major purpose is to open the language of the heart to complement the dominance of the language of the head.

If we appreciate "the unconscious" as poetic language, then we can become curious about other poetic terms as well. Each will carry a different nuance for the client, and each is associated with a different tradition of acting and understanding. From this perspective, a good therapist will be skilled in finding and using those poetic terms that are most helpful in a given situation.

For example, consider the Japanese martial art of aikido. In this situation, one is faced with physical attacks from all directions. The challenge is how to neutralize violence by receiving, harmonizing with, and redirecting the attack. Nothing is ever resisted or opposed; all behavior is blended with and utilized. (As I said earlier, Erickson was quite the aikido master.) To perform aikido, one does not talk about going into trance and trusting the unconscious, but instead emphasizes finding one's center. This mind/body center is not an esoteric or theoretical term, but a felt sense of an intelligence that allows relational creativity and calmness. Without it, one can only fight (dominate) or flee (submit); with it, the third choice of flow is possible (see Leonard, 1991).

Is the notion of a center relevant to therapy? I think so. For example, consider a therapy problem where a person is experiencing anxiety when criticized. Will it be more helpful to appeal to the client's unconscious in a trance, or to help the person find his or her center? Each tradition would share an interest in relaxing the grip of muscle-bound, head-oriented, control-based thinking. But they would go about it in different ways. The tradition of talking with the unconscious is associated with trance and related behaviors, such as eye closure, relaxed muscles, inward orientation, and resource images and stories. The tradition of working with one's center includes learning to drop one's attention below the navel as a primary focus, and then gently to open attention to a field-based perception without grasping on any fixed points (Palmer, 1994). The therapist who is skilled in both traditions will likely be more effective in finding what works best for a given client.

Other terms may also be helpful. For example, the idea of soulfulness may be quite relevant in various performance arts, such as music, poetry, oratory, and therapy. Yeats (in Jeffares, 1974) could have been talking about Erickson when he observed:

> An aged man is but a paltry thing
> A tattered coat upon a stick, unless
> Soul clap its hands and sing, and louder sing
> For every tatter in its mortal dress. (p. 104)

If Yeats had used the term "unconscious mind" rather than "soul," the poetry would have suffered. The point is that the unconscious mind belongs to a family of poetic terms referring to something quite knowable yet ineffable; other terms might be superior or complementary in various circumstances. My suggestion is that a therapist with a felt sense of the nuances of each of these poetic terms will be more effective than one who is stuck with a reified understanding of just one of them.

Thinking of this other-than-conscious self simply as the unconscious mind may lead us to ignore what Erickson (1980) referred to as "that vital sense of the beingness of the self [that] is often overlooked" (p. 345). It may suggest a mechanical or impersonal "thing" to be manipulated or programmed, rather than an integral human presence to be felt, honored, and cultivated.

Some may say that such words as heart and soul are too vague or too poetic, or that therapy should just deal "scientifically" with the mind or behavior. But, of course, the notion of the unconscious mind is even vaguer, and no loving parent or devoted artist would say that nurturing human life is done only via the unconscious mind. As a human encounter, therapy includes elements of both science and art, but must also go beyond them into the areas of love and psychological struggle. Language here must help the person go beyond language, touching on the soft, tender spots of being and interbeing. Access to multiple poetic terms can be helpful in this regard. Of course, it also carries the risk of making a mush of things, so the therapist must be skillful in activating felt senses within the client. How to do this is, I believe, one of the great contributions of the Erickson legacy to therapy.

2. *Is intelligence "in" the unconscious?* Erickson used the metaphor that the unconscious is intelligent. He failed, however, to explain why the patient was doing so poorly before meeting with him. After all, if this intelligence were so magnificent, how did the person end up in such a mess? It seems apparent that the intelligence of the unconscious, if we might call it that, began to become manifest only after Erickson started talking with the person. So we might say that the creative intelligence was in the conversation or relationship between Erickson and the client's unconscious.

In this regard, we might say that intelligence is a relational or field-based principle. To use Bateson's (1979) metaphor, it is the "pattern that connects," or the willingness to hold different views, descriptions, or truths within a deeper field. This echoes the Buddhist notion of interbeing (see Nhat Hanh, 1975), a nondualistic view that posits the interconnectedness and inseparability of each aspect of life.

This relational view challenges the traditional Western approach that separates and isolates mental process from its larger context, thereby making the mind a thing inside somebody's head rather than a process within relational space. In the relational view, mind is a sort of Great Internet, a web of patterns that flows through each of us, connecting all of us. It is not inside of us—we are inside of it. Each of us has a distinct place in the field, an ever-changing ecological niche with unique perspectives and specific knowledges, but the mental circuitry that moves through these vantage points is of a deeper, communal nature. We are individual, but not separate. When a person feels disconnected or separate—whether in inflated (grandiose, power-deluded) or deflated (depressed, frightened) ways—direct experience and creative responsiveness are lost. In the existentialist sense, pathology is precisely the study of loneliness (or the isolation of a process, truth, person, or experience from others). Thus, I believe a central goal of therapy is to reconnect experience and behavior to larger relational fields, rather than trying to fix something inside a person.

3. *Is the therapist really in charge of changing the client?* This Ericksonian view, especially espoused by Haley (1967, 1973), encourages therapists to be in control of the therapy and responsible for its outcomes, and to think in terms of manipulating the client. This view has been unhelpful to me. It reflects an exclusively hierarchical position that egoic intelligence, particularly that of the therapist, is the only game in town. It encourages therapists to become immersed in the principle of power rather than in a principle of cooperation with clients. Therapists are then faced with the problematic belief that they can and should "cure" clients.

These concerns about ideas of control were voiced by Bateson, who sent many students (including me) Erickson's way.[3] He repeatedly warned of what he called the pathological effects of conscious purpose on adaptation (Bateson, 1972), emphasizing that the myth of power is especially corruptive (Bateson, 1979). His concerns about Erickson's students were expressed in an interview with Brad Keeney (1977).

*Keeney:* You're saying that people who go to see Erickson come away with a craving for power?

*Bateson:* Yes! They all want power.

*Keeney:* Is there something about seeing [Erickson] that induces this power hungriness?

*Bateson:* Well, it's the skill which he has of manipulating the other person which really in the long run does not separate him as an ego dominant to the other person. He works in the weave of the total complex and they come away with a trick which is separate from the total complex, therefore goeth counter to it, and becomes a sort of power. I think it's something like that. (p. 49)

These comments encourage an alternative to the power principle that traditionally underlies our thinking (see Woodman, 1993). The power principle emphasizes intellect, unilateral manipulation, control, sin-

[3]The shortcomings of the ideas of power and control have been addressed by others, including Keeney (1983) and Hoffman (1985).

gular truth, and subjugation of nature. Addiction to this principle reduces relationship to stark contrasts: You either dominate or submit, are right or wrong, win or lose. In this either/or frame, the other-than-conscious self—whether it be the unconscious or another person or a group—is seen as an "it" that needs to controlled, rather than as a "thou" to be accepted and listened to.

A symptom is, in part, the breakdown of this power principle. It signals that a person no longer can maintain some ideological position, or isolated intellectual control, over the "other(s)" and the rest of his or her world. It suggests that a more integrated, less mechanical understanding of self and world be developed. From this perspective, the idea of power—whether it is the client's trying to control the problem or the therapist's trying to control and change the client—is part of the problem, not the solution.

Our images and understandings of cooperation are often undeveloped and limited, so it is easy to underestimate the value of this principle. We need to be clear that in rejecting the idea of power and the accompanying idea of the therapist's being in control, we are not left simply with the alternative of passive acceptance of the status quo. Gandhi used to say that if the choice was merely between passive submission to injustice and violent resistance, he would choose and encourage violence. But he articulated and walked a third path of nonviolent resistance.

Similarly, if the choice is only between passive acceptance of a person's suffering and deliberate manipulation to change the person, the latter would usually be a better choice. But a third path, originated but not completely developed by Erickson, involves actively accepting and cooperating with a person's ongoing process to reconnect with the natural process of change and healing that flows through each living system.[4]

[4]My personal view is that an admirable struggle existed in Erickson between the power principle, which reigned supreme and unchallenged during Erickson's time, and the cooperation principle, of which Erickson was a major originator. This struggle is similar to that of Morehei Ueshiba, the founder of the martial art of aikido, who was also known as the greatest martial artist in Japan's history. Ueshiba, like Erickson, gave birth to a vision of how to join nonviolently with an attacker to reconcile violence. Aikido is one of the traditions that has helped me to see symptoms as acts of violence against self and/or others.

This view is related to the Palo Alto Mental Research Institute group's notion that the attempted solution is often the problem (see Watzlawick, Weakland, & Fisch, 1974). The Milwaukee group, led by Steve de Shazer (1985, 1988), further developed this idea by encouraging attentiveness to already occurring (but nonarticulated) differences in the person's world as the basis for therapeutic change. For example, if the client complains of depression, the therapist might focus on exceptions (when the person is not depressed or feels less depressed) or the miracle question (what the person would do differently if, by some miracle, he or she were to wake up the next morning to discover that the problem had disappeared). The client is then directed to do more of the different-from-symptom behaviors. In this view, the therapist does not create change. Life does! It is more a matter of "being with" life, a fresh attentiveness to each moment, that allows new experiences (including desired changes) to emerge.

My approach of Self-Relations psychotherapy differs from these approaches in its strong emphasis on felt experience as well as behavior (see Gilligan, 1996). I am especially interested in what happens when the social/behavioral mind (the conscious mind) and the natural/experiential mind (the unconscious mind) are seen as different sides of the same coin. (I want to know the name of this coin!) Self-relations suggests that since every moment in life is different, experiencing the "same damn thing over and over" means that a person's conscious self is not "in life" at those times; it has dissociated from the experience of the present moment and is trying (with increasingly dismal failure) to control behavior from some satellite orbit. The social mind has split off from the natural world (including the body, its feelings and emotions) and is operating under the delusion that it is separate from it and can and should dominate it. The out-of-control nature of symptoms thus can be seen as an error-correction process that reveals the illusion of power as it attempts to establish a new mind/nature relationship based on cooperation.

Of course, the transition from control over to cooperation with the natural mind requires some workable practices of controlled surrender (Leonard, 1991). A first step is to be with experience as it is. For example, mental processes can harmonize with and bring attentiveness to natural processes, such as ongoing breathing, heartbeats, and physical behaviors. This method is similar to the pacing techniques of Ericksonian hypnosis (see Gilligan, 1987), but the intent is not so much to manipulate the behavior as it is to touch it with human awareness. It is like playing with young children, where relatedness and curiosity are crucial to developmental process. The therapist lets go of trying to reframe or change something in favor of properly naming and attentively being with what is present in a person's experience.

This is a piece of what the Buddhist mindfulness tradition calls the skillful means of love. The idea is that when human consciousness touches an experience or behavior with loving awareness, it is affirmed and grows, to paraphrase Rilke, a little bit more like itself. It is like helping a child learn to recognize, properly name, and respond to different natural states, such as hunger, sleep, and emotional needs. If these states are not properly named and attended to, suffering and acting out will result.[5] A symptom suggests a reoccurring natural state that has no mature human presence to be with it. This natural state might be the need to be seen or to have privacy, or the interest in relatedness, fear, and so on. The idea is that these natural states are not complete within themselves: without a mature human presence to "give them space," they will likely be experienced and expressed as negative forms with little redeeming value.

Mindfulness is, in part, a training of how to listen, be with, and allow the human nature of each of these states to unfold. It is a skill that offers a third choice of what might be called human sponsorship to the existing extremes of (1) repression of or (2) identification with an experience. Sponsorship, distinct from ownership, recognizes the autonomy of the other—whether it is a person or an emotional state or a symptomatic behavior—while also realizing the need for guidance, discipline, human social traditions, love, and relatedness. Since the experience or behavior of the other is unique and different in each moment, sponsorship needs considerable skill to practice. It requires that one cultivate listening deeply, opening fully, concentrating, tolerating, being flexible, understanding from the heart, challenging, naming, guiding, and, most of all, loving.

We generally accept the need for sponsorship as a given with children: Without a human presence to love, accept, and guide them,

[5]Interestingly, a major tool in 12-step recovery programs is the acronym HALT, for Hungry-Angry-Lonely-Tired. The idea is that these states, if active but unattended to, are triggers to addictive behaviors.

they will not develop in positive ways. As we mature, we develop the capacity to provide this sort of sponsorship for our own experiences, in addition to the continuing need to experience it from significant others in our community. *A repeating negative expression suggests that some natural experience is occurring without human sponsorship; for it to change, it must first be sponsored.* The skill of sponsorship is not simply behavioral, as in the Ericksonian concept of matching behavior; nor is it simply empathic, like the Rogerian concept of mirroring. It combines both skills into a third way of artfully being with a person. As it develops, change occurs on its own. The therapist then shepherds that change to fruition.

For example, imagine a four-year-old girl with her parents. Her normally charming self is replaced by a whining, unremitting, and unresponsive crankiness. Everybody in the vicinity feels affected by the child's mood, and the parents try nicely, then sternly, to get her to change. These tactics, which usually work, seem to be ineffectual. So the parents finally come around to listening and wondering what is going on. In this instance, knowing the child's world a bit, the parents realize she may be sad about her nanny's leaving and that her best friends next door are moving. So the question becomes how to acknowledge her sadness while also not letting the little girl act out too much or for too long. Again, a key idea is that the persistent negative behavior suggests a natural state (sadness and fear about people's leaving) that has not been properly named and responded to.

Let us compare this situation with that of an adult in a psychotherapy office, whining about childhood experiences or depressed about current relationships. The same feeling pervades the social context, and the same tendency to want to shut the person down prevails. But in the idea of sponsorship, the therapist begins to listen for an underlying natural state that is active but unnamed. This might involve simply listening, or asking questions about present and past social history. The proper naming of the experience is not a scientific classification process, but a touching of an experience with human consciousness. When the naming is accurate, the person will usually soften and become more responsive. The therapist then skillfully stays with the named experience, using language to "bless it" and bring it into the sphere of the person's normal competencies.

4. *Is trance really so common?* In the Ericksonian community, there is a view that trance is an everyday naturalistic state that is exceed-

ingly common. In the extreme version of this idea, trance is everywhere, all the time. Formal or even informal testing of trance may be seen as irrelevant, and client reports of not feeling trance may be disregarded, as the all-knowing "Ericksonian wizard" somehow knows the person is in a trance. In this view, powerful yet subtle indirect techniques can access a trance of which only the therapist is consciously aware.

The more traditional view is that hypnosis is a socially constructed state or relationship resulting from formal hypnotic induction. In this view, trance is not so common. It requires a situation defined as hypnosis and direct suggestions from a hypnotist. Even then, hypnosis tests indicate that only some persons can experience hypnosis.

While there are merits to both views, I would like to suggest a somewhat different approach. In its present form, this view is not so much a scientific fact as it is a clinical suggestion. It sees trance as part of the language of the natural mind, and hypnosis as one of the social rituals for naming, shaping, and giving meaning to its form and expression. This relationship is similar to the idea of sponsorship of other natural experiences: Trance is going to occur, like it or not. Without social traditions (such as hypnosis, art, religion, or ritual) to guide and artfully contain its expression, it will manifest as symptom(s) and be experienced as suffering.

What kind of natural state is trance? It is one that occurs when identity needs to preserved, transformed, or recreated. Identity is organic and impermanent, and undergoes major changes at certain times—for example, at such family events as births, deaths, marriages, illnesses, job changes, graduations, traumas, divorces, and leaving home. At such times, the old way of knowing one's self and one's world "dies" and a new identity must be born. This is a second-order, and occasionally a third-order, level of change (see Bateson, 1972). Since the normal conscious processes are designed to maintain the present order (they are conservative in nature), they must be relinquished for a different type of mental process.

Trance is precisely this type of process. In the experience of trance, time is suspended, logic is more flexible, focus is intensified, frames loosen, receptivity is deepened, and primary process is prominent (see Gilligan, 1987, 1988). This makes control secondary and change of perspective primary.

Thus, when a person or system is undergoing an identity change, trance will tend to show up spontaneously. Trance and trance rituals are present in virtually every culture, especially at transitional points. Symptoms also tend to occur around these transitional points; that is, a person is most likely to develop a symptom following significant life changes (Lazarus, 1966). This suggests that symptoms are spontaneous trances without good social rituals and human presence to sponsor and guide them. Thus, in therapy the point is not so much to introduce trance as it is to introduce hypnotic forms that allow the trance that is naturally occurring to be socially sanctioned and worked with.

From this perspective, it does not make much sense to think of trance merely as behavioral or simply as a social interaction between hypnotist and subject. This is like reducing love to the exchange of words or the experience of art to the commentary of critics. It makes trance too much about the therapist and not enough about the client's natural experience of growth and change. A minimal understanding of trance requires an appreciation of the inner and outer worlds, of natural mind and social mind, and especially an appreciation of how the altered states in a person's life are always occurring within a life stream of specific events. By seeing the symptom as a trance indicating an identity shift, hypnosis becomes a social ritual that provides a skillful means for connecting the change process to healing resources.

While this naturalistic view of trance is somewhat different from the traditional artificial or purely social view, it is also different from the Ericksonian view that sees trance as exceedingly common.[6] To confuse trance with the mental "spacing out" that takes place throughout the day is to miss its deeper clinical significance and potential.

5. *Is trance always such a good thing?* We in the Ericksonian community have sometimes naively approached hypnosis as the panacea for all that ails you. In its extreme version, the idea is that if we could only go into trance and stay there, happiness would be ours forever. This dangerous and seductive view makes certain things more diffi-

[6]There are, of course, other views on the nature of hypnosis. Lynn and Rhue (1991) provide an excellent summary of the current controversies. I do believe that the present view stands up well as a clinically helpful way to join and transform the client's suffering.

cult, such as being present as a spouse or parent or participating as a citizen in the community. Further, it assumes that trance is always a good thing. My view is that hypnosis, used wisely and in moderation, can be a wonderful and helpful experience. But it can be, and sometimes is, used as a narcotic, a druglike state to numb or turn one away from participation in life.

Trance is especially likely to be used as a dissociative tool among trauma survivors, to protect the self from further harm (Terr, 1994). But this dissociative skill may continue to be used long after the threatening conditions have dissipated, thereby turning the person away from the call to reenter the life of the community. For example, a person growing up in an alcoholic family may have learned to "trance out" when a parent was abusive or intoxicated, but now automatically uses the same strategy to avoid dealing with the fear of intimacy with a spouse. Then, what had been an ally becomes a hindrance to growth.

The value of trance is in the way it is used. You can be in trance and not "be with" your self or "in" life. Erickson had a wonderful capacity to sponsor trance and other psychological states; that is, he really connected the natural experience of trance to the person's well-being and learning. Whereas patients had previously learned to use trance to get away from the world, Erickson joined with where they were to help them use trance to come back into the community. This skill of being with a person's ongoing experience—what the Buddhists call mindfulness—is simple but elusive. It is far more important than whether a trance is present. In fact, when more attention is paid to mindfulness, trance will be used more effectively in therapy. It will be seen as a natural state that can be misused, and thus as something to approach with sensitivity and awareness. What is very important, it will not be seen as a panacea or a lifestyle, but as a resource available at various points in one's path. In this view, hypnosis is one member of a family of approaches that can promote peace of mind, relieve suffering, expand heartfelt understanding, and allow self-transformation.

6. *Is indirect communication such a good thing?* A hallmark of the Ericksonian approach is the use of indirect communication, ostensibly to enhance therapeutic responsiveness. To me, this is one of the most misunderstood and potentially harmful aspects of the Erickson legacy. Such misunderstandings arise partly, I believe, from a confu-

sion of signs with symbols. Signs are context-invariant descriptions; that is, they mean roughly the same thing in any situation. Symbols are context-variant, their meaning is contextually constructed (see Pribram, 1971).[7]

Signs and symbols may be seen as two poles on a dialectic. I believe the Ericksonian community is making the same mistake as traditional therapy by becoming too biased toward descriptions as context-invariant signals. A problematic behavior is seen more as a sign to be interpreted by the person in power, that is, the therapist. Thus, the meaning of a headache, a dream, or a marital fight is invariant, and is listed in the code book of the therapist's system. For example, a headache might "signal" sexual repression, which the therapist then takes as the "real" underlying problem to be defeated.

In this view, the therapist's superior training and expertise give privileged access to the deeper (problematic) meanings of the client's life. The therapist is justified in the decision to, and even ethically obliged to, technically operate on the client with a method, such as an indirect technique, that presumably will causally change the underlying problem. This "benevolent dictator" approach assumes that since the meaning (or deep structure) of a problem, such as a headache, is context-invariant, the method (e.g., story or indirect technique) used to treat the problem is also context-invariant (cf. de Shazer, 1994). This gives rise to popular practitioner "story books," similar to dream interpretation handbooks, in which the therapist can look up the proper story to be used to "cure" a given problem.

From a relational point of view, this is the power principle in action. The implicit premises are that (1) the therapist knows things about the client that the client does not and should not know (presumably because he or she could not handle this self-knowledge), (2) the therapist can and should use this information to influence the client deliberately without his or her permission or awareness, and (3) this deceptive practice actually works and is helpful to both the client's and the therapist's growth.

This is, I believe, a dangerous trend in the way the Ericksonian

[7]As Pribram notes, signs can sometimes be used symbolically and symbols can be used significantly, but this level of analysis is unnecessary for the purposes of the present discussion.

community has used the ideas and techniques of symbolic communication. It gets away from Erickson's cornerstone emphasis on the uniqueness of each person and each situation. Such an emphasis implies that meaning is never fixed; it is different for each person and, to some extent, for each moment. If nothing is fixed, the therapist has no ground to stand on, no code book to consult, no deep structure to discern.

This other pole on the dialectic suggests that problems, as well as the therapist's theories and responses to them, should be read more as poems than as scientific facts or entities. In poetry, as in hypnosis, the goal is to reconnect language to felt experiences or, to quote Rilke, "to feel closer to what language cannot reach." The idea is that descriptions become dysfunctional when they are no longer context-sensitive; that is, they no longer are connected to the pulsation of the present moment. When disconnected, descriptions function as fundamentalist texts that reject what is for what should be, thereby creating suffering (see Gilligan, 1996).

The repoetization of description is first and foremost a shift not in the content of the text, but in the relationship of the reader to the text. Thus, the magic is not in the story or its cleverly constructed details, but in the reengagement of consciousness to a story such that new meanings and experiences are unfolding. *This is the primary goal in experiential-symbolic communication: not cleverly to deceive but experientially to awaken the client's consciousness.*

Thus, the client with a headache complaint is seen to be rigidly attached to a frame of reference. The peculiar way that the client is holding on, no doubt in an effort to avoid further suffering, is shutting down the healing principle that permeates the present moment. The therapist is seeking to reconnect with that healing principle by joining with the client's process, listening to the "reified poem" of the headache complaint, feeling his or her own poetic responses ("It reminds me of...."), and then using therapeutic skills to feed back a related poem (such as a story, a paradox, or an indirect technique).

Such a poetic exchange is not an associational free-for-all where anything goes. Tremendous constraint and discipline are involved in any art. In the art of therapy, the therapist is committed to the emergence of new responses from the client, so considerable concentration is needed to stay engaged with the client at multiple levels. At the same time, the therapist realizes that he or she is not in control or has some privileged access to deep structures; the therapist is more trusting and is curious as to how this engaged poetic process can produce new meanings that are more vital and workable for the client.

The important point is that the meaning of the indirect communication is relationally derived. Just as sweetness is not a property of sugar (rather, it is an experience of the relationship between the sugar and the tongue's tasting it), the therapeutic meaning derives relationally from the connection between therapist and client. This leads to a more collaborative, indeterminate, curiosity-based understanding of indirect communication.

Thus, I believe the way in which indirect communication has been talked about in the Erickson community is misleading and unfortunate. I think it has led therapists to become more absorbed in their clever techniques than in connecting directly with the client. But as the dancer Isadora Duncan said when asked to explain the meaning of a particular performance, "If I could explain it, I wouldn't have to dance it!" So rather than plotting and planning to deceive clients, therapists should, like devoted artists, join the psychic field that allows the dancers to dance by the healing principle.

7. *Are failures important to admit?* One of the compelling aspects of Erickson's legacy is his success stories. As de Shazer (1994) has pointed out, every therapist has a persona, and Erickson (and especially his students) described his therapist persona from the point of view of Erickson-the-clever. Like Sherlock Holmes, Erickson-the-clever astounded the reader with a commonsense brilliance and remarkable creativity. Also like Holmes, Erickson seemingly never failed. While the work of Erickson-the-clever makes for fascinating reading and inspirational thinking, its value as a teaching style is less clear. Therapists (and clients) must find ways to accept and work with the differences between ideal and actual outcomes, especially failures. Surely Erickson failed many times, but we know little of how he struggled to learn from his failures.

In my own case, this type of omission has not been helpful to my development. For too long I downplayed my weaknesses and failures, and tried to act ever confident and always in charge. My taboo against failure especially compromised the capacity for disciplined not-knowing, that essential ingredient of curiosity and creativity.

I have come to believe that therapist failure is essential to therapy success. It is precisely when the client throws the theory back in the therapist's face or resists the therapeutic (or hypnotic) suggestion that therapy actually occurs. At that point, the client is discovering his or her own way, realizing that it is significantly different from the therapist's understandings. The therapeutic process that begins with the failure of the therapist's way must then be cultivated by following and gently giving human presence and structure to each successive expression of the client's way.

We see this process especially in working with hypnosis and with metaphor. Erickson used to encourage hypnotic subjects to translate his meanings, words, and images into their own meanings, words, and images. I believe the therapist should be quite concerned if the client is literally following each suggestion offered, as it suggests that the person is trying to be a "good boy" or "good girl" and follow the therapist's way, rather than discovering his or her own way. As clients develop openness and self-love, they discover increasing differences between them and the therapist. The inadequacy of the therapist's perspectives for the client's needs is realized, and the client learns that he or she must rely increasingly on his or her own thinking and feeling. Thus, the revelation of the therapist's failures becomes the basis for therapeutic progress.

8. *Is love a force to be reckoned with?* The discussion thus far has been somewhat critical of ideas of power, manipulation, and deception. It leads us to ask: Is the power of love greater than or equal to the love of power? Is love as a skill relevant to doing therapy? Can it be effectively used to absorb and transform the violence implicit in a symptom?

I believe the answer is Yes to each of these questions. Once we move beyond our immature and rigid understanding of love as a state that "happens to you" under favorable circumstances, we can appreciate it as a cultivated skill and force available under the most adverse circumstances (see Fromm, 1956) We see examples of this in the work of Gandhi, King, Christ, Mandela, and others. I think we saw it also in the work of Erickson. Love as a skill has many aspects, including opening, understanding from the heart, grounding, receiving, showing compassion (suffering with), protecting, being with, blessing, noticing growth, becoming committed, warning, and being flexible. I think therapy involves a great a deal of love, and that it is unfortunate that we talk so little of it. (Mother Theresa is fond of saying that there are no great acts, only small acts done with great love.)

I have been encouraged by Erickson's example to move from a place of trying to dictate, dominate, and control life to learning how to cooperate with it, in both the inner and outer worlds. I feel great love in Erickson's work, and find it a good example to remind me of what is possible. The core importance of thinking about therapy in terms of love, rather than of power or manipulation, is growing steadily clearer to me. Thus, I believe it is helpful to open discussions of what love as a skill is in therapy, and how to promote and cultivate the courage to love.

## SUMMARY

My development as a therapist has been strongly influenced by the example of Milton Erickson. His emphasis on the uniqueness of each person, accepting and cooperating with whatever the person offered, the restoration of balance, and the enjoyment of life, continues to light my path and to point onward. As this path has changed, my style has also changed. Some of the aspects of Ericksonian work that I leave behind include the emphasis on power and manipulation; the other-than-conscious self as a mental apparatus; intelligence as being "in" or "of" the unconscious; trance as always a good thing or an everyday event; the value of indirect communication; and a singular emphasis on success and a taboo on failures.

I am more curious about love as a skill; cooperation as a skill; heart, soul, center, inner self, and original soft spot as complementary terms to that of the unconscious; the intelligence in interbeing; the specialness of trance and its connection to "cousins," such as art and meditation; experiential-symbolic communication that bypasses both the therapist's and client's fixed frames; and the skill of being with failures.

I realize that others see Erickson's work differently. This was Erickson's enigma and strength; his work meant so many things to so many people. My major interest here is sharing how what I learned from him 20 years ago is still changing, for better or worse, in my work today. I hope that this remains true for all of us. As the Buddha said, "Be a light unto yourself."

## REFERENCES

Bateson, G. (1972). *Steps to an ecology of mind.* New York: Ballantine Books.
Bateson, G. (1979). *Mind and nature: A necessary unity.* New York: Dutton.
Buber, M. (1947). *Tales of the Hassidism.* New York: Schocken Books.
de Shazer, S. (1985). *Keys to solution in brief therapy.* New York: Norton.
de Shazer, S. (1988). *Clues: Investigating solutions in brief therapy.* New York: Norton.
de Shazer, S. (1994). *Words were originally magic.* New York: Norton.
Erickson, M. H. (1980). Basic psychological problems in hypnotic research. In E. L. Rossi (Ed.), *The collected papers of Milton H. Erickson on hypnosis, vol. 2.* New York: Irvington.
Erickson, M. H., & Rossi, E. L. (1979). *Hypnotherapy: An exploratory casebook.* New York: Irvington.
Erickson, M. H., & Rossi, E.L. (1981). *Experiencing hypnosis: Therapeutic approaches to altered states.* New York: Irvington.
Erickson, M. H., & Rossi, E. L (1989). *The February man: Evolving consciousness and identity in hypnotherapy.* New York: Brunner/Mazel.
Erickson, M. H., Rossi, E. L., & Rossi, S. I. (1977). *Hypnotic realities: The induction of clinical hypnosis and forms of indirect suggestion.* New York: Irvington.
Fromm, E. (1956). *The art of loving.* New York: Harper & Row.
Gilligan, S. G. (1987). *Therapeutic trances: The cooperation principle in Ericksonian hypnotherapy.* New York: Brunner/Mazel.
Gilligan, S. G. (1988). Symptom phenomena as trance phenomena. In J. Zeig & S. Lankton (Eds.), *Developing Ericksonian therapy: State of the art.* New York: Brunner/Mazel.
Gilligan, S. G. (1996). The relational self: The expanding of love beyond desire. In M. Hoyt (Ed.), *Constructive therapies, vol. 2: Expanding and integrating effective practices.* New York: Guilford.
Haley, J. (Ed.). (1967). *Advanced techniques of hypnosis and therapy: Selected papers of Milton H. Erickson, M.D.* New York: Grune & Stratton.
Haley, J. (1973). *Uncommon therapy: The psychiatric techniques of Milton Erickson, M.D.* New York: Norton.
Haley, J. (1985a). *Conversations with Milton H. Erickson, M.D., Vol. I: Changing individuals.* New York: Norton.

Haley, J. (1985b). *Conversations with Milton H. Erickson, M.D., Vol. II: Changing couples.* New York: Norton.

Haley, J. (1985c). *Conversations with Milton H. Erickson, M.D., Vol. III: Changing children and families.* New York: Norton.

Hoffman, L. (1985). Beyond power and control. *Family Systems Medicine, 3,* 381–396.

Jeffares, A. N. (Ed.). (1974). *W. B. Yeats: Selected poetry.* London: Pan Books.

Jung, C. G. (1916/1971). *The structure and dynamics of the psyche.* Section on the transcendent function reprinted in J. Campbell (Ed.), *The portable Jung.* New York: Penguin Books.

Keeney, B. (1977). On paradigmatic change: Conversations with Gregory Bateson. Unpublished manuscript.

Keeney, B. (1983). *Aesthetics of change.* New York: Guilford.

Lazarus, R. (1966). *Psychological stress and the coping process.* New York: McGraw-Hill.

Leonard, G. (1991). *Mastery: The keys to success and long-term fulfillment.* New York: Plume Books.

Lynn, S. J., & Rhue, J. W. (Eds.). (1991). *Theories of hypnosis: Current models and perspectives.* New York: Guilford.

Nhat Hanh, T. (1975). *The miracle of mindfulness.* Boston: Beacon.

Palmer, W. (1994). *The intuitive body: Aikido as a clairsentient practice.* Berkeley, CA: North Atlantic Books.

Pribram, K. H. (1971). *Languages of the brain: Experimental paradoxes and principles in neuropsychology.* Englewood Cliffs, NJ: Prentice-Hall.

Rilke, R. (1981). Moving forward. In R. Bly (Ed.), *Selected poems of Rainer Maria Rilke.* New York: Harper & Row.

Terr, L. (1994). *Unchained memories: True stories of traumatic memories, lost and found.* New York: Basic Books.

Trungpa, C. (1988). *Shambhala: the sacred path of the warrior.* Boston: Shambhala.

Watzlawick, P., Weakland, J., & Fisch, R. (1974). *Change: Principles of problem formation and problem resolution.* New York: Norton.

Woodman, M. (1993). *Conscious femininity: Interviews with Marion Woodman.* Toronto: Inner City Books.

Zeig, J. K. (Ed.) (1982). *Ericksonian approaches to hypnosis and psychotherapy.* New York: Brunner/Mazel.

Zeig, J. K. (Ed.) (1985a). *Ericksonian psychotherapy, Vol. 1: Structures.* New York: Brunner/Mazel.

Zeig, J. K. (Ed.) (1985b). *Ericksonian psychotherapy, Vol. 2: Clinical applications.* Brunner/Mazel.

Zeig, J. K. (Ed.) (1994). *Ericksonian methods: The essence of the story.* Brunner/Mazel.

# 2

# Brief Moments and Enduring Effects: Reflections on Time and Timing in Psychotherapy

*Michael J. Mahoney*

The dimension of time has always been a central one in psychotherapy, as it is in life itself. How should a client and therapist organize and use their time together? How much time do they have? How much time is required for a person to make important changes? Like other psychotherapists, these are issues that I continue to ponder. My goal in this chapter is not to answer such questions, or even adequately to elaborate the complexities that they entail. Rather, I shall reflect on a few selected issues related to time and close with some remarks on how my ideas about time and psychotherapy have changed over the course of my career.

## THE ENDURING EFFECTS OF BRIEF MOMENTS

I shall begin with a personal illustration of how brief moments in psychotherapy can lead to powerful changes in a life. The life involved was my own and the year was 1967. Following my graduation from a community college in Joliet, Illinois, I was in the throes of a major life transition. A respiratory illness had left me literally breathless and often bedridden for much of the preceding winter. My physician had cautioned me about the dangers of spending another winter in the Midwest. He recommended Arizona as a more hospitable environment for my breathing. I was reluctant to leave my home and family, but the prospect of hospitalization was an ominous one. My wife and I packed our meager belongings into our old Rambler station wagon and headed toward the Arizona desert.

An important theme in this story was my need for direction. I was painfully naive about the "college process." I found mention of two state universities in a book, one in Tucson and one in Tempe. Not knowing how to choose between them, the decision was made by a coin toss. We set out for Tempe. My naiveté was such, however, that I did not realize that I first had to apply for admission. Thus—after surviving the long trek, car problems, and terrible storms in New Mexico—I arrived only to learn that there was more to becoming a student at Arizona State University than simply registering for classes. After reviewing my transcript, the registrar accepted my application. But a second and more serious dilemma immediately ensued. Because I had been accepted as a beginning third-year student, I was required to declare a major. At Joliet Junior College, I had enjoyed the freedom of a broad liberal arts curriculum. Now I was told that I had to specialize.

"But I don't know what I want to be yet," I told the woman in the registrar's office.

"Well, you have until Monday to make up your mind," she said, "but you can't take any summer classes until you declare a major."

I drove from Tempe to downtown Phoenix, fighting an existential panic that felt overwhelming. What was I to do? How should I decide? This was a choice I could not settle with a coin toss. After hours of agony, I chanced on the thought of asking an expert for help. I stopped at a phone booth on Central Avenue and thumbed through the yellow pages. There were hundreds of listings for psychologists, psychiatrists, and psychotherapists. I had no idea how to choose among them, and I still don't know why I chose the one I did—perhaps it was the long list of specializations he listed after his name.

When his receptionist answered, I introduced myself and briefly described my dilemma.

"I have $60 in life savings and I need to talk to someone right away. I have to make a major life decision by Monday, and I don't know how to do it." She put me on hold briefly and then returned to inform me that the doctor could see me for two hours that afternoon. I received directions to his office, which was in his home, and arrived promptly at the appointed time. I was very nervous as I waited, but his house and the waiting room felt safe and comforting. When the receptionist, his wife, showed me into the doctor's office, I was struck by his frailty. His face was thin, almost gaunt, and his eyes stood out. He sat in a wheelchair behind a large desk. I remember his voice as gentle and reassuring.

He didn't ask me why I was there, and at first I did not tell him. I don't remember what I said exactly, but he began to talk. He told me stories. Stories about his children. Stories about their adventures in the Superstition Mountains east of Phoenix. The two hours went by quickly and I suddenly realized that I only had a few minutes left. I awkwardly stammered out my predicament.

"Well, Doctor, the reason I am here is that I have to declare a major at the university on Monday and I don't know what I should do." He nodded for me to continue. "I've always wanted to be a writer—novels and poetry—but I don't think there is much security in that. And the only other thing is psychology—my introductory instructor told me to consider it." He looked at me, waiting patiently. "Well," I continued, "I don't know. I mean, most of my writing *is* about what goes on inside people, but I've heard that you have to go past a bachelor's degree to be able to do anything in psychology and I'm not even sure I will be able to get my bachelor's. Besides...."

My voice trailed often in hesitation. "Yes?" he said, nodding encouragement. "Well," I said anxiously, "sometimes I get anxious and depressed myself, and what right would I have to tell other people what to do in their lives when I don't have my own life together?" The words came out quickly and I could feel my heart pounding at the sound of hearing myself say them. I waited for his response, but he was silent. He rubbed the late-afternoon gray stubble on his cheeks and chin with his long thin fingers, and then he lifted himself with his arms and shifted his position in the wheelchair. Leaning toward me and looking directly into my eyes, he finally said quietly, "You know something, Michael? Some of the best football coaches in this country have never played the game." In that moment, it was clear to me that he was encouraging me to go into psychology. He didn't say that, but I knew. I stood up and thanked him. He smiled, and we shook hands. "Good luck," he said as I left.

Two years later I saw him again, but this time from a distance and in a different role. I was finishing my bachelor's degree in psychology and serving as vice-president of the campus chapter of Psi Chi, the national honor society in psychology. He was our guest speaker. Imagine my surprise when I heard him introduced as a world-famous therapist! Without knowing who he was or what he was famous for, I had randomly selected the name of Milton Erickson from the Phoenix yellow pages. Many times in the ensuing years I have reflected on those two hours and those last few minutes. His response to my dilemma was not a straightforward prescription or even a logical translation. But it was a powerful experience that influenced the trajectory of my life.

When I have related my experience to friends over the years, those familiar with Erickson's work have had some interesting questions. Did I feel hypnotized? What was he like? What do I think he meant by that analogy? What was his therapeutic strategy? An honest response to all four questions would be, "I don't know." We did not go through a hypnotic induction procedure, but I certainly came away in a very different state of consciousness than when I entered. I remembered the details of his stories for quite some time, but I did not rehearse them into conscious memory, and I certainly did not realize at the time what a profound impact that experience was to have on my life. He was like a wise old eagle, but hardly as mystical and magical as some of the caricatures I have read in the ensuing years. As to his analogy, I have not plumbed its microgenetic meanings. I don't remember being confused about its meaning at the time; to me it meant that I didn't have to have my personal life totally together to be helpful to others involved in that process. But I didn't analyze the logic or psychologic of his analogy. From my self-description over the phone, he probably knew that I was at an important decision point in my life. I suspect that this knowledge might have made it more likely that he would have been listening for the sources of my ambivalence or reluctance to move in different directions. However, my sense was that he was not acting out a planned strategy of influence. He seemed relaxed and spontaneous throughout our session, flowing from story to story in a way that made it feel as though each might have some lessons for me in my situation. I was the one who brought the session to a focused question, and he responded, after thoughtful reflection, with an indirect but powerful analogy.

In 1995, 28 years later, I got another glimpse of how enduring an effect that session had had on me. I was attending the annual meeting of the American Psychological Association in New York City and was on my way to meet with an editor from one of the publishing companies. Running late, I tried to make my way through the crowded exhibits area. I was focused on moving quickly and reaching my destination when I suddenly stopped in midstride. People were pushing past in both directions, and I stood there puzzled. I didn't know why I had stopped, but there was a lingering intuition that I had meant to. I looked around and saw nothing but crowds of people and book displays. All I could hear was the din of multiple simultaneous conversations. Then I turned around and walked slowly back along the path I had just followed. A few yards back, I felt a sense of recognition. It was a voice that I somehow had distinguished among the many that were audible. I looked to the side, and there was a video monitor with Milton Erickson demonstrating hypnotic induction techniques. I smiled and lingered for a while. He was much younger in that film, but his voice was the same, and it had definitely "gone with me" (Rosen, 1982).

During my two years at Arizona State, I pursued an interesting mixture of studies. At that time, the psychology department was predominantly Skinnerian. I took animal laboratory courses that had been organized by Fred Keller, and I read the classics on behaviorism and positivism. On the other side of campus, I pursued my philosophical interests, primarily in epistemology and the philosophy of religion. I became increasingly interested in the area of self-control in psychology. At that time, there was very little research on the topic, and most of it pointed toward cognitive processes. My undergraduate adviser, David Rimm, recommended that I apply to his alma mater, Stanford, to work with Albert Bandura. Bandura gave a colloquium on self-regulation at Arizona State while my application was under review, and he later told me that his only reservation in accepting me as his student had been the possibility that I might be a bit too Skinnerian. When he later wrote about "chance encounters" and their effects on life paths (Bandura, 1978), my session with Milton Erickson was one of the first examples that came to my mind.

At Arizona State University, I had been immersed in an enthusiastic culture of behavior modification. People's behavior, we were taught, could be changed quickly and predictably by changing the contingencies and controlling stimuli in their immediate environments. In rat and pigeon laboratories, I learned to "successively approximate" or "shape" desired responses or patterns of responding. Both courses had been designed by Fred Keller, who was a master on many levels. I remember how impressed I was by our final exam in the pigeon laboratory. The teaching assistant randomly selected a cumulative response curve with three or four distinguishably different phases of response patterning (e.g., a steady but slow rate of responding, a steady high rate, an intermediate and variable ["troughed"] rate, and a declining rate). Our task was to take our pigeon to an experimental chamber and have it duplicate the test pattern by engineering the discriminative stimuli in the appropriate sequence. At the time, of course, I did not realize how much latitude the teaching assistants had in accepting our birds' variable compliance, let alone the extent to which my own behavior (thinking and feeling included) was being shaped by these structured experiences.

My graduate studies at Stanford offered incredible opportunities for expansion of my vistas and acceleration in my theoretical development. Bandura and I collaborated on several research projects that moved me into a cognitive social learning perspective and an interest in self-organizing processes. I learned clinical behavior therapy from Gerald C. Davison and John Marquis and I began some interactions with B. F. Skinner that led to a book (Mahoney, 1974) and a series of exchanges on the nature of science, psychology, and cognitive studies (Mahoney, 1989, 1991a; Skinner, 1987, 1990). It was a time of exciting change in the field. The cognitive revolution was gaining momentum, humanistic psychology was differentiating, and transpersonal approaches were emerging.

When I went to Pennsylvania State University for my first academic appointment, I was still a believer in brief therapy and a critic of the prolonged treatments associated with psychoanalysis and the insight-oriented therapies. But I was changing, and in ways that I had not anticipated or engineered. In the early 1970s, I realized that, despite a wonderfully enriching experience in graduate school, I was not well prepared for the diversity of challenges that I was encountering in my roles as a psychotherapist and clinical supervisor.[1] In the late 1970s, I decided to go into personal therapy (Mahoney, 1996), and I started enrolling in workshops focused on experiential approaches and alternative conceptual scaffoldings for psychotherapy. These experiences, combined with research and teaching, became a diversified and expanding base for my thinking, feeling, and practice. My clients and students have invaluably supplemented my personal experience, teaching me lessons that extended far beyond those I learned in libraries and laboratories.[2]

In the 1980s, I began to find myself differentiating between the rationalism that dominated North American cognitive therapies and the self-organizing constructivism that was more apparent in some Asian, European, and South American approaches. The main difference, it seemed, was that the rationalist therapies assumed that irrational, unreasonable, or unrealistic thinking lay at the heart of psychological dysfunction, which was equated with "feeling bad." Their main therapeutic strategy was to identify and change such patterns

[1]This should not have been surprising, since I had gone to Stanford University soon after the school had transformed its clinical program into one focused on "personality and experimental psychopathology." Hence, my coursework was not designed or intended to prepare me as a practitioner. I was fascinated by applied issues, however, and had sought out opportunities to develop my skills in psychological services by living in a community-based treatment center for children and volunteering for a noncompensated internship at the Palo Alto VA Medical Center.

[2]To accelerate and deepen my learning, I decided to confine my private practice to "difficult" clients, all of whom had previously been in therapy (two to eight times) and who presented with chronic patterns of distress or dysfunction. Since 1985, I have concentrated my private practice on practitioners in the health sciences, with special emphasis on psychotherapists at various stages in their careers.

of thinking, thereby allowing their clients to "feel good." The constructivists, on the other hand, were embracing more holistic and developmental metaphors that seemed to be less corrective and authoritarian in emphasis. Feelings and private phenomenology were not the effects of right or wrong (good or bad) thinking for constructivists. Indeed, they challenged the assumed boundaries between thoughts, emotions, behaviors, and somatic experiences. I found (and still find) myself more resonant with the constructivist perspectives (Mahoney, 1995, in press; Neimeyer & Mahoney, 1995). The distinction between rationalist and constructivist themes in the cognitive therapies has not gone unchallenged (Ellis, 1994), however, and there is continuing dialogue about its usefulness. At this time, I can only say that it has been helpful to me in clarifying and organizing my own experience as a psychotherapist.

## TIME AND CHANGE

How does this relate to my ideas about time? My time with Milton Erickson convinced me that a single session of psychotherapy can influence the course of a person's life. But what about the broader and deeper issues of time and timing in psychotherapy? Can a human life or a personal lifestyle be abruptly transformed? Does enduring change require a long time? How permanent can revolutionary changes be? These are questions that have fascinated me throughout my career as a psychotherapist. I still do not feel as though I have given anything resembling a final and satisfactory response, but I do feel increasingly more comfortable with some evolving approximations.

Can people change abruptly? Yes, I think so, but this kind of change is much more complex and difficult than I had originally thought. The issue here is not only one of plasticity—the magnitude of possible change—but also one of acceleration, or the rate of change. If that sounds complicated, it is because it is. I believe that time is important primarily as the dimension in which development unfolds. Humans are complex, self-organizing systems who strive to maintain their coherence (systemic integrity) while they deal with the challenges that emerge for them (Mahoney & Moes, in press). Among other things, this means that they are always in motion and striving for an elusive and dynamic balance between old and new patterns of experiential activity. They (we) are always changing in the sense that maintaining, regaining, or elaborating their sense of balance depends on lifelong exchanges within themselves and between themselves and the complex systems in which they are participants. This is, incidentally, a convergent implication of constructivism, feminist studies, and the sciences of complexity (Goldberger, Belenky, Clinchy, & Tarule, 1996; Kauffman, 1995; Masterpasqua & Perna, in press). The emergence of new patterns in complex, self-organizing systems is simultaneously resisted and yet virtually inevitable. From such a perspective, resistance to change is not an expression of self-defeating neuroticism. Rather, it is a natural expression of self-protection by a system struggling to maintain itself. The conditions affecting that dynamic attempt at self-maintenance are always changing, of course, and there are inevitable and unpredictable novelties that must be negotiated. Strategically, this means that psychotherapy is a collaborative endeavor in which therapists try to help clients to maintain their balance while they are dealing with or seeking new ways of being themselves. The demands on the therapist can be formidable, partly because each client's needs (for order or stability versus challenge and novelty) may vary considerably over both brief and extended periods of time.

Change takes time or, more accurately, change takes place over time. Indeed, there is no time in which we are not changing, even though we may not be aware of it. But there are also some times when we are changing more rapidly than at other times. This is the essence of the concept of acceleration, which was introduced by Isaac Newton to describe the rate of change in the velocity of an object. Humans are not objects in the Newtonian sense, however, and we should be careful not to confuse acceleration with improvement. Faster change is not necessarily better, and it is almost always riskier. My own changes, personally and professionally, have borne this out.

Likewise, there are important differences between relatively superficial and deep changes. For most people, changing clothes is easier than changing personal habits, and the most difficult changes are those involving self-concept. The more core the change is—the more central it is to personal meaning and a sense of personal coherence—the more there will be natural, healthy, and vigorous resistance. This is, perhaps, the cardinal paradox of complex self-organizing systems. We simultaneously seek both order (familiar structure) and novelty (new experience). We are open systems seeking a closure that, if it were achievable, would end our viability. While trying to maintain some semblance of a moving balance of the forces within and those impinging upon us, we lean into a hopeful posture that welcomes the kinds of peace and pleasure that are largely elusive. No matter, it seems. We are passionately intent on seeking them, and we glimpse them often enough in the meteorology of our moods that we remain not only faithful to the belief in their existence, but also devoted to finding them again and becoming their captors or captives. As the complexity scientists put it, we live precariously within a turbulent sea of chaos that is partly created by and sustaining of the ordering processes that are our essence.

To paraphrase, then, I believe that significant change takes significant time. The significance of the change and the significance of the time are not readily measured in chronological parameters. In other words, it is not the amount of time shared so much as the personal significance and, if you will, the timing of that time that are most important in determining its effects on interacting humans. I am an advocate neither of brief therapy nor of "interminable analysis" (Malcolm, 1980). Indeed, the actual number of hours logged in psychotherapy is much less important to me, and to many other therapists, than is the significance of the experiences that transpire during that time (Mahoney & Craine, 1991). Clients may well need years to elaborate the personal significance of the moments that they have helped to create in psychotherapy, but this is hardly an indictment of psychotherapy.

The time it takes to change—the time that people need to explore and ultimately enact new ways of being—is probably unrelated (or, at most, marginally related) to the length of therapy. What is important are those moments, whatever their content and form. It is in those moments that new patterns of experiencing are given opportunities to express themselves, and this is, after all, the primary goal of most psychotherapies.

## CONCLUSION

Brief encounters of the closest kind, human encounters, are undoubtedly capable of being life-changing events for the participants. In my session with Milton Erickson, the life-changing potential of our meeting was almost guaranteed by the fact that I was facing an imminent career decision, the consequences of which were neither clear nor calculable.[3] But brief moments that have nothing to do with imminent choices may endure as formative experiences. Words of encouragement, looks of compassion, moments of tense confrontation, shared observations, suggested working metaphors, maxims, smiles, hugs—all may become important moments in clients' and therapists' lives. In follow-up contacts with my own clients, I have often been surprised by what they considered most important in our interactions. They were often things I did not remember. I have seen some clients for single sessions only, some for a few sessions spanning several months, some for weekly sessions over two or three years, and many "episodically" (single sessions separated by long time intervals). Perhaps not surprisingly, I feel that I have learned the most from those clients whom I got to know very well and who stayed in contact for a long time. I also hope and believe that I was helpful to those whom I saw only once or very briefly.

Finally, what is, or should be, the relationship between the personal life of the psychotherapist and the quality or merit of his or her professional services? In my session with Dr. Erickson, I was worried that my own developmental struggles would get in the way of my helping other people. His words to me, which I construed as reassurance and encouragement, changed the course of my life path. What I did not know then was how deeply my life would be changed by that choice and that path. My concern had been about how a therapist's personal life might influence his or her clients. I had not even begun to fathom the other direction of influence—that is, how clients' stories and struggles might influence the therapist's personal life. There

[3]Milton Erickson's impact on my life and my style as a therapist is probably much more extensive than I realize. Like him, for example, I have preferred to see my clients at a home office. Moreover, I have often been gratified to be told by other practitioners that my therapeutic style is reminiscent of his.

is a reciprocity in human relationships that is undeniably present in psychotherapy. I am reminded here of Bugental's (1978) reflections on this theme:

> I am not the person who began to practice counseling or psychotherapy more than 30 years ago in an army hospital. And the changes in me are not solely those worked by time, education, and the life circumstances shared by most of my generation. A powerful force affecting me has been my participation in so many lives. A psychotherapist had best recognize that the profession will continually press on her or him to change and evolve. (p. 149)

Bugental's writings on authenticity and existential-humanistic issues have been both instructive and inspirational in my continuing development as a person and as a psychotherapist (Bugental, 1965, 1976, 1987, 1990; Mahoney, 1996). Indeed, the personal life of the psychotherapist has become one of my research and practice interests over the past decade (Guy, 1987; Mahoney, 1991b; Mahoney & Fernandez-Alvarez, 1995; Skovholt & Rϕnnestad, 1992). Survey data and clinical experience point toward the fact that being a psychotherapist is, indeed, a demanding challenge that places unique stresses on the practitioner. At the same time, however, there is also considerable warrant for the assertion that many psychotherapists experience accelerated psychological development and a deep sense of satisfaction deriving from their professional work. We do not yet know whether there are different stresses and benefits for therapists who practice brief as compared with prolonged psychotherapies, and the oversimplifications of these contrasts are important to bear in mind. We do know, however, that intimate participation in other people's lives is likely to change all of the participants, therapists and clients alike. The psychotherapy practitioner is, therefore, wise to acknowledge this complexity and to prioritize self-care and personal development in his or her own life.

I am grateful to Milton Erickson for his role in my life. Even though our interaction was brief, its effects were powerful and enduring. They were also positive in the sense that I have never regretted my decision to major in psychology or to become a psychotherapist. As I hope to have conveyed here, I am still so becoming, and I have been deeply enriched in the process.

## REFERENCES


Bandura, A. (1978). The psychology of chance encounters and life paths. *American Psychologist, 37,* 747–755.

Bugental, J. F. T. (1965). *The search for authenticity: An existential-analytic approach to psychotherapy.* New York: Holt, Rinehart & Winston.

Bugental, J. F. T. (1976). *The search for existential identity: Patient-therapist dialogues in humanistic psychotherapy.* San Francisco: Jossey-Bass.

Bugental, J. F. T. (1978). *Psychotherapy and process: The fundamentals of an existential-humanistic approach.* Reading, MA: Addison-Wesley.

Bugental, J. F. T. (1987). *The art of the psychotherapist.* San Francisco: Jossey-Bass.

Bugental, J. F. T. (1990). *Intimate journeys: Stories from life-changing therapy.* San Francisco: Jossey-Bass.

Ellis, A. (1994). *Reason and emotion in psychotherapy: Revised and updated.* New York: Birch Lane Press.

Goldberger, N. R., Belenky, M., Clinchy, B., & Tarule, J. (Eds.) (1996). *Knowledge, difference, and power: Essays inspired by women's ways of knowing.* New York: Basic Books.

Guy, J. D. (1987). *The personal life of the psychotherapist.* New York: Wiley.

Kauffman, S. (1995). *At home in the universe: The search for the laws of self-organization and complexity.* Oxford: Oxford University Press.

Mahoney, M. J. (1974). *Cognition and behavior modification.* Cambridge, MA: Ballinger.

Mahoney, M. J. (1989). Scientific psychology and radical behaviorism: Important distinctions based in scientism and objectivism. *American Psychologist, 44,* 1372–1377.

Mahoney, M. J. (1991a). B. F. Skinner: A collective tribute. *Canadian Psychology, 32,* 628–635.

Mahoney, M. J. (1991b). *Human change processes: The scientific foundations of psychotherapy.* New York: Basic Books.

Mahoney, M. J. (Ed.) (1995). *Cognitive and constructive psychotherapies: Theory, research, and practice.* New York: Springer.

Mahoney, M. J. (1996). Authentic presence and compassionate wisdom: The art of Jim Bugental. *Journal of Humanistic Psychology, 36,* 58–66.

Mahoney, M. J. (in press). *Constructive psychotherapy: Principles and practice.* New York: Guilford.

Mahoney, M. J., & Craine, M. H. (1991). The changing beliefs of psychotherapy experts. *Journal of Psychotherapy Integration, 1,* 207–221.

Mahoney, M. J., & Fernandez-Alvarez, H. (1995). The personal life of the psychotherapist. Unpublished manuscript, University of North Texas.

Mahoney, M. J., & Moes, A. J. (in press). Complexity and psychotherapy: Promising dialogues and practical issues. In F. Masterpasqua & P. A. Perna (Eds.), *The psychological meaning of chaos: Self-organization in human development and psychotherapy.* Washington, DC: American Psychological Association.

Malcolm, J. (1980). *Psychoanalysis: The impossible profession.* New York: Random House.

Masterpasqua, F., & Perna, P. A. (Eds.) (in press). *The psychological meaning of chaos: Self-organization in human development and psychotherapy.* Washington, DC: American Psychological Association.

Neimeyer, R. A., & Mahoney, M. J. (Eds.) (1995). *Constructivism in psychotherapy.* Washington, DC: American Psychological Association.

Rosen, S. (Ed.) (1982). *My voice will go with you: The teaching tales of Milton H. Erickson.* New York: Norton.

Skinner, B. F. (1987). Whatever happened to psychology as the science of behavior? *American Psychologist, 42,* 780–786.

Skinner, B. F. (1990). Can psychology be a science of mind? *American Psychologist, 45,* 1206–1210.

Skovholt, T. M., & Rϕnnestad, M. H. (1992). *The evolving professional self: Stages and themes in therapist and counselor development.* New York: Wiley.

# Ethics

# 3

# Ethics and Hypnosis: Unorthodox or Innovative Therapies and the Legal Standard of Care

*Alan W. Scheflin*

Hypnosis has enjoyed more than three decades of favor since the American Medical Association first endorsed it in 1958 as a valuable therapeutic technique (Council on Mental Health, American Medical Association, 1958). Only a few years earlier, *Time* (March 30, 1953) had reported the struggles of hypnosis to achieve respectability.

> Hypnosis has been a hard-luck kid among medical techniques. A century ago, it was just beginning to win acceptance as a pain-killer when ether anesthesia was discovered, and hypnosis was discarded. It was making a comeback 60 years ago when Freud hit upon the idea of psychoanalysis, and the experts again lost interest in hypnosis. Now, the third time around, it is once more winning the support of reputable men in both the physical and psychic areas of medicine. (p. 34)

Interest in the therapeutic uses of hypnosis grew in the 1960s and swelled in the 1970s, and by the 1980s, interest in hypnosis in the medical and mental health communities had never been greater. Zeig is correct in noting that "Ericksonian methods are probably the fastest-growing field of psychotherapy in the western world" (Zeig, 1985a). Today, however, although the numbers of people attracted to learning hypnosis is still growing, it no longer enjoys the virtually unblemished reputation it had established.

## HYPNOSIS UNDER SIEGE

In the 1990s, hypnosis has been under attack by several main assaults (Scheflin, 1994). The first began in the courts in the late 1970s (Scheflin & Shapiro, 1989), but because so far it has had no major impact on practicing therapists, its implications as yet have not been fully understood. The criticism here was primarily directed at the use of hypnosis for refreshing the memory of witnesses and victims of crimes. Police departments praised hypnosis as an investigative tool that could play a major role in solving crimes. Many hypnosis experts, however, argued that hypnosis inevitably contaminated memory and thereby resulted in tampering with or destroying evidence. After hundreds of court battles, most judges came to adopt a rule that automatically disqualifies a witness or victim from testifying about any matters remembered during or after hypnosis. This per se exclusion rule is based on the judicial perception that hypnosis always causes subjects to confabulate and to develop excessive self-confidence in the validity of their hypnotically refreshed recollections. Courts do not have a favorable impression of hypnosis when used with memory.

The second assault on hypnosis logically follows from the first, but it appeared more than a decade later. It claimed that therapists who work with hypnosis for memory retrieval have been unwittingly, and sometimes willfully, implanting memories of childhood sexual abuse that never actually happened. The hypnotic subjects then filed lawsuits against family members they now "remember" as molesting them as children. This false-memory attack broadened beyond hypnosis to include an assault on virtually all aspects of psychotherapy, with an emphasis on those therapists who work with dissociative disorder and/or trauma cases.

If hypnosis continues to draw disfavor in the courts and the media, therapy that utilizes the technique, especially with memory, will come under increasing forensic attack, an attack that already has scared, and may eventually frighten off, potential innovators.

At this crossroads in the history of hypnosis, this chapter seeks to make three points. First, innovators and unorthodox practitioners have never been given adequate legal protection in their efforts to advance the science and art of healing. That is still true today. More frightening, however, is the second point for those practitioners of mainstream hypnosis. The standard of care is rapidly changing, sometimes to the detriment of hypnotic interventions. In other words, every person who uses hypnosis must now be aware of ethical and legal dangers that were nonexistent a short time ago. Finally, for hypnosis ultimately to weather the attacks, the concept of manipulation by therapists will have to be addressed directly.

## THE NATURAL HISTORY OF FADS AND FASHIONS*

Sociologists have long recognized the value of studying fads and fashions in subcultures. As Meyersohn and Katz (1957) have noted:

> The study of fads and fashions may serve the student of social change much as the study of fruit flies has served geneticists: Neither the sociologist nor the geneticist has to wait long for a new generation to arrive.
>
> Fads provide an extraordinary opportunity to study processes of influence or contagion, of innovative and cyclical behavior, and of leadership. (p. 594)

Psychiatric diagnoses, treatments, and techniques, including hypnosis, have not been immune from the same rules of fads and fash-

*I would like to thank Dr. Edward M. Opton, Jr., a psychologist and a lawyer, for many insights in understanding fads and fashions in psychiatry. I have drawn upon two pages of notes that Dr. Opton (1974) prepared for revision, rewriting, and ultimate inclusion in Scheflin, A. W., and Opton, E. M. Jr. *The Mind Manipulators* (Paddington Press, 1978). The notes eventually were not used in that book.

ions that govern clothing styles or musical tastes because they, too, are fueled by prevailing social events. In the history of understanding and communicating about the brain, for instance, the influence of Darwin and hydraulics and quantum mechanics led psychiatrists to talk about unconscious stresses, breaking points, repression, and similar physical properties. The early 20th century introduced the new social phenomenon of widespread electricity and mass communication by telephone. Prevailing metaphors of the mind referred to it as a gigantic "switchboard" system with miles of electric currents handling incoming and outgoing messages. The computer age has brought its own perspective, with the brain now conceptualized as sophisticated hardware playing a nearly infinite variety of software programs. One judge (*Logan v. New Jersey Division of Mental Health and Hospitals,* 1995) recently noted that:

> An infant science in the modern world, psychiatry's growth and evolution has been rapid. Freud, the father of psychoanalysis, lived less than sixty years ago. Now, each decade brings with it new concepts, new classifications, and new or altered nomenclature. (p. 91)

These major shifts in paradigm bring major changes in thinking about old problems (Kuhn, 1962). As this thinking refines into treatments and interventions, the laws of fashion come into play. These laws are especially crucial when unorthodox or innovative therapies are challenged in court. Any fad in general, and psychiatric treatments in particular, must proceed according to a seven-step process.

1. *Invention (innovation).* The process of inspiration, or creativity, that generates the new idea normally begins with an insight based on (a) previous error, (b) an idea generated from the social or physical sciences now transposed by analogy to the study of the mind, (c) the presentation of an entirely new problem or phenomenon requiring explanation, or (d) a hunch.

Innovations in psychiatry often have come from people working at relatively elite institutions, or from those with sufficient resources or power to "sell" their ideas. Innovators generally must have a boldness to take risks and a sense of security to afford those risks. They must work under conditions where the ambiance encourages and rewards risk taking and the resources are sufficient to permit the necessary experimentation.

But innovators in psychiatry and hypnosis have also been people who were relatively unknown and without resources. This may be especially true with hypnosis, and it may account, in part, for why the hypnosis field is divided into two not fully integrated camps—the clinicians and the experimentalists. Especially recently, with regard to the attacks on hypnosis, these two camps have often been on opposing sides. The experimentalists lament the lack of anecdotal proof and the absence of structured control in the treatments offered by clinicians, whereas the clinicians resent the ivory tower lack-of-real-world experience in the artificial laboratories of the experimentalists. It is no surprise that at recent meetings of the American Society of Clinical Hypnosis (March 1996) and the Society of Clinical and Experimental Hypnosis (November 1995), special programs were presented to bring these factions together.

When innovation comes from the ranks, and not from the elite, it often faces a tougher struggle in its efforts to unseat the prevailing wisdom. The forces of the establishment rally against the upstart, who must then hope to have enough sustaining power to prevail. In this regard, the achievements of a genius like Milton H. Erickson are doubly remarkable.

When Erickson was an infant, his family traveled *east* by covered wagon (Haley, 1993a). From that auspicious beginning, he never stopped traveling against the current. In a moving tribute to his late friend, therapist Jay Haley has written that "Erickson's cases were as distinctive as a Picasso painting" (Haley, 1993b). His solutions to his patients' disturbances were so unique that therapists immediately recognize his singular stamp on them. What other therapist would have ordered his patients to get worse? To have relapses? To fail at certain tasks? (Haley, 1973).

Therapists swap Erickson stories with the same gusto that young boys trade baseball cards. "Did you hear about the time he had that man urinate through a tube?" "How about the time he had the mother sit on her son?" "Remember the phobic man who had to ride in an elevator with a very seductive young woman?" And the stories go on because there are so many of them, each more absorbing and baffling than the last.

While mainstream psychiatrists followed strict rules about dual relationships, Erickson would frequently have social contacts with patients outside the therapy room. Indeed, he would often arrange social situations to have a beneficial impact on his patients, and he would engineer to have friends, family, or other patients participate in therapeutic cures. At a time when psychiatrists were studiously taught to avoid making expressly direct suggestions to patients, Erickson could be quite authoritarian. The opposite is even more true. Part of Erickson's acknowledged genius was in his ability to influence people around him "indirectly."

Haley (1993b) has effectively shown that Erickson's contributions to hypnosis and therapy are so original that they appear to have no direct predecessors, despite the fact that most science rests on the shoulders of those who came before. The new generation alters, modifies, expands, contracts, and adapts old procedures into new techniques. But no one worked the way Erickson worked. He used hypnosis 30 years before medical associations validated the technique; he applied family therapy procedures decades before family therapy was created; he utilized techniques of sex therapy and systems therapy that were not officially recognized until long after he had developed them; he concentrated on quick solutions rather than long-term psychoanalysis; he attached great significance to presenting problems rather than searching for historical causes; he rejected the negative image of the unconscious and instead made it an ally in the healing process; and he developed techniques that are still being discovered and discussed.

During Erickson's career, legal actions against therapists were exceedingly rare (Brown, Scheflin, & Hammond, 1997). In today's litigious climate, however, pioneers are at great risk, even if their patients prosper. My fear is that the law will stifle future Ericksons by imposing too heavy a price on innovation. As already noted, storm clouds are gathering around hypnosis, thus making the therapeutic landscape more hostile where ethics, law, and innovation meet at the crossroads.

2. *Promotion.* Innovations become fads or fashions after they have been successfully promoted. Fame and fortune ride on the successful circulation of information about the process or technique. Initially, promotion begins with the selling of the idea to the profession's elite, who may then pass judgment on this new treatment. In many cases, however, fads and fashions may sweep through the therapy community despite the lack of endorsement of the profession's top figures,

who are often experimentalists and not clinicians. Thus, success at promotion depends on attracting the attention of either the elite or the masses. As Meyersohn and Katz (1957) have noted:

> The birth of a fad is really accompanied by two labels; the phenomenon is given a name, and it is named as a fad. The fad is defined as real and in consequence becomes so. (p. 600)

3. *Dissemination.* Fads generally follow a "trickle-down" process from the few who have "authenticated" it to the masses who will now use it. In the world of mental healing, there is great human pressure to innovate. As Opton (1974) has noted:

> The desperation of suffering patients and the felt responsibility of the physician/psychiatrist to "do something" combine to produce a readiness on the part of both to adopt new therapies even if—or especially if—they are poorly understood, unauthenticated, and smacking of magic or mysticism.

4. *Acceptance and routinization.* Once the fad has been disseminated, it becomes fashionable, if not necessary, to use it. This widespread use, however, often alters the original insight in order to tailor it for mass consumption, as Opton (1974) has observed:

> As a therapy becomes widely or universally accepted, it loses its charisma, its "magic" or "miracle" potency and much of its placebo effect. But although expectations shrink, the use of the therapy continues or even grows through routinization, the automatic employment of the remedy without much attention to its effects.

5. *Fading from grace.* By the time a new treatment has reached the average practitioner and has become a matter of routine, it has lost much of its glimmer. Meyersohn and Katz (1957) have observed that "when a fad has reached full bloom, its distinguishing features become so blurred that some are totally lost" (p. 601). Opton (1974) has expressed similar thoughts:

> When a therapy is no longer pushed as an innovation, when its promotion is no longer a route to professional prestige, when its dissemination no longer produces substantial profits, when

> expectations of its potency are no longer inflated, then it must stand or fall on its merits against the merits of older and newer therapies.

6. *Abandonment.* An old therapy that has been shown to be ineffective may still not be abandoned if there is no older or newer therapy to take its place. It is better to do something, even if unproductive, than to do nothing, as Opton (1974) has observed:

> The process of routinization usually prevents the displacement of a therapy by an older therapy, but it leaves the therapy vulnerable to displacement by newer therapies. The important exception occurs when an older therapy becomes so obscure and forgotten that its reinvention appears as a genuine novelty.

7. *New innovation.* Dissatisfaction with the innovation begins almost as it is first announced. Its birth triggers the necessity for its ultimate abandonment. After the older innovation gains acceptance and then becomes routine, "the self-conscious among the class-conscious will want something new for themselves" (Meyersohn & Katz, 1957, p. 601). Necessity will then once again become the mother of innovation.

While the progress inevitably entails innovation, for the first time in history, the legal threat to innovators, which has been steadily increasing, is now capable of stifling future innovators. In order to appreciate how the law may inhibit creativity, we must first explore how the law sets the applicable standard of reasonable care when unorthodox or innovative therapies are devised and practiced.

## UNORTHODOX THERAPIES

At what cost may a mental health professional use unorthodox or innovative therapies? In general, traditional practitioners in any discipline are held by the law to a standard of care reasonable for their profession (Shea, 1978). However, these standards of reasonable care have developed from the fact that a majority of practitioners have validated certain practices. In other words, a healer on trial for malpractice will win if she or he can show that a majority of healers would have done exactly what she or he did in that case. But what if a majority would not have so acted? By what standard can the law measure that which is not yet a generally accepted procedure?

Medicine, psychiatry, and psychology all have mainstream practitioners as well as avant garde theorists. This latter group raises a legal issue as to the proper standard of care for practitioners who utilize minority, or unorthodox, therapies. At the turn of this century, and for several decades thereafter, the law in general forced the unorthodox practitioner to deviate from majority doctrine at his or her own risk (Shapiro & Spece, 1981; Note, 1974). Thus, a complaining patient, or mental health review board, needed only show that the procedure or treatment was not one commonly practiced. This threat of absolute liability is indeed stifling, but it was offset by the fact that lawsuits against therapists for talking cures were virtually unknown. Healers occupied a position of respect and authority. Lawsuits against them were, from our current perspective, exceedingly rare. In today's litigious climate, however, the standard of absolute liability places a heavy hand on innovation and unorthodoxy.

To this rule of absolute liability, there was, however, one recognized important exception. The "two schools of thought" doctrine has been acknowledged in law since the last century. In *State v. Mylod* (1898), a Rhode Island Supreme Court opinion noted that "it is a matter of common knowledge that among medical men there are defined differences regarding the treatment of disease. These differences have resulted in different schools or systems of medicine." The injustice of measuring one school by the standards of the other was addressed in *Remley v. Plummer* (1922).

> The practitioners of a reputable school of medicine are not to be harassed by litigation and mulcted in damages because the course of treatment prescribed by that school differs from that adopted by another school.

The problem is well stated in a case involving a claim for medical malpractice. In *Chumbler v. McClure* (1974), the plaintiff, who was injured in an electrical explosion, was treated with Premarin by a Dr. McClure, a neurosurgeon. The plaintiff claimed that the drug treatments caused him injury and that the prescription of Premarin fell below the appropriate standard of care. The trial judge found in favor of the doctor, and the Court of Appeals, in affirming this judgment, noted that the trial testimony, at best, showed only that there was a difference of medical opinion about Premarin, and that Dr. McClure was the only neurosurgeon in Nashville using it. The court then formulated a test for evaluating unorthodox therapies.

> The test for malpractice and for community standards is not to be determined solely by a plebiscite. Where two or more schools of thought exist among competent members of the medical profession concerning proper medical treatment for a given ailment, each of which is supported by responsible medical authority, it is not malpractice to be among the minority in a given city who follow one of the accepted schools.
>
> Were this not true, an anomaly might occur where nine neurosurgeons in Memphis, Tennessee, prescribed Premarin for cerebral vascular insufficiency and where nine neurosurgeons in Nashville prescribed other treatment. Should one Memphis neurosurgeon move to Nashville and continue to prescribe Premarin, he might be liable for malpractice. Such a result would impose a standard of practice upon the medical profession which would be totally unsupported by logic and unreasonable in concept.

The two-schools-of-thought doctrine, also known as the respectable minority rule, acts as a complete defense in medical malpractice cases. In order to be able to assert the defense, however, a school of thought must prove that it is "respectable," which means that it has adherents who enjoy good reputations. One respectable school may not be judged by the standards of another respectable school. Thus, Freudians could not use Freudian theory to show that Jungians were mistaken in their treatment methods. As long as the school of Freud and the school of Jung are both respectable, the tenets of one cannot be used to evaluate the other.

Surprisingly, many states have not yet resolved the central question of whether the respectable minority rule, or two-schools-of-thought doctrine, is a quantitative or a qualitative analysis. If it is the former, an unorthodox practitioner would have to show that a "considerable number" followed the same approach. If the latter, the unorthodox practitioner would have to show that "respectable" people followed the same approach, even if their numbers were small. The Pennsylvania Supreme Court, in a survey of national law, recently answered the issue for that state by making the law tougher on unorthodox practitioners. Under the new test, the court combined the quantitative and qualitive analyses into a formula that states that the unorthodox practitioner would have to show that a "considerable number of recognized and respected professionals" endorsed the approach (*Jones v. Chidester,* 1992). Thus, unorthodox practitioners in Pennsylvania now must satisfy both a qualitative and a quantitative analysis before being deemed legally acceptable.

Courts have recently had several opportunities to evaluate warring schools of thought in the courtroom. In *Underwager v. Salter* (1994), two specialists in child sexual abuse and repressed memory sued for defamation when manuscripts and speeches were presented by the defendant-psychologist that disagreed with their viewpoint and criticized their scientific methods. The court concluded that the defendant honestly believed her criticisms of the plaintiffs to be true, and that she had a mountain of evidence to support that conclusion.

> Psychologists Ralph Underwager and Hollida Wakefield have written two books: *Accusations of Child Sexual Abuse* (1988), and *The Real World of Child Interrogations* (1990). They conclude that most accusations of child sexual abuse stem from memories implanted by faulty clinical techniques rather than from sexual contact between children and adults. The books have not been well received in the medical and scientific press. A review of the first in the *Journal of the American Medical Association* concludes that the authors took a one-sided approach: "It may be that the adversarial system has so influenced this discussion [about child abuse] that objectivity no longer has value.... When a given reference fails to support their viewpoint they simply misstate the conclusion. When they cannot use a quotation out of context from an article, they make unsupported statements, some of which are palpably untrue and others simply unprovable." David L. Chadwick, Book Review, in 261 *JAMA* 3035 (May 26, 1989).

• • •

> The monograph [by defendant Salter] is highly critical of the 1988 book and of Underwager's testimony. Like Dr. Chadwick's book review, the monograph states that the book misrepresents the studies, rips quotations from their context (and misleadingly redacts them), attributes to scholars positions they once held but have repudiated in light of more recent research, and ignores evidence contradicting its thesis.
>
> • • •
>
> [A]ll of the other reviews we could find take Salter's side rather than plaintiffs'.... Some judges have reached a similar conclusion. For example, the Supreme Court of Washington held that Underwager's analysis and conclusions are not accepted by the scientific community, making it appropriate for a trial judge to preclude him from testifying.... It may be that Salter, the judges, and the book reviewers all err in evaluating the Underwager–Wakefield work. Scientific truth is elusive. Nothing in this record suggests, however, that Salter either knew that she was writing falsehoods or feared that she might be doing so but barged ahead without checking.

The Court of Appeals was not comfortable with deciding scientific disputes between warring factions, and it expressed this discomfort in the following language.

> Underwager and Wakefield cannot, simply by filing suit and crying "character assassination," silence those who hold divergent views, no matter how adverse those views may be to plaintiffs' interests. Scientific controversies must be settled by the methods of science rather than by the methods of litigation.... More papers, more discussion, better data, and more satisfactory models—not larger awards of damages—mark the path toward superior understanding of the world around us.

Other courts have reached the same conclusion. In *Underwager v. Channel 9 Australia* (1995), the Ninth Circuit Court of Appeals upheld the right of scholars to use rhetorical phrases and hyperbole when discussing the viewpoints of other scholars on controversial issues. Even factual errors are permissible (not defamatory) if they are made without malice. In *Dilworth v. Dudley* (1996), the Seventh Circuit Court of Appeals held that the inclusion of the plaintiff's work in a book about mathematical "cranks" was not defamatory. According to the court:

> But anyone who publishes becomes a public figure in the world bounded by the readership of the literature to which he has contributed.... By publishing your views you invite public criticism and rebuttal; you enter voluntarily into one of the submarkets of ideas and opinions and consent therefore to the rough competition of the marketplace. (p. 309)

Another attempt to use the judiciary to debate issues of competing scientific views may be found in *Singer v. American Psychological Association* (1993), involving two specialists in religious cult mind control activities. Margaret Singer and Richard Ofshe sued the American Psychological Association (APA) and the American Sociological Association (ASA) in New York, and then in California alleging improper conduct leading to the apparent rejection by the APA and the ASA of the Singer–Ofshe viewpoint on cult brainwashing. Although the lawsuits were thrown out of court, they indicate an increasing willingness to draw judges into conclusions as to which school of thought is "best."

Yet another attack over warring philosophies may be found in the $40 million defamation suit brought by the Landmark Education Corporation against the Cult Awareness Network (*National Alliance,* 1994). The plaintiff was a San Francisco-based company that runs training seminars for businesses and groups. The defendant described itself as "a national nonprofit organization founded to educate the public about the harmful effects of mind control as used by destructive cults." In essence, the plaintiff claimed that the defendant labeled it a cult and spread materially misleading stories about its activities. At the heart of the case was a dispute about the legality and validity of cult indoctrination procedures.

A final example of the ongoing war of schools of thought in court may be found in the hundreds of cases filed involving "repressed" memory, "false" memory, childhood sexual abuse, ritual abuse, and/or multiple personality disorder (Brown, Scheflin, & Hammond, 1997).

These suits, which are ideological battles over which scientific theory is actually correct, are causing great harm. In the first place, judges are now deciding, inconsistently across the country and often within a particular state, which scientific theory is best. Thus, in one state an expert will be permitted to testify about repressed memory, and yet in the neighboring state, the same explanation of repressed memory will be excluded as "unscientific"! In some states, including New Hampshire, experts will be permitted to testify in one city and rejected in another. Second, because of this legal uncertainty and contradiction, practitioners of all minority schools now face a greater risk of legal liability than ever before. This enhanced risk unduly inhibits the practice of the healing arts.

Real pioneers, such as Erickson, face an even tougher legal battle because their methods, at the beginning, have no followers and no school. Their work must be tested as that of innovators.

## INNOVATIVE THERAPIES

Before a therapeutic treatment gets to be unorthodox, it must first be innovative. In other words, it must be invented, and then tested—somebody had to do it the first time to see what happened. Some pioneer must take the first step, but at what risk?

As noted earlier, the law has had a simple rule for healers using innovative therapies—deviate at your peril. During a less litigious era, this harsh rule might not deter bold experimenters whose innovations are essential for progress. Modern litigiousness, however, could serve as a deterrent to the evolution of new therapeutic techniques, especially if any deviation automatically results in a form of strict liability. Until a technique is fully tested, who may judge whether it was reasonable to use it? Indeed, if all other cures fail, is it not unreasonable to do nothing else? But what should be the standard of care for something previously untried and untested?

All the cases attempting to set a standard of care for innovative or unorthodox therapies have involved the practice of medicine, not psychiatry. Those cases that did involve psychiatric treatments also involved the use of physical force, such as beatings (*Hammer v. Rosen,* 1960), thereby triggering either intentional tort theories, such as battery, or complaints about the absence of informed consent (*Rains v. Superior Court (Center Foundation, 1984)*. No appellate court in the country has articulated a test for the standard of care that must be met by an innovator who does not use physical methods of treatment.

It may be suggested that therapeutic innovations should be measured by a standard that includes the elements represented by the following questions: (1) Are more mainstream treatments or procedures available? (2) Is this innovative procedure based on sound scientific principles? (3) Has this experimental procedure met ethical requirements? (4) Are experts available to testify that this innovative procedure is sensible under current knowledge? (5) Has the procedure addressed the patient's needs and best interests? (6) Has all care been taken to minimize harm to the patient from the new innovative procedure? It should be noted that the success or failure of the innovative procedure is a poor legal standard. Science progresses by reexamination of its failures. Theories become the basis of experiments (innovations), which then produce data that, in turn, suggest possible alterations in the original theory. The success of the innovation is too harsh a test for innovators, or for the patients who must rely on innovators for new cures.

Because clinicians face, as Erickson repeatedly emphasized, the uniqueness of each patient, Simon (1993) has suggested that "most clinicians are innovators, attempting novel treatment interventions according to the clinical needs of patients" (p. 473). Clinicians, therefore, as well as experimentalists, need a legal rule that does not stifle or smother therapeutic innovation.

## INNOVATION AND HYPNOSIS

The current attacks on hypnosis are accelerating the pace for resolving some of the more fascinating issues concerning therapeutic hypnosis. Perhaps the first constraint on innovators is the legal requirement of informed consent, a significant heritage from the Nuremberg trials in the late 1940s, which crafted the informed consent doctrine in the wake of Nazi medical atrocities. The doctrine now stands as a formidable monument to individual autonomy.

## INFORMED CONSENT AND THERAPY OUTSIDE THE PATIENT'S AWARENESS

The doctrine of informed consent works well with regard to physical medicine. A strong argument may be made, however, that it is antitherapeutic and unworkable when applied to mental medicine.

In a seminal article on informed consent with strategic therapies and hypnosis, Zeig (1985a) begins by noting the special ethical posture of hypnotic interventions.

> The field of hypnosis has been subject to more sensationalism and mystification than any other therapeutic methodology in the history of psychotherapy. This is due in part to both the fact that hypnosis has been associated with the loss of self-control, and the fact that hypnotic methodology often provides an opportunity for patients to change without conscious insight or rational understanding.

Should therapy be practiced outside the awareness of the patient? As psychologist and hypnosis authority Michael Yapko (1983) has noted, "Maneuvering the client into a position of accepting offered suggestions is evidence of the skilled use of hypnosis." This point is quite right and quite important. Just as a patient needs to be made ready for surgery, a patient also needs preparation for effective psychotherapy. This preparation is often outside the awareness of the patient. Because the therapist must subtly persuade the patient to accept the therapist's solutions, some therapists have recognized that patients are more likely to obtain lasting relief if they believe that they have solved their own problems.

The effectiveness of what Zeig (1980) calls "covertly eliciting unconscious processes," has been noted by Alan Mitchell (1960), a British psychiatrist.

> My main mistake was over-eagerness to tell the patient what was wrong with him. For instance, if I believed the paralysis of his arm was caused by hostile impulses, I would say so immediately. But the secret of successful treatment is entirely the reverse. It is better, even if many hours are required, to give the patient sufficient clues, so that, eventually, he will suggest the cause himself. (p. 50)

This point is well illustrated by a comment made to me in the late 1960s by Adrian Fisher when he was dean of the Georgetown University Law Center. Dean Fisher, who had negotiated treaties with the Soviet Union on behalf of the United States government, observed that the secret of international negotiations was "to get the other side to make an offer you could accept." If the offer came from those on the other side, they were much more likely to follow through. The art, or trick, is to maneuver the other side into making the right offer. A definition of diplomacy found on a T-shirt makes the same point, although rather more bluntly: "Diplomacy is the ability to let someone else have your way."

As Yapko (1983) observes, "Direct approaches increase the likelihood of arousing resistance to therapeutic maneuvers.... By dealing directly with a client's fears, doubts, and self-esteem, the risk of threatening the person is high and may arouse the need for some defense—'resistance.'" While direct approaches allow clients to feel involved in the therapy and cure, they also may tend to prolong, and perhaps defeat, the therapy by increasing the resistances to it. Consequently, it may be argued, the most successful therapy is therapy that is conducted outside of the awareness of the patient so as to prevent the creation of new resistances. The indirect methods of therapy, facilitated by indirect suggestions, are designed to bypass conscious resistance by working primarily on the unconscious level. As Zeig (1985a) has noted:

> Many clinical situations are not logical. Informed consent is based on the morality of logical, conscious self-control. However, symptoms by their very definition happen autonomously. It does not make sense to initially demand of the patient that they take logical, conscious responsibility for their symptoms when that is diametrically opposed to what they describe in their presentation. (p. 467)

Zeig's provocative article challenges the assumption that the informed consent model is beneficial in therapy. If his point is persuasive, with what can we replace the informed consent model as a standard of control?

The law provides an answer with the concept of "fiduciary relationships." The therapist–patient relationship is contractual and also one of fiduciary responsibility. A fiduciary owes undivided loyalty to the patient and must not do anything to harm the interests of that patient. Replacing the informed consent model with the fiduciary relationship model would impose but a single test on innovators, unorthodox practitioners, and mainstream therapists alike: Was the therapy performed in the best interests of the patients?

Another ethical issue involved in the discussion of informed consent and indirect suggestions is worth mentioning. Zeig (1980), in an article describing some indirect techniques, wrote: "If a patient is going to follow suggestions, then indirection is not necessary. In general, the amount of indirection necessary is directly proportional to the anticipated resistance."

While this point certainly makes sense, it also raises a question as to how a client can effectively communicate "No" when the therapist interprets every negative as the very resistance that must be overcome. Paradoxically, the more the client might *really want to resist,* the more hidden from awareness the therapeutic procedures become.

## IMPLANTING FALSE MEMORIES FOR THERAPEUTIC PURPOSES

One of the current attacks on hypnosis is that it encourages the implantation of false memories (Hammond et al., 1994; Scheflin, 1997a). In these instances, the complaint usually is not about the falsity of the memory, but rather about the use of this false memory to bring criminal or civil charges against someone who in the memory committed unlawful acts, such as sexual molestation. Thus, a false memory for a negative and unresolved experience moves from the narrative truth of the therapy room to the historical truth of the courtroom (Scheflin, 1996).

But what if the reverse situation took place? May positive memories, or memories that help resolve past conflicts, be hypnotically implanted for therapeutic purposes? Consider the following case related to me by world hypnosis authority Herbert Spiegel. During World War II, a soldier was brought to Dr. Spiegel for treatment. The soldier had been on the front line where he saw his best friend hit by bullets and then heard the friend call out to him, "Save me, save me." Meanwhile, the troop was retreating and the soldier was faced with the immediate choice of either saving his friend or going back with the retreat, leaving his friend there to die. He chose the latter course and became so depressed and guilt-ridden that he was dysfunctional. Spiegel used hypnosis to implant in the soldier's mind the sensation and visualization that he saw his friend actually die before the retreat. The treatment was successful, the issue of failing to save his friend no longer existed, and the soldier was soon fit enough to return to combat.

The treatment was successful, but it raises many profound questions. Was it also ethical? Is the implantation of false memories for therapeutic purposes ever ethical? Should it require informed consent? Is it possible to give consent to have false memories implanted? Naturally, if the soldier later went into a court of law, the false memories might produce false testimony. Should the narrative therapeutic session be limited or restrained by the possibility that a forensic hearing might be held sometime in the future? Must patients be forced to choose between their mental health and their legal rights?

These are hard questions, but important ones. Erickson's (Erickson & Rossi 1979; 1989) use of hypnotically implanted memories in the case of "the February man" has inspired some negative commentary (O'Hanlon, 1990; Singer, 1990), even though the technique had been widely known and used since at least the 1880s (Scheflin, 1997b). Gravitz (1994) has defended the practice in an article that traces its historical roots and discusses three current applications in which hypnotically implanted pseudomemories proved therapeutically beneficial. Gravitz concludes that the technique is very valuable in cases of severe trauma, but that it should be used with caution and not with certain patients.

Implanting false memories for therapeutic purposes may open up innovative avenues for handling severe trauma problems, especially in an age of brief therapy. Such implantation also raises some fascinating issues about the essence of the therapy relationship and the importance of historical truth versus narrative truth.

The recent attacks on hypnosis and innovation have come at precisely the point when hypnosis was beginning to address some of the most profound and important questions regarding its use.

## CONCLUSION

Modern attacks on hypnosis and on therapy all have an underlying objection—therapeutic manipulation. Therapists have been reluctant to admit their power over patients, and the need for their knowledge and skills in exercising this power. In a courageous and important article, Edgette (1989) faces directly the issue of manipulation by therapy. As she correctly observes, what else do therapists do? What else do patients want? Edgette observes that it would be impossible for therapists *not* to manipulate the therapeutic relationship. Her principle of therapeutic fidelity and benevolence, which is quite similar to the law's notion of fiduciary relationship, leads her to conclude that attacking therapists for being manipulative is a completely wrong approach. Instead, efforts should be made to develop guidelines for channeling the manipulation necessarily inherent in the therapeutic relationship along constructive pathways that always benefit patients. The interesting but formidable questions of assessing innovative treatments, working outside conscious awareness and informed consent, and implanting false memories for therapeutic purposes are worthy of a more extended discussion than can be given here.

During this era of attacks on therapy as manipulation, and the involvement of courts of law in how therapy is practiced, it may appear paradoxical to argue for thinking about permitting even greater manipulation. But the questions about legitimate innovation and treatment will not go away. It is time we all began to work on some very good answers.

## REFERENCES

Brown, D., Sheflin, A., & Hammond, D. C. (1977). *Memory, trauma treatment and law.* New York: Norton.

*Chumbler v. McClure.* (1974). 505 F.2d 489 (6 Cir.).

Council on Mental Health, American Medical Association. (1958). Medical use of hypnosis. *Journal of the American Medical Association. 168,* 186–189.

*Dilworth v. Dudley.* (1996). 75 F.3d 307 (7th Cir.).

Edgette, J. S. (1989). Tempest in a teapot: Ethics and Ericksonian approaches, In S. Lankton, (Ed.), *Ericksonian hypnosis: Application, preparation and research, Ericksonian Monographs No. 5.* New York: Brunner/Mazel.

Erickson, M. H., & Rossi, E. L. (1979). *Hypnotherapy: An exploratory casebook.* New York: Irvington.

Erickson, M. H., & Rossi, E. L. (1989). *The February man: Evolving consciousness and identity in hypnotherapy.* New York: Brunner/Mazel.

Gravitz, M. A. (1994). Memory reconstruction by hypnosis as a therapeutic technique. *Psychotherapy, 31,*687–691.

Haley, J. (1973). *Uncommon therapy.* New York: Norton.

Haley, J. (1993a). Milton H. Erickson: A brief biography, In *Jay Haley on Milton H. Erickson.* New York: Brunner/Mazel.

Haley, J. (1993b). Typically Erickson, In *Jay Haley on Milton H. Erickson.* New York: Brunner/Mazel.

*Hammer v. Rosen.* (1960). 7 N.Y.2d 376, 154 N.E.2d 756, 198 N.Y.S.2d 65.

Hammond, et al. (1994). *Clinical hypnosis and memory: Guidelines for clinicians and for forensic hypnosis.* Des Plaines, IL: American Society of Clinical Hypnosis Press.

*Jones v. Chidester.* (1992). 531 Pa. 31, 610 A.2d 964.

Kuhn, T. S. (1962). *The structure of scientific revolutions.* Chicago: University of Chicago Press.

*Logan v. New Jersey Division of Mental Health and Hospitals.* (1995). Superior Court of New Jersey, Mercer County, Law Division Docket No. MER L 001126-94 PW, Opinion of the Court, Judge Delehey.

Mitchell, A. (1960). *Harley Street psychiatrist.* London: G.G. Harrop.

Meyersohn, R., & Katz, E. (1957). Notes on a natural history of fads. *American Journal of Sociology, 62,*594–601.

*National Alliance.* (1994, October 6). CAN sued by Landmark Education Corporation. p. 4.

Note. (1974). Standard of care in administering non-traditional psychotherapy. *University of California, Davis Law Review 7,*56–83.

O'Hanlon, W. (1990). Book review: Erickson's shadow side: Is the pedestal crumbling? *Family Therapy Networker,* pp. 65–67.

Opton, E. M., Jr. (1974). Draft outline: The natural history of medical therapies. Unpublished Manuscript.

*Rains v. Superior Court (Center Foundation).* (1984). 150 Cal. App.3d 933, 198 Cal. Rptr. 249 (2nd Dist.).

*Remley v. Plummer.* (1922). 79 Pa. Super. Ct. 117.

Scheflin, A. W. & Opton, E. M., Jr. (1978). *The mind manipulator.* London: Paddington Press.

Scheflin, A. W. & Shapiro, J. L. (1989). *Trance on trial.* New York: Guilford.

Scheflin, A. W. (1994). Hypnosis: 1994 and beyond. *Hypnos, 21,*196–204.

Scheflin, A. W. (1995). The current assaults on hypnosis and therapy. Canadian Society of Clinical Hypnosis, Alberta Division. *News & Views* (Fall/ Winter).

Scheflin, A. W. (1997a). Hypnotic coercion: The CIA experiments. *American Journal of Clinical Hypnosis.*

Scheflin, A. W. (1997b). Narrative truth, historical truth and forensic truth: Implications for the mental health professional in court, In Lifson & Simon,(Eds.), *Practicing psychiatry without fear: A clinician's guide to liability prevention.* Cambridge, MA: Harvard University Press.

Shapiro, M. H., & Spece, R. G. (1981). *Bioethics and law.* St. Paul: West.

Shea, T. E. (1978). Legal standard of care for psychiatrists and psychologists. *Western State University Law Review. 6,* 71–99.

Simon, R. I. (1993). Innovative psychiatric therapies and legal uncertainty: A Survivalguide for clinicians. *Psychiatric Annals. 23,*473–479.

Singer, M. T. (1990). Book review of Erickson, M. H. & Rossi, E. L., *The February Man: Evolving consciousness and identity in hypnotherapy. American Journal of Clinical Hypnosis, 33:* 56–59.

*Singer v. American Psychological Association.* (1993). 1993 WL 307782 (S.D.N.Y. 1993) (not reported in F. Supp.).

*State v. Mylod.* (1898). 40 Atl. 753 (R.I.).

Time. (March 30, 1953). The uses of hypnosis. p. 34.

*Underwager v. Channel 9 Australia.* (1995). 69 F.3d 361 (9th Cir.).

*Underwager v. Salter.* (1994). 22 F.3d 730 (7th Cir.), cert. denied 115 S.Ct. 351, 130 L.Ed.2d 306 (1994).

Yapko, M. (1983). A comparative analysis of direct and indirect hypnotic communication styles. *American Journal of Clinical Hypnosis. 25,* 270–276.

Zeig, J. (1980). Symptom prescription techniques: Clinical applications usingelements of communication. *American Journal of Clinical and Experimental Hypnosis, 23,* 23–33.

Zeig, J. (1985a). Ethical issues in hypnosis: Informed consent and training standards. In J. Zeig (Ed.), *Ericksonian psychotherapy, Vol. I: Structures.* New York: Brunner/Mazel, pp. 459–473.

Zeig, J. (1985b). *Experiencing Erickson: An introduction to the man and his work.* New York: Brunner/Mazel.

# Conversations

# 4

# How Does a Non-Ericksonian Integrate Ericksonian Techniques Without Becoming an Ericksonian?

*Peter B. Bloom*

As creative therapists, we work by fusing the scientific underpinnings of our disciplines with our intuitive understanding derived from our clinical experiences. As we mature, we find our own voice as a therapist. Ericksonian techniques in trance induction and therapy are rich in nuance and complexity. Many therapists have hesitated to integrate Milton Erickson's work into their practices in fear that they might have to abandon the style and colouring of their own develop-

---

An earlier version of this Keynote Address given in Rome, Italy in 1991 is now published: Bloom, P. B. (1995). Come un ipnotista non-ericksoniano puo adottare tecniche ericksoniane senza diventare ericksoniano. Emanuele Del Castello & Camillo Loriedo (Eds). Tecniche Dirette Ed Indirette In Ipnosi E Psicoterapia. Milan, Italy: FrankoAngeli.
Also published in the *Australian Journal of Clinical and Experimental Hypnosis, 22*(1), 1–10 (1994).

ing therapeutic posture. This paper examines a variety of Ericksonian techniques and compares them with some examples of my own work over the years. I conclude that these techniques are easily identified and adapted to a variety of clinical approaches and that abundant opportunities exist for Ericksonians and non-Ericksonians to learn from each other's work.

Early in my training in internal medicine, before becoming a psychiatrist, I developed a strong interest in the doctor–patient relationship. I became intrigued with how to maximize bedside manner, how to create a therapeutic alliance, and how to understand common sense in these matters. My teachers had said, "One deals with patients by just following common sense." While I had such a sense, it seemed to be of a different kind and far from common when compared with the sense of some of my colleagues working with the psychological aspects of medicine. In those early years, moving from my residency in internal medicine to my residency in psychiatry, I continued to experiment with a variety of approaches to patient care that felt natural and were centered on my own developing ideas of how therapy works.

In the United States (and possibly Australia), many psychiatrists are leaning more and more toward the biological basis of medical psychiatry. We risk failing to teach our resident psychiatrists how to do psychotherapy. It was with great interest and enthusiasm, then, that I met with a group of psychiatrists, psychologists, and other interested professionals to talk about creative therapy at an Ericksonian symposium during the 5th European Congress in 1990 in Constance, Germany. In recent years, I have been watching the Ericksonian Foundation spread the name of Milton H. Erickson around the world and so I wanted to gain, at first hand, an impression of Ericksonian hypnosis because I was unsure of its relationship to Erickson's own work, with which I was quite familiar (Haley, 1967, 1973). I was surprised. This was not so much a symposium on hypnotic techniques, per se, as I had expected, but rather a creative discussion of clinical methods of psychotherapy. I was pleased because I had not been able to account for the immense popularity of the Ericksonian movement if it were, as I had believed, just based on popularizing Erickson's and his followers' own hypnotic techniques. It occurred to me, following this workshop, that the popularity of the Ericksonian movement was based primarily on offering a way of looking at and enhancing psychotherapy.

If this is so, why are Ericksonian and non-Ericksonian or traditional hypnotherapists at apparent odds with each other, seeming to describe different therapeutic strategies when both groups emphasize the value of psychotherapy?[1]

My interest in these issues peaked when I reviewed Michael D. Yapko's book, *Trancework: An Introduction to the Practice of Clinical Hypnosis* (1990). As I read his description of Ericksonian techniques and Yapko's own effective methods of psychotherapy, it occurred to me that the apparent differences between non-Ericksonian hypnosis and Ericksonian hypnosis become less obvious when perceived from the common ground of effective psychotherapy. Nonetheless, it continued to trouble me that the seemingly idiosyncratic Ericksonian nomenclature, which labels universal hypnotic techniques, is peculiarly distancing to me. It seems the Ericksonians are suggesting that we are talking about different things when I believe we are not (Bloom, 1991). The real danger, I believe, is that traditional hypnotherapists will not be willing to learn from Ericksonian hypnotherapists because of their perception that one must embrace an ideology, a school of hypnosis, and a radically unfamiliar frame of reference regarding psychotherapy. I hope I can argue the point that, in all our creative work, we are at our best when we use both Ericksonian and traditional approaches to hypnosis and psychotherapy.

I shall present four of my early cases, which I believe integrate therapeutic strategies from both the traditional and Ericksonian points of view. I shall argue that the clinical methods are similar despite the seeming differences in terminology. If they are similar, as I believe them to be, what conclusions can we reach in sharing our work about the true nature of psychotherapy more comfortably?

In the following, I present my cases in several categories. In the heading for each category, the hypnotic techniques associated with traditional hypnosis precedes the hypnotic technique associated with Ericksonian hypnosis. It is my hope that these cases will illustrate the effectiveness of hypnosis and psychotherapy, which depends more on the unique therapeutic needs of the patient than on the differences in

[1]Since 1979 when the term "Ericksonian" was first used in print in conjunction with the International Congress on Approaches to Hypnosis and Psychotherapy (Zeig, personal communication, 1991), the term "non-Ericksonian" or "traditional" has been used to describe those unfamiliar or unidentified with Erickson's own approach to hypnosis and psychotherapy. I use the terms interchangeably, although I recognize the inherent restrictions such labels may present for therapists who wish to develop their own creative styles.

terminology. I believe non-Ericksonians and Ericksonians alike can learn from each other to be more effective therapists without regard to the various ways each has of describing the process of therapy.

## CASE PRESENTATIONS

### PARADOXICAL INTENTION AND/OR NEGATIVE SUGGESTION

Paradoxical intention usually involves telling a patient to continue a behavior he or she already is doing in order to extinguish it. Negative suggestion involves telling a patient not to respond in a desired way in order to elicit the desired behavior (Yapko, 1990, p. 163). Indirect suggestions, currently popular in the Ericksonian movement, are by no means the only effective way to deliver a therapeutic message to our patients. Equally elegant and powerful in their effects are direct suggestions, such as paradoxical intention or negative suggestions. When a patient is confronted with a direct request to continue to do what he or she is already doing or to not respond in a desired way, such as trying to stay out of trance in order to go into one, he or she usually responds by stopping the behavior and adopting a more adaptive behavior to meet his or her primary needs. No one likes to be controlled and one is often willing to recover emotionally in order to remain in control of one's thoughts, mood, and behaviors. Thus, when used clinically, paradoxical intention, or its related term "negative suggestion," can be a powerful therapeutic modality. I will describe this process as I used it with one of my daughters and then with one of my patients.

My (then) three-year-old daughter was pounding her spoon on her dinner plate and screaming loudly while sitting with the family at the dining room table. Wishing to intervene for all our sakes. I smiled and said, "Diana, scream again, louder." She looked at me for a moment, and proceeded to scream and hit her plate with her spoon, but not quite as loud this time. When she caught her breath, I said, "Diana, scream again, louder!" She looked at me once more, and started to get down out of her high chair while screaming, again less loudly. We repeated this exchange a few more times until she had slowly made her way over to me and was cuddling in my arms, whispering a little scream. The results were clear. She got what she wanted, which was more close attention from me, and I got what I wanted, some relief from her screaming at dinner.

Paradoxical intention seldom, if ever, drives people actually to continue what they are already doing to their detriment. Most patients do not follow the commands literally, nor do patients paradoxically do the opposite of what they are currently doing with no more personal or psychological involvement. What this intervention does do is directly force the patient to face the issue of control and power, so that he or she finds it necessary to adopt a more adaptive means of coping with the actual need expressed within the behavior. My daughter perceived that a better adaptation to her screaming for attention would be to ask directly for the attention she wanted by coming to me for it. Whether it be called paradoxical intention or negative suggestion, this kind of "reverse psychology"—asking for more of the same behavior in order to extinguish it and to create the opportunity for more adaptive behavior—is a powerful tool and, incidentally, has been used by most successful mothers throughout the ages.

Another example of this kind of direct suggestion comes from my practice. I treated a young woman who weighed 180 pounds. She was single and beginning graduate school. When she came to my office, she said she felt like a "green-headed monster," a term representing her low self-esteem. We began psychotherapy and soon turned our attention to her excess weight, which she felt prevented her socializing with men. After six months of psychotherapy with no resulting weight loss, I was preparing to go on a long Christmas vacation. During our last session, I looked at her and said, "I am going to end my therapy with you unless, when I return from vacation, you have gained 20 more pounds and weigh 200 pounds. This new weight of 200 pounds will be my criterion for our continuing psychotherapy. If you will not lose, I insist you gain weight to demonstrate your ability to change." We looked at each other and, of course, talked it through thoroughly. The therapeutic alliance remained strong and, despite this very direct and demanding confrontation, a constructive sense of mutual collaboration was maintained. Nonetheless, it was serious therapeutic business. I was firm and I meant what I had said, and she knew it.

Was actual hypnosis involved? I am becoming less clear about when hypnosis is utilized and when it is not. I have thought for a long time that in all our psychotherapy, we use hypnotic techniques whether the patient is in or out of trance to help us through certain kinds of impasse. I suggest that this kind of direct suggestion has applications throughout our work. In any event, I went on vacation.

Today, I am sure I would never use the direct suggestion of paradoxical intention with a patient just before I was leaving town and so would be unavailable to her. I did leave, though, and when I returned, she was grotesque. She had acne on her face, she was swollen, and she weighed 198 pounds. She told me she had weighed 200 pounds two days before my return and she had become so upset she felt it imperative to lose weight. Even so, at 198 pounds, she could barely sit in my office chair. As she looked at me, she said she would never, never weigh that much again in her life. She then began to work in psychotherapy in earnest. It was a fascinating experience for me. I suppose I had not been fully aware of the risks that I had imposed on her, but as therapists, we do risk: we risk ourselves, we risk our patients. One hopes that these risks are in the service of the patient's care and not in the service of one's own ego.

Four months later, she weighed 135 pounds. Now thinner, she "discovered" in her apartment house a young man who had lived across the hallway for the past two years. He began talking to her and invited her to dinner. A year later, they were married and now have a child, and my patient practices social work. This intervention marked the turning point in our therapy: a direct suggestion to gain weight, and not just a simple suggestion, but a complex one involving paradoxical intention utilized in the context of a strong therapeutic alliance. I do not ever recommend taking a technique that works in the unique individual context of one patient and applying it to all patients. Suggesting weight gain is not a generic technique for weight-loss programs. But in some patients for specific reasons inherent in their psychotherapy, both non-Ericksonians and Ericksonians have techniques that can be enormously effective in working through therapeutic impasses.

## REORIENTING A PATIENT WITH ADDITIONAL USUALLY POSITIVE, OPTIONS AND/OR REFRAMING

Reframing is an Ericksonian word for, I believe, nothing more and nothing less than reorienting a patient with positive options. However, things are not always as they seem. In reorienting or reframing, entirely new perspectives on living can evolve.

## TELLING STORIES AND/OR USING METAPHORS

Telling stories or using metaphors that have meaning for patients is another powerful psychotherapeutic intervention that is enhanced in hypnosis. Both non-Ericksonian and Ericksonian therapists tell stories that have meaning and speak directly or symbolically to patients' problems. I am concerned when Ericksonians call stories metaphors, thereby creating different labels. Two labels describing the same process can create difficulties in communicating our experiences because it may be assumed by some that we are describing different phenomena.

## PATIENT OR CLIENT-CENTERED AND/OR NATURALISTIC APPROACHES; ACCEPTING RESPONSES, BEHAVIORS, AND RESISTANCES AS COOPERATION AND/OR UTILIZATION

These two techniques described by both non-Ericksonians and Ericksonians were used in the next case. A naturalistic approach involves taking cognizance of a patient as he or she presents, an idea Carl Rogers (1951) called client-centered therapy. The Ericksonian term "utilization" refers to resolving resistance to therapy by defining the patient's response and behavior as cooperation. To illustrate the use of these universal hypnotic techniques in the course of psychotherapy, I will present another case from my early practice.

I saw a 52-year-old black male accountant in a hospital consultation after his third heart attack. The first heart attack had almost cost him his life. His second heart attack had left him with hiccups, but he eventually recovered and reported taking his medications by a stopwatch during the day. He was an accountant who kept track of all the financial records at our local Veterans' Administration Hospital in Philadelphia. He was always on time and felt in complete control of his life. However, despite his sense of mastery and control, he suffered a third, his current, heart attack. Once again, he presented with intractable hiccups so severe that his physicians were considering surgically crushing his phrenic nerves in order to paralyze his diaphragm to prevent his hiccups, as everything else they had tried had been ineffective. Two days before his scheduled surgery, he asked for a trial of hypnosis.

When I went to see him, he told me he did not believe in hypnosis, but had asked for my consultation in order to delay and perhaps avoid the surgery. When I asked him what he did believe in, he said, "The only thing I believe in is my accounting skill and my ability to control my life with discipline." In the consulting room, I was joined by several residents in medicine waiting to see me use hypnosis with this patient. I felt awkward having to explain the challenge now presented to me.

In utilizing the patient's responses and behaviors while remaining aware of his resistances, I elected to alter my interventions accordingly. Keeping in mind his strengths and assets, I asked him if he were truly good at keeping records, and he said he was, of course. I asked the medical resident to obtain a stopwatch from the hematology department, and I requested the patient to write down every single hiccup he had during the day. He explained to me he had "singles" (which would be one hiccup), "doubles" (which would be two at a time), and occasionally "triples." I asked him to record with the stopwatch each and every hiccup he had during the day: singles, doubles, and triples. I looked him in the eyes and in a slow, steady hypnotic voice, I said, "And at the end of the day, *when you are finished* [emphasis mine], I would like you to add up all the time you have recorded that you have spent hiccupping: all the singles, the doubles, and the triples." He looked at me, absorbed in the process, and nodded his agreement. I told him I would return in two days to look at his record of his hiccup experience.

I had learned from interviewing the hospital personnel caring for the patient that his hiccups stopped whenever a nurse patted him on his back or shoulder. I also had learned that he did not hiccup at night while sleeping, thus supporting my sense that this symptom was a plea for attention, not solely a presentation of the damaged heart muscle irritating the adjacent phrenic nerve. When one empathized with this patient, his stress was easily understood: having three heart attacks despite following his physician's orders impeccably, and then learning he might have to undergo bilateral phrenic nerve crushes. Anyone would require attention and support, but this man could not ask for it directly. His need for attention was my working dynamic and provided the rationale for my intervention.

Two days later, I returned to his room to see how he was doing. I asked him how he had recorded his hiccups with the stopwatch and he replied that he had not used it. I asked to see his graph of his recorded hiccups and he showed it to me. It had only one entry: "Tried one more time with the nasogastric tube to tickle the back of my throat, hiccups stopped." He had recovered from his hiccups, avoided surgery, and avoided the onerous recording task I had given him. Was it a fortuitous last attempt with the previously prescribed therapy or was it related to my own intervention?

How might we understand his response? To the very end, he resisted our interaction. However, he knew psychologically from the moment I left his room on the first day that every future hiccup would be in "my presence"; that is, I would see the record in two days and review every recorded hiccup. Thus, he could imagine I would be with him all the time, lending my interest and support. My response to his need for attention would be nearly absolute. To maintain control over his freedom from recording his hiccups, his only solution was to give up the hiccups. Certainly, this was easier than the hiccup-recording work I had required of him. Most important, the hypnotic/behavioral message was clearly given in the phrase "at the end of the day when you are finished hiccupping." It was a powerful suggestion given this particular man in this naturalistic approach utilizing his every response to my intervention.

In the final analysis, patients utilize many resources offered them in critical times. The immediacy of surgery, the behavioral paradigm recognizing his need for attention, his disbelief in hypnosis, and the continued availability of the nasogastric tube all played a role. I believe, however, it was the psychological/behavioral/hypnotic intervention that tipped the scale toward recovery in this patient.

## THE MESSAGE WITHIN THE MESSAGE, OR METAMESSAGE AND/OR EMBEDDED MESSAGES

Human communication occurs on many levels. An interesting exercise in teaching hypnosis to professionals is to encourage practicing inductions without saying a word. Participants quickly learn to use breathing, body movements, and expressions better to convey hypnotic intentions to their subjects. Communication among family members often contains embedded messages that create great difficulty for our patients, requiring our interventions to promote healing. Treatment in these cases can also rely on using complex messages within the usual therapeutic interactions to promote a return to health. Let us examine another case in which traditionalists and Ericksonians would find common ground in understanding the presenting problem and choosing the treatment paradigm.

I saw an electrician who reported driving to another city to see his mother, who had suffered a stroke. After observing how ill she was and consulting with her doctors, he immediately sold her home and made a reservation for her in a long-term nursing home. Unexpectedly, she partially recovered, and when he came back to visit her, he told her what he had done. She said, "Can't you *see* what you've done?" Of course, in English, the word "see" also means "understand." Following this confrontation with his mother, feeling increasingly guilty for what he had done, he began to drive home from his mother's hospital to his own city many miles away. En route, the lights of the oncoming cars began to "break up," he experienced tunnel vision, and by the time he arrived at his home, he was hysterically blind. Shortly thereafter, he was admitted to our psychiatric hospital. First, his eyes were examined by a qualified ophthalmologist, who found them normal. Then we turned our attention to his mother's statement, "Can't you *see* what you have done?" The message within the message or the embedded message is always a challenge and of interest to tease out. Treatment was designed to reverse the development of his psychosomatic presentation by symbolically treating his eyesight and helping him integrate his mother's new physical status. We began by preparing some very warm saline soaks. I put them on his eyes and held them there for about 20 minutes. Later that day, the nurse followed my example and told him that, gradually, with these warm saline soaks, he would be able to regain his vision. Simultaneously, I began talking with him about how reasonable his actions had been in putting his mother into the nursing home. On integrating this insight and in response to our ministrations, he recovered both his vision and his composure and went home. Messages within messages: One doesn't need to be either a traditionalist or an Ericksonian to utilize these techniques that are common to all effective therapy, no matter what the particular persuasion of the therapist.

## ACCEPTING RESPONSES, BEHAVIORS, AND RESISTANCES AS COOPERATION AND/OR UTILIZATION

I was asked to see a young woman who heard her mother's voice saying "No" each time she tried to consummate her sexual relationship with her fiance. While this was her only hallucination, she was in her third engagement. As a strict Roman Catholic, she was ambivalent about sex before marriage, but was eager to resolve this difficulty before her wedding.

During the third month of therapy, she began her session saying, "Two men at work have asked me to go to bed with them." As she was sitting down, I turned away from her chair and "imagined" I saw a ticker tape machine (those machines that had a thin strip of paper coming out, allowing one to read the news or the stock market reports). I "reached" for the pretend tape noting she was in trance and was staring at it too. As I "pulled" it out, I "read," "The United Stated Public Health Service has warned all young women not to sleep with these two men because they have contracted the most severe case of syphilis ever reported." After continuing to note her full absorption and involvement in this spontaneous process, I "took" the tape in my hand, while she continued to stare at it in trance. I then "reached" for a pair scissors and cut the ticker tape. As I held it toward her, she spontaneously opened her purse, I dropped it in and she closed the purse.

When we do this kind of spontaneous work, when we follow our own creative impulse, we should constantly check, in a secondary process, to see if it fits the context of the overall therapy. My plea is to encourage us not to block these moments of creativity, but to see if what transpires seems right for that particular patient at that particular moment and that the process of therapy seems to flow by using this intervention.

Two minutes of therapy had elapsed and we had 58 minutes left in the hour. I decided not to discuss this interaction. We talked about the Christmas holidays and how, as an airline flight attendant she could fly at no cost from Philadelphia to Dallas to do her shopping. We managed to get through the therapy hour without referencing this earlier therapeutic interaction. As she got to the door, she turned, patted her purse, and looked at me and said, "Thank you."

The shared image of the ticker tape was a symbol for saying "No": a symbol she accepted and received in her purse. Once she had the inner resources to freely say "No" to the men at work, she could tap the same resources freely to say the more desired "Yes" to her fiance. Over the next several weeks, her mother's hallucinated voice began to recede, then finally disappeared. My patient began an emotional and physically balanced relationship with her current fiance. They were married six months later and my wife and I danced at their wedding. In a long-term follow-up, 12 years later, she called to ask for a referral to a good pediatrician for her children. I asked if she remembered the session in my office involving the ticker tape. She said she did not remember much of anything that we did, but felt much better and thanked me. It seems the patients with whom we are most successful will not be able to describe their therapy in detail. Often, there are no remembered techniques, only the awareness of intensely shared experiences that helped (Bloom, 1989, 1990).

## CONCLUSION

These examples from my early practice highlight the power and complexity of direct suggestion, indirect suggestion, and the use of a shared imagery and shared trance. Therapy is based on the use of observation and the freedom to be creative with each patient, irrespective of technique. During a visit with Milton Erickson in 1972, I asked him for the one word he would suggest that I remember for my lifetime in order to enhance my ongoing growth as a psychiatrist. Erickson immediately replied, "*Observation.*" He said, "*If you observe your patients and yourself, you will have all the data you will ever need.*"

It is my opinion that the Ericksonian labels describing the various interventions of psychotherapy have little to do with real differences, but constructively serve to organize certain kinds of thinking for some clinicians about how therapy works. "How a non-Ericksonian therapist can use Ericksonian techniques without becoming an Ericksonian" contains a deep admonition that none of us should become traditionalists and none of us should become Ericksonians. We can learn from our own feelings and insight what therapy is, based always on the context of our rigorous training. When training and intuition fuse, my understanding of how to do therapy becomes "just opening my mouth and letting it come out" (Bloom, 1989, 1990).

I encourage each of you to have the freedom from doctrine to be yourself and to learn directly from your patients. Ericksonian techniques are useful. We should learn from them and adopt those that fit our style. We should do this, not in the service of becoming an

Ericksonian or in the belief in Erickson's special importance, but in the ever-evolving free application of our knowledge and art in the service of each patient who seeks our care.

## REFERENCES


Bloom, P. B. (1989). The art of medical hypnosis and therapy. *Hypnos, 26,* 64-75.

Bloom, P. B. (1990). The creative process in hypnotherapy. In M. L. Fass & D. Brown (Eds.), *Creative mastery in hypnosis and hypnoanalysis: A festschrift for Erika Fromm* (pp. 159-168). Hillsdale, NJ: Erlbaum.

Bloom, P. B. (1991). Some general comments about Ericksonian hypnotherapy: *American Journal of Clinical Hypnosis, 33,* 221-224.

Haley, J. (1967). *Advanced techniques of hypnosis and therapy: Selected papers of M. H. Erickson.* New York: Grune & Stratton.

Haley, J. (1973). *Uncommon therapy.* New York: Norton.

Rogers, C. R. (1951). *Client centered therapy: Its current practice, implications and theory.* Boston: Houghton Mifflin.

Yapko, M. D. (1990). *Trancework: An introduction to the practice of clinical hypnosis* (2nd ed.). New York: Brunner/Mazel.


# Discussion: How does a Non-Ericksonian Integrate Ericksonian Techniques ... ?

## *Comments by Stephen Lankton*

My first thought is that you are correct in believing that your presentation is an important contribution for uniting an unnecessary schism in the field. On the other hand, it does serve to perpetuate the schism in at least two subtle ways. These are subtle because one is probably due to something akin to an unconscious bias and the other to a trend in misunderstanding that still exists. Here is how I view it.

The most distressing thing I read was the thread of bias that you continue to perpetuate while trying to reduce the same consciously. It seems as if you have an unconscious bias that is a bit like the bias that was evident in my speech when I told a story to my supervisor regarding a fearful incident I had in 1968. The supervisor confronted me and helped me correct the way I spoke so as to eliminate the implied bias. For example, you comment: "I am concerned when Ericksonians call stories metaphors, thereby creating different labels." Are you not concerned when non-Ericksonians do this? There are several books by professionals who do this very thing and do not identify with Erickson's work at all. When someone who never met Erickson criticizes Erickson's students and Erickson himself, and is most certainly non-Ericksonian by any account, calls stories metaphors, are you not concerned? If you are equally concerned, then why the use of the term "Ericksonians"? Is it not promoting an unconscious bias in favor of the unnecessary schism? That is my primary concern.

The basic point of calling techniques Ericksonian is that he, more than anyone else I know (and, as you recall the reference, even Margaret Mead knew), brought techniques of rhetoric into therapy and kept such oral traditions alive in this century in a medical and therapeutic context. His major contribution did not lie in technique, however, but in the approach he provided to understanding people and their problems.

My second concern is that most people seem to trivialize Erickson's contribution as a set of techniques concerning which they have some fear and about which they question the research (as if everything they said was supported by research) while blindly labeling clients, hiding behind the barriers of "resistance" they themselves build, and taking authoritarian/expert stances with their clients, and doing so unknowingly without research to support their efficacy. Nevertheless, Erickson's approach is not built on a set of techniques. It is easily and often recognized by a set of techniques. But techniques alone will not a good clinician make and "Ericksonian" techniques will not an Ericksonian therapist make. So, the paper distresses me a little since you blur this issue and perpetuate the misunderstanding that "Ericksonian equals some sort of unique techniques." Then you show that the techniques are not unique, thus making the distinctions between versatile therapists and Ericksonians vanish in a puff of logic. However, the logic is based on some false premises. It seems that you yourself recognize this in the latter part of the paper, but it did not prevent you from exploiting the misunderstanding to make your comparisons throughout most of the text.

A few technical aspects need some correction. The term "utilization" is a broader term as defined and demonstrated by Erickson. However, one of the uses of the term is as you have stated. Yet another meaning is the retrieval and reliance on existing experiential resources that may not be "on the surface" of the immediate moment in therapy.

Another point is that the idea of paradoxical intention was a therapeutic intervention that seems to have been developed independently by Milton Erickson, John Rosen, and Viktor Frankl. It does embody more than merely negative suggestion, as I understand the interventions. I also think the term "reframing" is slightly more meaningful than orienting the client in a positive direction, but it does include this aspect.

It might be better to rest your arguments on the works of some others beyond those presented by Dr. Yapko. Although he is very thoughtful, well meaning, and articulate, there are many other discussions of Erickson's approach that would round out the picture.

Again, the major departure point is how the techniques fit into an overall approach to helping people change and conceptualizing problems in the main. Erickson was goal oriented, future oriented, health (nonpathology) oriented, participation oriented, change (not insight) oriented, interpersonal (not intrapsychic) oriented, and so on. Of course, others were so as well—perhaps Rogers and Sullivan, among many others. Yet, in one single package, he seemed to have integrated these values and perspectives in a remarkably focused manner and carried that package to the fields of hypnosis and individual and marital/family therapy. I realized after about three years of study with Dr. Erickson that one could fairly well predict the outcome of the interventions he used with clients (or you used, say, with the hiccuping client). Certainly, it is easier to notice the therapeutic effect after the client responds and then to hypothesize why the client responded to the intervention.

The difference in Erickson's approach lies, in part, in the high degree of accuracy of the prediction. That is, conceptualizing how the client will respond to the intervention and why the client will so respond before the intervention is made (and being willing to be wrong and readjust, of course) is a difference in approach. This assessment skill is the result of a paradigm shift in how clients and problems were viewed in the therapist's mind—and this is the major difference between Erickson's approach and the prevailing approach in therapy. It is based on how one prioritizes such things as client resources, needs, and developmental demands. This is the most important aspect of Erickson's contribution to therapy, in my opinion. The so-called Ericksonian techniques come quite naturally when the client and the problems are viewed through such a lens. That is why I say that the techniques are secondary to the paradigm.

The reliance on the term "Ericksonian" seems to have frightened some clinicians because of its unfamiliarity; scared some owing to economic, territorial, and political threats; and left many others simply awaiting clarification. The obfuscation created by those who attacked his work out of fear has successfully, or almost successfully, left its mark on the psyche of many. The unconscious bias of your paper in attempting, on the one hand, to heal and, on the other, to perpetuate bias is an example. But overall, I think you have done a great service in taking this step to bridge the gap. Perhaps it is best bridged by dealing with the true misunderstandings whenever the professional community can actually discuss things in a spirit of nonthreatened cooperation in working toward the common goal of promoting health for clients.

In closing, I again want to put these comments in perspective. Most readers will analyze your paper with less rigor. Your cases are handled very creatively. I agree with your analysis. Readers should applaud your earnest attempts to help heal the rift that you set out to heal. I hope my comments can improve your future ability to reach that goal.

## *Comments by Carol Lankton*

First, I applaud your undertaking. This matter of being Ericksonian has always presented quite a paradox. Erickson, himself, would probably be the first to reject any such notion. For me, the beauty of what is called "Ericksonian" is that it celebrates the unique, the positive, and the creative problem-solving, health-seeking resources of all, clients and therapists alike. There is no one way to be Ericksonian. It is, moreover, a permission and encouragement to be oneself. You say that therapists fear they would have to abandon the style and coloring of their own developing therapeutic posture in order to integrate Erickson's work. I think the opposite is more realistic—they would have to abandon blind reliance on any preconceived or prearranged way of doing therapy and instead develop their unique style and coloring and therapeutic posture. This would in effect, be different with each client due to the uniqueness therein and the necessity to alter one's style to best discover that client's needs and resources. This could seem somewhat daunting, however—a pressure to be oneself.

That ties into your comment that "traditional hypnotherapists would not be willing to learn from Ericksonian hypnotherapists because of their perception that one must embrace an ideology, ... and a radically unfamiliar frame of reference regarding psychotherapy." Steve's comments emphasized the point that it wasn't so much Erickson's techniques that make his work so important, but the legacy of his approach and his way of perceiving people and how they learn, grow, and change. And in a manner of speaking, this way of thinking about people and psychotherapy does constitute a frame of reference that is radically different from tradition. It is, in fact, the paradigm shift that is much bigger and encompasses much more than Erickson or Ericksonian. However, it is impossible to integrate a few of Erickson's techniques or to do therapy in an Ericksonian manner without embracing that paradigm shift. This ideology, as it is called, or paradigm shift is sometimes and loosely used synonymously with the label "Ericksonian" simply because Erickson was a key figure who embodied, represented, and called attention to it. But when he was guided by those expectations and beliefs about people, their resources, and how they could change, he wasn't calling it Ericksonian. And I don't call myself Ericksonian when I'm doing that either, although Erickson's work was the key piece that inspired my developing those foundation beliefs about people, no matter which, if any, "technique" of therapy I am using.

I agree that there needs to be a deemphasis on labels for interventions, whether Ericksonian or otherwise generated. Also useful would be a deemphasis on techniques that therapists of any persuasion use with clients, in favor of a cocreation between clients and therapists to create a unique and mutually desirable outcome. And while I respect the preference not to call ourselves anything, "traditionalists" or "Ericksonian," somehow the title of the paper seems to suggest that it is a problem to be Ericksonian—almost as though it is a disease of some sort, rather than just an unnecessary label that unduly restricts and reduces (like most labels do). Perhaps you simply refer to reluctance to glorify an individual or to the fear therapists might have that it is complex or difficult to become Ericksonian. But it is a little ambiguous and stimulates the question: What would be so wrong with becoming an Ericksonian?

I basically agree with the thrust of your presentation and know that Erickson would join you in encouraging everyone to have the "freedom from doctrine to be yourself and learn directly from your patients." You add that Ericksonian techniques are useful and that we should learn from them and adopt them, but I would edit that to read that the mind-set or world view that has been characterized as Ericksonian is useful and we should adopt that into our personal style. The techniques will logically flow from that, guided by each unique circumstance. And I heartily agree that the purpose of such a shift is in no way to believe in Erickson's special importance. Again, I am sure he would be the first to reject that and to instead emphasize that the purpose is to believe in, expect, and respect the special importance and capabilities of each individual—just as you did.

## *Response by Dr. Bloom*

In preparation for this response to your thoughtful comments, I read the cited chapters in both the *Handbook of Clinical Hypnosis* (Matthews, Lankton, & Lankton, 1993) and the *Handbook of Family Therapy* (Lankton, Lankton, & Matthews, 1991). I have also given a great deal of thought to how best to express my enthusiasm for what you both have said, while retaining some of the freshness of my initial critical reactions and what I subsequently learned from them.

Your first point, Steve, is that I might be perpetuating an unconscious bias in that I seem to suggest that Ericksonians may be unique when I suggest they call stories metaphors while not being concerned that "non-Ericksonians (might) do this (too)."

I had initial trouble with this paragraph when I wrote it. I ran the whole article past Roxanna Erickson Klein, who wrote me, saying, "Metaphors are different from stories. Stories can be distractions, entertainment, time fillers, and so on. Metaphors (on the other hand) speak to the unconscious by directly or indirectly addressing issues that need (tending to). All metaphors are stories, but some stories are just stories. Dad used both stories and metaphors. . . ." (October 1993).

While I like her response, I admit I am still confused about the many definitions of metaphors. When you yourself go beyond the dictionary definition and define metaphor as "a story with dramatic devices to capture attention and provide an alternative framework for the listener to develop novel experience," additional elements are introduced that for me do not address the dictionary definition that a metaphor is "a figure of speech in which a word or phrase that ordinarily designates one thing is used to designate another, thus making an implicit comparison. . . ." (*American Heritage Dictionary,* 1992).

Even though you state that you and Carol have made a "clearly stated definition that (you) are using the term beyond that of a dictionary definition," I am leery to go beyond dictionary definitions for fear of developing neologisms, that is, words with special meanings that only a few may understand. I know that implicit comparisons may allow new learning in patients, but do they lead to novel experiences per se? While we are probably closer than we imagine to saying the same thing, I try always to remain grounded in everyday language to enhance my communication with my patients and nonhypnosis colleagues. I empathize with your own editors in your family therapy chapter when they, too, state, "It fascinates us to see how (and how often) linguistic differences between therapists can lead to the impression of actual differences in clinical conceptualization." (Lankton et al., 1991, p. 247)

But one thing truly bothers me more than learning to appreciate what the others mean in these special instances. My first reading of your initial point angered me. Your suggesting an unconscious bias on my part felt out of place in an academic discussion. But, on reflecting further on what actually made me feel so strongly, I came to realize that you may have inadvertently hit one of my sensitive "buttons," which you could not have anticipated.

For many years working integrally as a senior psychiatrist in a very psychoanalytic institution, I have always been concerned that we mental health clinicians, perhaps especially those of us who are psychiatrists, may believe we know what is best about the unconscious drives, motivations, and therapeutic goals of our patient/clients. I now use the word, "unconscious" as my analytic colleagues would, and as I believe you did in your example to me, and not in Erickson's use of the word that is more comfortable to you and me in our clinical work. The "I know more about your unconscious mind that you do" stance that much of analytic therapy is built on simply appears to be a form of therapists' arrogance in their relationship with their patient/clients and colleagues.

While I will be happy to elaborate on these concerns in the future if you like, may I suggest that, in our future discussions (which I hope will be many), you just say to me, "Hey, Peter, I think you are missing something here that may be very important to consider, or do you have some ideas or reasons you would like to expand on or share?" There were indeed many contextual reasons for writing the paper as I did, which I would like to share with you. But, even so, I do value your comments and regret even a "subtle" perpetuation of the "schism" that it may have engendered.

Regarding the context in which the original article was written, several opportunities shaped my presentation immensely. Jeff Zeig and I were on the same panel for the first time ever in Rome in 1991, when I first gave the paper. We were debating "Direct and Indirect Techniques in Hypnosis and Psychotherapy" organized by Camillo Loriedo. It was a vigorous discussion and I was to take the role in support of direct techniques. I decided to identify myself for the sake of the panel as a member of the "traditionalist camp" and be provocative for discussion. My hidden agenda was to use this opportunity to reach out with an olive branch, as it still is. Yet I really do not like to be identified primarily with either group. I wrote that the title itself "contains a deep admonition that none of us should become traditionalists and none of us should become Ericksonians. We can learn from our own feelings and insight what therapy is, based on the context of our rigorous training." (See p. 76 in this chapter.)

Regarding your next concern, I must agree that the use of the word "technique" rather than the more proper emphasis on "process" of the therapeutic interactions is well taken. As I explained earlier, it came out of Camillo Loriedo's conference title, which was in fact, comparing direct and indirect techniques. While I had to respond to the conference title and did so in the paper, I believe therapy is a seamless moment-to-moment interaction involving many attributes of the therapist and the patient. So-called techniques that work for one patient often are not useful for other patients. Erickson was a master at this and I hope my own case examples suggest that I practice what I am now preaching.

When you suggest that this awareness on my part did not stop me from "exploiting the misunderstanding to make (my) comparisons throughout most of the text," I must disagree. However, I do agree that the title is provocative. It was purposeful to get the attention of both groups. Yet, when I give the paper in person, the audience can see the affection I have for Erickson and for those who creatively model themselves on his work, and the affection I have for all the other therapists who are also on their own journey as maturing clinicians. Exploiting is just too harsh a word. I think most readers will not be confused about issues of writing style and accept my true views about the role of techniques when I state, "Therapy is based on the use of observation and the freedom to be creative with each patient, irrespective of technique."

Your description Erickson's work is beautiful. In fact, in your chapter in the *Handbook of Clinical Hypnosis,* the concluding paragraphs are the best description of Erickson's therapy I have ever read. On a personal note, my own work was heading in that direction and fortunately I found a personal therapist who embraced the same philosophy. When I first heard a tape of Erickson presented by Jay Haley to a group in Philadelphia, I rejoiced that I was not alone anymore. When my wife, Marcia, and I visited him in 1972, Erickson expressed his pleasure that we had so much in common while encouraging me to continue developing my own unique style. Your description of his style rings very true to me and I thank you for verbalizing it so nicely.

Steve, I will save your three additional technical points for later discussions for the sake of brevity. I was very happy you took what I said seriously. I will take what you said constructively.

Now to you, Carol. Your letter begins with a beautiful statement that to be Ericksonian is to declare you are "abandoning blind reliance on any preconceived or prearranged way of doing therapy...." If the term "Ericksonian" could more explicitly embrace the concept that it means becoming more your own self, what a beautiful tribute to him. Perhaps I am taking the debate more literally than necessary, but I think for me it may be easier to encourage people to be themselves without involving Erickson's work. It seems that too many young clinicians do not want the hard work it entails. However, for those who are willing to become more fully themselves as therapists, Erickson can become a major life inspiration—as he was for me.

I like what you said about Erickson's legacy lying not in techniques but rather in his "approach and his way of perceiving people and how they learn, grow, and change.... the paradigm shift that is much bigger and encompasses much more than Erickson or Ericksonian." I wish I had said that!

You suggest that my discussion stimulates the question: What is wrong with becoming an Ericksonian? That goes to the heart of it, doesn't it? Let me try a first answer, but I will need more time to think about it. I work in a psychiatric hospital with over 285 psychiatrists! We have about 200 mental health beds and very large private outpatient practices, both on campus and in Philadelphia and surrounding area suburbs. We have three analytic institutes and there are six medical schools in our city. In the various Philadelphia universities, behavior therapy with Joseph Wolpe, cognitive therapy with Aaron Beck, marriage and family therapy with Emily Mudd, and structural family therapy with Salvador Minuchin began (although marital and family therapy may have been developed elsewhere too, but I think we did it first in a university setting).

In this rich and diverse psychotherapeutic community, I have seen, over the years, many young people cling to and identify with these various leaders, as well as to Jung and Freud, resulting in an ultimate detriment to their own creative unfolding as therapists. Unwilling to explore new ideas, to take risks in treating difficult patients, or to cross interdisciplinary boundaries as, for instance, I do when I take my psychotherapy work into internal medicine and gastroenterology (in which I was originally trained), these young people risk struggling with the role of perpetual student as they search for self-definition all their professional lives.

My goal for many years when I directed a large continuing education program for our hospital and university was to shift this pedagogic paradigm to one of adult education: to treat each participant as an equal who comes to learn with a rich life and work experience that must be respected and shared in the service of his or her own maximal growth and learning. I have developed these ideas further in the *Handbook of Clinical Hypnosis* (Bloom, 1993), but let me just say here that promoting the idea of becoming Ericksonian is seemingly counter to my basic belief in how we enhance the development of our own art. I think the answer may lie even deeper in terms of encouraging autonomy in one's professional life.

In conclusion, I would like to point out the deeper purpose of my writing the original article, which I hope does not get lost in this discussion. I simply wanted to share some exciting cases I have worked on and the wonder I have for the creative process that runs through some of my work. I truly believe therapy is an art and that Erickson was one of the greatest psychotherapists I have ever known. But for myself, the privilege in experiencing in my own work glimpses of this ultimate fusion of knowledge and intuition is a joy for which I am forever grateful. How to encourage others to develop their own artistry is the focus of all my teaching these days. In the future, I would welcome your ideas on the creative process and how you think it may have worked in the cases I presented and in your own. This could be a very rich exchange of ideas and concepts.

## REFERENCES

*American heritage dictionary of the English language* (1992). (p. 1134). Boston: Houghton Mifflin.

Bloom, P. B. (1993). Training issues in hypnosis. In J. Rhue, S. Lynn, & I. Kirsch (Eds.), *Handbook of clinical hypnosis* (pp. 673–690). Washington, DC: American Psychological Association.

Lankton, S. R., Lankton, C. H., & Matthews, W. J. (1991). Ericksonian family therapy. In A. S. Gurman & D. P. Kniskern (Eds.), *Handbook of Family Therapy,* vol. II. (pp. 239–283). New York: Brunner/Mazel.

Matthews, W. J., Lankton, S. J., & Lankton, C. H. (1993). An Ericksonian model of hypnotherapy. In J. Rhue, S. Lynn, & I. Kirsch (Eds.), *Handbook of clinical hypnosis* (pp. 187–214). Washington, DC: American Psychological Association

## *Further Comments by Stephen Lankton*

I want to apologize if I offended you by suggesting that I knew anything about your unconscious motive. I did not mean to suggest that you had some pathology or that I know about your unconscious dynamics. I thought that you had used an unexamined habit of thought and speech (which is unconscious).

Readers only can know about the author from what they read. If you consciously are worried about Ericksonians and not non-Ericksonians using the word "metaphor," then yours was not an unconscious selection for emphasis and my comment was entirely wrong. If you are concerned about Ericksonians using the word "metaphor" when they mean story and not concerned when non-Ericksonians do it, then your words were well chosen. But I still don't know why any Ericksonian's using the word gives concern to someone when others are not concerned. My question is still unanswered: Are you not concerned when "non-Ericksonians" do this? I just find it offensive when someone consciously singles out a group of which I am thought to be a member (Ericksonians' using the word "metaphor") when others are exempt from the same scrutiny for reasons invisible to me. If, on the other hand, you did not wish to continue the schism, then what was it if not an unconscious habit that led you to develop it in that phrasing? So I prefer not to be offended and to attribute the phrasing to unexamined (unconscious) habit. I assumed that you had only good intentions in writing and that this unconscious usage went undetected by your editing mind. Word selection throughout, beginning with the title, perpetuated the schism as I documented.

## *Further Response by Dr. Bloom*

It seems we are now working on finding agreement on the word "unconscious." I have never heard it used to mean "an unexamined habit of thought and speech (which is unconscious)." A Freudian slip is always significant in some circles. You would have been angered if you were told that you were denying deeper feelings. That is what I thought you were doing to me, and I was wrong.

As I mentioned, you could not have anticipated the background from which I was responding. Having now read what you mean, I must plead guilty. I did intend to be provocative and to create tension. Perhaps, paradoxically, more people will learn of Erickson's contributions from the way I presented the material than if I were less risk taking, especially in the title. I believe that it is equally important to attract the attention of the larger non-Erickson groups to Erickson's rich ideas. And one way to do that was by throwing a little fuel on the fire. In light of your subsequent comments, and hopefully with future opportunities for me to speak further on this subject, I will lay this sort of provocation to rest and push harder for a greater sense of "us" rather than "we/them."

In my heart, I am "worried about Ericksonians *and* [emphasis mine] non-Ericksonians' using the word 'metaphor' ... when they mean story." I would certainty clarify this in the future. I truly dislike sloppy language and therapy in any "camp," and the non-Ericksonians have enormous problems in this area that go beyond anything we have discussed. Most of the time, both groups lack a precision for the meaning of the terms they use, I am no exception. Is your question ("Are you not concerned when non-Ericksonians do this?") now answered?

# 5

# The State of the Altered State Debate

*Irving Kirsch*

In the 1970s, everyone seemed to agree that the question of whether hypnosis is an altered state was the most contentious issue in the field. In the 1980s, the state debate mysteriously disappeared. It was pronounced a dead issue, and some editors insisted that references to it be deleted from manuscripts before they could be accepted for publication (Coe, 1987). This came as quite a surprise to nonstate theorists, and in his presidential address to Division 30 of the American Psychological Association (Division of Psychological Hypnosis), Bill Coe (1987) suggested that if the issue had been resolved, someone ought to have informed him as to how it had turned out.

The magical disappearance of the state controversy was accomplished through a very clever, verbal sleight of hand. The term "state" was redefined to be "a kind of shorthand, with no causal properties

This chapter was originally published in *Contemporary Hypnosis, 9:* 1–6. (1992). Reprinted with permission.

or defining features associated with it" (Kihlstrom, 1985, p. 405).[1] When defined in this way, it was pointed out "the question of whether hypnosis is a special state of consciousness disappears as a substantive issue." The logic of this argument is unassailable. When something has no defining features, hypotheses about it are untestable, and untestable hypotheses cannot be substantive issues.

In conventional philosophy of science, there is a term that is used to describe untestable propositions; if a statement about the world is untestable, it is considered meaningless. We are now in a position to answer Coe's question about the outcome of the state debate. Based on this so-called "weak" version of the state concept, the proposition that hypnosis is an altered state is meaningless.

It is metaphysical mumbo jumbo masquerading as science, and it ought to be stricken from scientific discourse. The editors were right, but they didn't go far enough. Not only should references to this dead issue be deleted from experimental reports, but also references to "trance" and phrases like "deeply hypnotized" should be stricken from clinical articles.

Before I am quoted out of context, I hasten to point out that the state issue cannot really be disposed of so easily. Most state theorists use the term in a much stronger sense. According to Erickson (1980), Fromm (1979), Gill and Brenman (1959), Orne (1959), Weitzenhoffer (1989), and even Hilgard (1986), hypnotic inductions produce in susceptible subjects one or more distinct states of consciousness that are introspectively distinguishable from waking consciousness and from other altered states. There are differences among these theorists as to the defining characteristics of the hypothesized hypnotic state or states, but all agree that they do have defining characteris-

[1]Kihlstrom (1985) attributed this weak version of the state view to Hilgard (1969). However, Kihlstrom's presentation of this position differs from Hilgard's in some important respects. Hilgard proposed that there may be hypnotic states, but those states may not cause hypnotic responding. He did not propose that hypnotic states have no defining features, however. On the contrary, he continues to specify what some of those features are (increased suggestibility, enhanced imagery, subsidence of the planning function, and reduction in reality testing; Hilgard, 1986) and has advanced the hypothesis that defining physiological features of hypnotic states will someday be established (Hilgard, 1969).

tics and that heightened suggestibility is one of them. This notion of hypnosis as a state has the virtue of being testable, and therefore it is not meaningless.

## TESTING THE ALTERED STATE HYPOTHESIS

The strongest possible evidence for the existence of a distinct hypnotic state would be the discovery of clear physiological markers of that state. In 1969, Hilgard hypothesized that such evidence might be found within the ensuing 20 years. Although he was at least wrong about the timing, it is still possible that unique physiological markers of a hypnotic state will someday be found, if not in the next 20 years, then maybe in the next 50 or 100. The possibility of someday uncovering evidence of a unique state means that the altered state hypothesis can never be disproved. But it is potentially confirmable, and it is this fact that makes it testable and meaningful.

In the absence of physiological markers of a trance state, we must rely on the evidence of behavior and self-report as evidence of its existence. Unfortunately, behavioral differences between hypnotized and unhypnotized subjects have also been difficult to come by. The heightened suggestibility that follows a hypnotic induction can be duplicated or even surpassed by a variety of other procedures, including placebo pills (Glass & Barber, 1961), task-motivation instructions (Barber, 1969), and imagination training (Comins, Fullam, & Barber, 1975; Katz, 1979; Vickery, Kirsch, Council & Sirkin, 1985). This leaves us with the self-reports of responsive subjects who say that they were in an altered state of awareness. These reports have been accepted as "primary data about the presence or absence of hypnosis" (Tart & Hilgard, 1966, p. 253).

If self-reported changes in experience constitute evidence of a hypnotic state, then introspective reports of hypnotized subjects ought to be distinguishable from those who are not hypnotized. My colleagues and I have tested that hypothesis by administering hypnotic procedures (conventional and "alert" inductions) or nonhypnotic procedures (relaxation training and didactic instruction in goal-directed imagery) and asking subjects to provide detailed descriptions of their subjective experiences (Kirsch, Mobayed, Council, & Kenny, 1992).

Subjects were asked to provide these descriptions immediately after the hypnotic induction or control procedure and also after the administration of test suggestions. They were asked to describe their general states of awareness, and also their experience of particular suggestions.

These descriptions were recorded verbatim, and those produced by relatively responsive subjects were then given to well-known experts in the field of hypnosis, who were asked to determine which of the subjects had been hypnotized. Our expert judges are an exceptionally distinguished group of scholars, including some of the best known and most widely cited contemporary hypnosis theorists. Fourteen of them are Fellows of APA Division 30, eleven are Fellows of the Society for Clinical and Experimental Hypnosis, nine are on the editorial board of the *International Journal of Clinical and Experimental Hypnosis,* and eight are diplomates of the American Board of Psychological Hypnosis. Most identified themselves as "state" theorists, and most of the state theorists (including some who are identified with "weak" versions of the altered state view) predicted that they would be able to distinguish hypnotized from nonhypnotized subjects on the basis of reports obtained after the administration of hypnotic test suggestions.

Despite these predictions, experts were not able to distinguish the self-reports of subjects who had experienced hypnotic inductions from those who had not. This was true regardless of when the self-reports were obtained (before or after the administration of suggestions) and regardless of what subjects were describing (general state of consciousness or experience of specific suggestions).

Many state theorists maintain that subjects can slip into a hypnotic state without any formal induction procedure. Might that not have happened in the nonhypnotic conditions, and could that not account for the inability of our experts to discriminate hypnotic from nonhypnotic conditions? Our study permitted a test of that hypothesis. Besides attempting to postdict the procedure that subjects had experienced, the judges were asked to estimate subjects' depth of hypnosis from their descriptions of their states of consciousness. If subjects had slipped into hypnosis, and if the hypnotic state is associated with enhanced suggestibility, then those estimates should be correlated with their suggestibility scores, as measured on Form C of the Stanford Hypnotic Susceptibility Scale (Weitzenhoffer & Hilgard, 1962).

In fact, the experts were very accurate in determining how suggestible the subjects were, but only when those estimates were based on subjects' descriptions of their responses to suggestions. When the judgments were based on descriptions of general states of consciousness, correlations between expert judgments of suggestibility and actual suggestibility scores were close to zero. Thus, not only were the states of consciousness described by our subjects unrelated to the hypnotic induction or control procedures that preceded them, but they were also unrelated to suggestibility.

It is important to stress that these data do not disconfirm the altered state hypothesis. Had we used a different set of questions to obtain our descriptions of states of awareness, perhaps the experts would have been able to discriminate hypnotic from nonhypnotic conditions. Or maybe a different set of experts could have made more accurate distinctions, although given the caliber and representativeness of our judges, we doubt this. Even if introspective reports of hypnotized subjects cannot be distinguished from those of control subjects, some physiological or behavioral markers of a trance state may someday be discovered, and data of that sort could provide strong evidence for the altered state hypothesis. As noted above, the altered state hypothesis is not falsifiable. Nevertheless, continued failure to find confirmatory evidence should lead one to consider it unlikely.

## DOES IT MATTER?

To say that a hypothesis is testable and, therefore, meaningful is not the same as saying it is interesting or important. Some proponents of the so-called weak version of the state view claim that whether or not hypnosis is an altered state is irrelevant. Because altered states do not cause hypnotic responding, in their view they look elsewhere for answers to the more interesting question, "What are the processes and mechanisms by which subjective and behavioral responses to suggestions are produced?" This brings them closer to the views of nonstate theorists, who have always looked elsewhere for an answer to this question.

I suspect that some adherents of "weak" versions of the state position are actually nonstate theorists who are reluctant to identify themselves as such, even to themselves. Their reluctance may be due to antagonisms and allegiances associated with the ferocity with which the state debate has been waged. It may also be associated with a persistent tendency to misread nonstate positions as proposing that hypnotic responses can be understood as simple compliance, less euphemistically known as faking. Although compliance has been emphasized by Wagstaff (1981) and in some of Spanos's more recent work (e.g., Spanos, Perlini, Patrick, Bell, & Gwynn, 1990), most nonstate theorists recognize that suggestions produce genuine changes in experience and see these changes as special enough to constitute an important field of study (Barber, Spanos, & Chaves, 1974; Kirsch, 1985, 1990; Sarbin & Coe, 1972). Rather than casting doubt on the reality or importance of hypnotic phenomena, most nonstate theorists seek to explain them in terms of the same factors that account for nonhypnotic experiences and behaviors. In their view, hypnotic experiences are not due to an altered state of consciousness. Instead, they are produced by people's beliefs and expectations (Kirsch, 1990, 1991), role involvement (Sarbin, 1950; Sarbin & Coe, 1972), and imaginative strategies (Barber et al., 1974; Lynn, Rhue, & Weekes, 1990).

The state issue is important for a number of reasons. For one thing, most people think of hypnosis as an altered state in the conventional sense of the term, that is, in the same sense that sleep and drug intoxication are altered states. If hypnosis is not an altered state in this sense of the term, the easiest way to correct this misconception is to acknowledge that the traditional view of hypnosis as an altered state is wrong. Continuing to refer to it as an altered state, while occasionally explaining that one does not really mean anything of substance by the term, merely perpetuates misinformation.

There is a second reason why the state issue is important. Many contemporary hypnosis theorists have a notion of the hypothesized hypnotic state that is similar to some of the views held by the general public. They, too, liken hypnosis to sleep and intoxication, and they see the relationship between hypnotic responding and the hypnotic state as analogous to that between dreaming and sleep or staggering and drunkenness. Some deny that this relationship is causal (Hilgard,

1969, 1973), but even if it is not causal, does it not require an explanation?[2] Also, if hypnosis is a state, like sleep or intoxication, then establishing its essential characteristics is an important task for hypnosis researchers (Orne, 1959). Conversely, if the state hypothesis is false, these questions are meaningless and research should be directed elsewhere.

Besides affecting the focus of research, the validity of the altered state hypothesis affects how that research is conducted. Some of the conventions of hypnosis research do not make sense unless one assumes that hypnosis is an altered state in a relatively "strong" sense of the term. For example, because hypnotizable subjects might inadvertently slip into hypnosis, nonhypnotic control subjects are carefully selected for their presumed inability to be hypnotized (Orne, 1979). It does not make much sense to think that a person might slip into "a label representing some domain of characteristic phenomena" (Kihlstrom, 1985, p. 405). Furthermore, if the hypothesized state does not *cause* changes in experience or behavior, it cannot possibly affect the outcome of a study, and it need not be controlled.

Finally, the altered state hypothesis has implications for public policy. If hypnosis is not an altered state, we should lay to rest the recurring attempts at regulating who is allowed to induce it. Why should we prohibit people from using particular labels when inducing relaxation and asking people to imagine things?

Perhaps we can look forward to the resurrection of the state controversy in the decade ahead. In fact, it was never dead; it was merely

---

[2]Maintaining the analogy to sleep, Hilgard (1969) argued that sleep does not cause or explain dreaming or snoring. But is there really no causal relation between sleep and dreaming or between sleep and snoring? Hilgard's reason for denying that there is a causal relation between these events is the fact that it is possible to sleep without snoring or dreaming. A tacit assumption of this argument is that if a variable is not a *sufficient* cause of a phenomenon or does not explain it *completely,* then it is not causally related to that phenomenon at all. If we accept this argument, then we must also conclude that smoking does not cause cancer, that drunk driving does not cause auto accidents, that auto accidents do not cause death, and so on. Having then decided that these relations are not causal or explanatory, we might go on to decide that the debate about smoking and cancer is irrelevant and proclaim it to be a dead issue (which in a sense it is).

concealed by various euphemisms, such as "special process," "social psychological," "cognitive," and "cognitive-behavioral," terms that were never clearly defined with respect to their bearing on hypnosis. I suspect that if these euphemisms are replaced and the term "state" is used in its traditional meaningful sense, just the way people outside of the field of hypnosis use it, some hypnosis scholars may be surprised to discover that they are, in fact, nonstate theorists, and that without knowing it, they have been so all along.

## REFERENCES


Barber, T. X. (1969). *Hypnosis: A scientific approach.* New York: Van Nostrand Reinhold.

Barber, T. X., Spanos, N. P., & Chaves, J. F. (1974). *Hypnosis, imagination, and human potentialities.* New York: Pergamon.

Coe, W. C. (1987, August). *Hypnosis, wherefore art thou?* Paper presented at the meeting of the American Psychological Association, New York.

Comins, J., Fullam, F., & Barber, T. X. (1975). Effects of experimenter modeling, demands for honesty, and initial level of suggestibility on response to hypnotic suggestions. *Journal of Consulting and Clinical Psychology, 43,* 668–675.

Erickson, M. H. (1980). *The nature of hypnosis and suggestion.* New York: Irvingtons.

Fromm, E. (1979). The nature of hypnosis and other altered states of consciousness: An ego-psychological theory. In E. Fromm & R. E. Shor (Eds.), *Hypnosis: Developments in research and new perspectives* (rev. ed., pp. 81–103). New York: Aldine.

Gill, M., & Brenman, M. (1959). *Hypnosis and related states: Psychoanalytic studies in regression.* New York: International Universities Press.

Glass, L. B., & Barber, T. X. (1961). A note on hypnotic behavior, the definition of the situation, and the placebo effect. *Journal of Nervous and Mental Diseases, 132,* 539–541.

Hilgard, E. R. (1969). Altered states of awareness. *Journal of Nervous and Mental Disease, 149,* 68–79.

Hilgard, E. R. (1973). The domain of hypnosis: With some comments on alternate paradigms. *American Psychologist, 28,* 972–982.

Hilgard, E. R. (1986). *Divided consciousness: Multiple controls in human thought and action* (expanded ed.). New York: Wiley.

Katz, N. (1979). Comparative efficacy of behavioral training, training plus relaxation, and a sleep/trance induction in increasing hypnotic susceptibility. *Journal of Consulting and Clinical Psychology, 47,* 119–127.

Kihlstrom, J. F. (1985). Hypnosis. *Annual Review of Psychology, 36,* 385–418.

Kirsch, I. (1985). Response expectancy as a determinant of experience and behavior. *American Psychologist, 40,* 1189–1202.

Kirsch, I. (1990). *Changing expectations: A key to effective psychotherapy.* Pacific Grove, CA: Brooks/Cole.

Kirsch, I. (1991). A social learning theory of hypnosis. In S. J. Lynn & J. Rhue (Eds.), *Theories of hypnosis: Current models and perspectives.* New York: Guilford Press.

Kirsch, I., Mobayed, C. P., Council, J. R., & Kenny, D. A. (1991). *Expert judgements of hypnosis from subjective state reports: New data on the altered state controversy.* Unpublished manuscript, University of Connecticut.

Lynn, S. J., Rhue, J. W., & Weekes, J. R. (1990). Hypnotic involuntariness: A social-cognitive analysis. *Psychological Review, 97,* 169–184.

Orne, M. T. (1959). The nature of hypnosis: Artifact and essence. *Journal of Abnormal Psychology, 58,* 277–299.

Orne, M. T. (1979). On the simulating subject as a quasi-control group in hypnosis research: What, why, and how. In E. Fromm & R. E. Shor (Eds.), *Hypnosis: Developments in research and new perspectives* (2nd ed., pp. 519–601). New York: Aldine.

Sarbin, T. R. (1950). Contributions to role-taking theory: I. Hypnotic behavior. *Psychological Review, 57,* 225–270.

Sarbin, T. R., & Coe, W. C. (1972). *Hypnosis: A social psychological analysis of influence comuniation.* New York: Holt, Rinehart & Winston.

Spanos, N. P., Perlini, A. H., Patrick, L., Bell, S., & Gwynn, M. I. (1990). The role of compliance in hypnotic and nonhypnotic analgesia. *Journal of Research in Personality, 24,* 433–453.

Tart, C. T., & Hilgard, E. R. (1966). Responsiveness to suggestions under "hypnosis" and "waking-imagination" conditions: A methodological observation. *International Journal of Clinical and Experimental Hypnosis, 14,* 247–256.

Vickery, A. R., Kirsch, I., Sirkin, M. I., & Council, J. R. (1985). Cognitive skill and traditional trance hypnotic inductions: A within-subject comparison. *Journal of Consulting and Clinical Psychology, 53,* 131–133.

Wagstaff, G. F. (1981). *Hypnosis, compliance and belief.* New York: St. Martin's Press.

Weitzenhoffer, A. M. (1989). *The practice of hypnotism* (Vol. 1). New York: Wiley.

Weitzenhoffer, A. M., & Hilgard, E. (1962). *Stanford Hypnotic Susceptibility Scale: Form C.* Palo Alto, CA: Consulting Psychologists Press.

# Discussion: On the Road of Hypnosis Research: Kirsch's View of Altered Conditions

*Comments by Kevin M. McConkey*

On the road of hypnosis research, there are occasional signposts that help us know where we have come from, where we are now, and where we could go next. The chapter by Kirsch (1992), on which his current chapter is based, together with a more extensive treatment by Kirsch and Lynn (1995), follows the signpost tradition of, among others, Hilgard (1973, 1975), Spanos and Barber (1974), Kihlstrom (1985, 1992), and Spanos (1986). Moreover, the article is timely since, in the first half of the 1990s, hypnosis research was going through a process not only of change within its own boundaries, but also in its interactions with other areas of psychology (e.g., see Fromm & Nash, 1992; Kihlstrom & McConkey, 1990; Lynn & Rhue, 1991; Rhue, Lynn, & Kirsch, 1993; Lynn, Rhue, & Weekes, 1990). In this exciting time for those in the area of hypnosis, it is important that the major gains of the last few decades be advanced rather than wasted, and the major questions of the next few decades be identified and addressed.

Kirsch looks back over the road of the last few decades, points to how we have been using different road maps—including some that change language—and highlights the need to be clear in our thinking and speaking about hypnosis in the next few decades. The words that we use matter, and Kirsch tells us that "state" (altered or not) is one word that matters more than most when thinking and speaking about hypnosis. Some in the area of hypnosis are said by Kirsch to consider that hypnosis involves an altered state (in either its weak or its strong version; see also Kihlstrom, 1985), and others are said to

Preparation of this comment was supported in part by a grant from the Australian Research Council.

not consider this, but rather to focus on the processes and mechanisms associated with changes in experience; moreover, some are said to think that they are weak-state theorists when they are really nonstate in orientation.

Kirsch presents a number of key points that underscore why we should think carefully about the altered conditions on the road of hypnosis research. For example, he reminds us that the public typically thinks of hypnosis as being an altered state that is very different from everyday functioning, and asks whether we should allow the public to believe this if it is not the case. Also, he tells us that an assumption that hypnosis involves an altered state underlies in part legislative attempts to regulate its use in clinical and applied settings, and asks whether we should be involved with attempts to limit the use of hypnosis if it simply invloves one person (the hypnotist) speaking to another (the subject) and if there is nothing special about its effects. Moreover, he tells us that assumptions about the state or nonstate of hypnosis will determine in large part the central issues that we think need to be investigated, and also how we will frame those issues in operational terms. In this respect, focusing on the wrong issues or framing the questions inappropriately will be of little use. Finally, he tells us that some methods of investigation in hypnosis research carry tacit assumptions about what should be controlled and what needs to be compared; of course, controlling or comparing the wrong variables will be of little use at best and totally misleading at worst.

Although Kirsch (see also Kirsch & Lynn, 1995) gives us a clear insight into the way in which he would like us to think and speak about hypnosis, there are various issues that need to be dealt with further. I would like to make brief comment on three of these. First, although Kirsch points to some of the differences that have existed among state theorists, he does not convey fully enough the differences that have existed among nonstate theorists (e.g., see Spanos & Chaves, 1989); the lack of consensus among those theorists on some issues has been substantial. In this respect, Kirsch and Lynn (1995; see also Lynn & Rhue, 1991) have noted that theoretical views about hypnosis now fall on a continuum, with different investigators emphasizing different variables and adopting different views about the relative importance of those variables. Second, although Kirsch highlights how different assumptions shape different experimental questions and research methods, he does not indicate what questions, methods, and answers we all agree on. Kirsch and Lynn (1995) usefully presented 10 "unresolved questions" about hypnosis, and also offered 10 "resolved questions." For these, it would be particularly useful if we could not only agree on these 10 "facts" about hypnosis, but also lay out clearly their explanation from different theoretical orientations; this would allow us to determine the precise ways in which theories differ in terms of their explanation of accepted factual information. Third, although Kirsch focuses on the relevance of views about the state or nonstate of hypnosis for investigation and explanation, the issues that he raises are relevant to the application of hypnosis in various practice settings, and clarifying the relevance of theoretical orientation for the use of hypnosis in clinical and other applied settings would be useful. Even more useful would be the identification of the 10—or seven, or three—applications of hypnosis that can be said to be based in evidence that is acceptable to everyone regardless of theoretical orientation. Although those who are primarily involved in hypnosis research may be getting closer, as it were, those who are primarily involved in the application of hypnosis appear to be exceptionally diverse in their views about hypnosis and in their distance from empirical evidence about hypnosis; a more active rapprochement between the experimental and clinical aspects of hypnosis is one direction that needs to be followed in the next few decades (e.g., see Rhue et al., 1993; Sheehan & McConkey, 1993; Zeig & Rennick, 1991).

There are a number of other issues that could be canvassed in any discussion of the state or nonstate of hypnosis. I would like to make brief comment on three of these. First, hypnotized individuals' beliefs that their suggested experiences have reality value would seem to be fertile ground not only for addressing core questions about the nature of hypnosis, but also for seeking similarities between hypnosis and other phenomena that involve delusions and self-deceptions (e.g., see McConkey, 1991, 1995; Noble & McConkey, 1995). Greater understanding of the processes involved in the private experiences of hypnotized individuals, and the attributions that they make about the source of those experiences, is needed to better define the characteristic (if not unique) qualities of hypnosis. Second, the effect of hypnosis on, and the parallels of hypnosis with, the processes associated with other psychological phenomena needs to be more fully explored. For instance, there are some clear findings about the way in which hypnosis affects confidence in reported memory that carry implications for how we should think about both hypnosis and memory (e.g., see McConkey, 1992, 1995; McConkey & Sheehan, 1995). A more detailed appreciation of the way in which hypnosis affects such phenomena and processes would help us not only to understand more about hypnosis, but also to specify whether and how the explanation of hypnosis needs any appeal to distinct variables. Third, a part of the domain of hypnosis that has been relatively neglected in the last few decades has been self-hypnosis, and this is unfortunate given its theoretical interest and assumed clinical utility (e.g., see Orne & McConkey, 1981). A more precise questioning and a more systematic consideration of the many issues that exist about self-hypnosis—and its similarity or otherwise to heterohypnosis—would be important not only for its own sake, but also because it would seem to throw into bold contrast many of the issues that Kirsch highlights about (hetero)hypnosis.

As an investigator who seeks to understand the role of both cognitive and social influences in hypnosis and to recognize the complexity of the experience and behavior of the hypnotized individual, it is a challenge for me to walk a line that provides a reasonable balance of description and explanation while staying true to the primary data (e.g., see McConkey, 1991, 1995; Sheehan & McConkey, 1982). Each investigator of hypnosis should know the nature of the vehicle in which he or she is traveling on the road of hypnosis research, and Kirsch reminds us of that. Most important, perhaps, we all need to recognize that our questions and methods of inquiry should allow data to speak for themselves as much as possible, but we should all be mindful of how paradigms, theories, and models—formal and informal—limit as much as they guide our investigations and interpretations.

## REFERENCES

Fromm, E., & Nash, M. R. (Eds.) (1992). *Contemporary hypnosis research.* New York: Guilford.

Hilgard, E. R. (1973). The domain of hypnosis: With some comments on alternate paradigms. *American Psychologist, 28,* 972–982.

Hilgard, E. R. (1975). Hypnosis. *Annual Review of Psychology, 26,* 19–44.

Kihlstrom, J. F. (1985). Hypnosis. *Annual Review of Psychology, 36,* 385–418.

Kihlstrom, J. F. (1992). Hypnosis: A sesquicentennial essay. *International Journal of Clinical and Experimental Hypnosis, 50,* 301–314.

Kihlstrom, J. F., & McConkey, K. M. (1990). William James on hypnosis: A centennial reflection. *Psychological Science, 1,* 174–178.

Kirsch, I. (1992). The state of the altered state debate. *Contemporary Hypnosis, 9,* 1–6.

Kirsch, I., & Lynn, S. J. (1995). The altered state of hypnosis: Changes in the theoretical landscape. *American Psychologist, 50,* 846–858.

Lynn, S. J., & Rhue, J. W. (Eds.) (1991). *Theories of hypnosis: Current models and perspectives.* New York: Guilford.

Lynn, S. J., Rhue, J. W., & Weekes, J. R. (1990). Hypnotic involuntariness: A social cognitive analysis. *Psychological Review, 97,* 169–184.

McConkey, K. M. (1991). The construction and resolution of experience and behavior in hypnosis. In S. J. Lynn & J. W. Rhue (Eds.), *Theories of hypnosis: Current models and perspectives* (pp. 542–563). New York: Guilford.

McConkey. K. M. (1992). The effects of hypnotic procedures on remembering: The experimental findings and their implications for forensic hypnosis. In E. Fromm & M. R. Nash (Eds.), *Contemporary hypnosis research* (pp. 405–426). New York: Guilford.

McConkey, K. M. (1995). Believing in hypnosis. In G. D. Burrows & R. O. Stanley (Eds.), *Contemporary international hypnosis* (pp. 63–67). Chichester: Wiley.

McConkey, K. M., & Sheehan, P. W. (1995). *Hypnosis, memory, and behavior in criminal investigation.* New York: Guilford.

Noble, J., & McConkey, K. M. (1995). Hypnotic sex change: Creating and challenging a delusion in the laboratory. *Journal of Abnormal Psychology, 104,* 69–74.

Orne, M. T., & McConkey, K. M. (1981). Toward convergent inquiry into self-hypnosis. *International Journal of Clinical and Experimental Hypnosis, 29,* 313–323.

Rhue, J. W., Lynn, S. J., & Kirsch, I. (Eds.) (1993). *Handbook of clinical hypnosis.* Washington, DC: American Psychological Association.

Sheehan, P. W., & McConkey, K. M. (1982). *Hypnosis and experience: The exploration of phenomena and process.* Hillsdale, NJ: Erlbaum.

Sheehan, P. W., & McConkey, K. M. (1993). Forensic hypnosis: The application of ethical guidelines. In J. W. Rhue, S. J. Lynn, & I. Kirsch (Eds.),

*Handbook of clinical hypnosis* (pp. 719–738). Washington, DC: American Psychological Association.

Spanos, N. P. (1986). Hypnotic behavior: A social-psychological interpretation of amnesia, analgesia, and "trance logic". *Behavioral and Brain Sciences, 9,* 449–502.

Spanos, N. P., & Barber, T. X. (1974). Toward a convergence in hypnosis research. *American Psychologist, 29,* 500–511.

Spanos, N. P., & Chaves, J. F. (Eds.) (1989). *Hypnosis: The cognitive-behavioral perspective.* Buffalo, NY: Prometheus Books.

Zeig, J. K., & Rennick, P. J. (1991). Ericksonian hypnotherapy: A communications approach to hypnosis. In S. J. Lynn & J. W. Rhue (Eds.), *Theories of hypnosis: Current models and perspectives* (pp. 275–302). New York: Guilford.

# What We Know and Do Not Know About Hypnosis

## *Response by Dr. Kirsch*

There is nothing with which I can disagree in McConkey's very thoughtful comments. This in itself is a commentary on the changes that have taken place in the field. Although some sharp theoretical differences remain, careful research has established a body of factual knowledge about hypnosis. We may disagree about how to interpret these facts, but not about what they are. In this amplification of McConkey's comments, I summarize what we know about hypnosis and draw further attention to some of the things that we very much need to learn.

### DEFINING HYPNOSIS

There was a time when agreement on such a basic question as the definition of the term "hypnosis" was a matter of dispute. The lack of an agreed-upon definition made fruitful discussion next to impossible and was one factor that made the altered state debate so acrimonious. When people understand their words to mean different things, their communications bypass each other frustratingly (Kuhn, 1970).

With that in mind, the executive committee of the Division of Psychological Hypnosis (Division 30) of the American Psychological Association (APA) assembled a definition and description of hypnosis that has been endorsed by leading hypnosis scholars of all theoretical persuasions (Kirsch, 1994). It is not copyrighted, and its reproduction is both permitted and encouraged. Among other things, it can be used as a handout for clients. The APA definition and description are as follows:

> Hypnosis is a procedure during which a health professional or researcher suggests that a client, patient, or subject experience changes in sensations, perceptions, thoughts, or behavior. The hypnotic context is generally established by an induction procedure. Although there are many different hypnotic inductions, most include suggestions for relaxation, calmness, and well-being. Instructions to imagine or think about pleasant experiences are also commonly included in hypnotic inductions.
>
> People respond to hypnosis in different ways. Some describe their experience as an altered state of consciousness. Others describe hypnosis as a normal state of focused attention, in which they feel very calm and relaxed. Regardless of how and to what degree they respond, most people describe the experience as very pleasant.
>
> Some people are very responsive to hypnotic suggestions and others are less responsive. A person's ability to experience hypnotic suggestions can be inhibited by fears and concerns arising from some common misconceptions. Contrary to some depictions of hypnosis in books, movies, or on television, people who have been hypnotized do not lose control over their behavior. They typically remain aware of who they are and where they are, and unless amnesia has been specifically suggested, they usually remember what transpired during hypnosis. Hypnosis makes it easier for people to experience suggestions, but it does not force them to have these experiences.

> Hypnosis is not a type of therapy, like psychoanalysis or behavior therapy. Instead, it is a procedure that can be used to facilitate therapy. Because it is not a treatment in and of itself, training in hypnosis is not sufficient for the conduct of therapy. Clinical hypnosis should be used only by properly trained and credentialed health care professionals (e.g., licensed clinical psychologists), who have also been trained in the clinical use of hypnosis and are working within the areas of their professional expertise.
>
> Hypnosis has been used in the treatment of pain, depression, anxiety, stress, habit disorders, and many other psychological and medical problems. However, it may not be useful for all psychological problems or for all patients or clients. The decision to use hypnosis as an adjunct to treatment can only be made in consultation with a qualified health care provider who has been trained in the use and limitations of clinical hypnosis.
>
> In addition to its use in clinical settings, hypnosis is used in research, with the goal of learning more about the nature of hypnosis itself, as well as its impact on sensation, perception, learning, memory, and physiology. Researchers also study the value of hypnosis in the treatment of physical and psychological problems.

Two important points are worth noting about this definition. First, hypnosis is defined as a procedure, rather than as a condition of the person being hypnotized. It is this feature that allows widespread agreement and facilitates meaningful communication between people with different theoretical orientations. Whether hypnosis produces altered states of awareness, the nature of those hypothesized states, and their relation to responses to suggestion are empirical questions. Making empirical questions part of a definition begs the question and hinders meaningful communication.

The second important feature of this definition is that it is not all-encompassing. Some people in the field have attempted to define hypnosis so broadly that it covers any communication between a client and therapist. We already have a term with that meaning. It is "psychotherapy." Making hypnosis synonymous with psychotherapy renders it redundant. Overly broad definitions are useless.

## WHAT WE KNOW

Beyond the consensually adopted definition of hypnosis, Lynn and I identified the following 10 facts that have been established about hypnosis (Kirsch & Lynn, 1995).

> It is now known that (a) the ability to experience hypnotic phenomena does not indicate gullibility or weakness; (b) hypnosis is not related to sleep; (c) hypnotic responsiveness depends more on the efforts and abilities of the subject than on the skill of the hypnotist; (d) subjects retain the ability to control their behavior during hypnosis, and they are aware of their surroundings and can monitor events outside of the framework of suggestions during hypnosis; (e) spontaneous posthypnotic amnesia is relatively rare; (f) suggestions can be responded to with or without hypnosis, and the function of a hypnotic induction is merely to increase suggestibility to a minor degree; (g) hypnosis is not a dangerous procedure when practiced by qualified clinicians and researchers; (h) most hypnotized subjects are neither faking nor merely complying with suggestions; (i) hypnosis does not increase the accuracy of memory; and (j) hypnosis does not foster a literal reexperiencing of childhood events. (pp. 846–847)

Some of these facts are addressed in the APA definition and description. I will amplify two of them here.

### HYPNOSIS AS AN EMPIRICALLY VALIDATED PROCEDURE

The rise of managed care has created numerous problems for clients, patients, therapists, and physicians. It provides at least one benefit, however. It has given fresh urgency to the need to validate our clinical methods empirically. Because of the power of the placebo effect, clinical experience and case reports are not sufficient for this task. Even the most misguided therapeutic procedures generate positive clinical outcomes. Therapies go in and out of style as often as do changes in fashion and more often than the symptoms of hysteria.

Fortunately, some clinical uses of hypnosis are well supported by controlled data. Hypnosis compares favorably with alternative treatments for severe and persistent pain and may be effective even for people who are not highly hypnotizable (Holroyd, 1996). Also, the addition of hypnosis to cognitive-behavioral treatments for weight reduction, anxiety, phobias, hypertension, and duodenal ulcers enhances the effectiveness of treatment (Kirsch, 1996; Kirsch, Montgomery, & Sapirstein, 1995). The benefit of hypnosis is particularly evident in weight-reduction programs. Unlike people treated without hypnosis, those in hypnotic treatment maintain their weight loss over relatively long periods of time.

Most other clinical uses of hypnosis have not yet been verified empirically. This does not mean that they are ineffective. The problem is that they have not yet been sufficiently tested. It is incumbent on the proponents of these treatments to provide reliable efficacy data. History teaches that if this is not done, the treatments will eventually be discarded.

## THE MISUSE OF HYPNOSIS

Although most applications of hypnosis have not been adequately tested, there is one that has clearly failed the test—the use of hypnosis to uncover or enhance memory, whether in a clinical or forensic setting (McConkey, 1992). Hypnosis increases the amount of information that is reported, but it does not increase the accuracy of that information. It does, however, increase the confidence with which the memories are held. These effects can be found among low suggestible people, as well as among the more responsive.

It seems likely that these effects are due to people's beliefs about hypnosis. Beliefs have always shaped hypnotic experiences. When people believed that convulsions were the sine qua non of mesmerism, they convulsed. When they thought it required a trance, they went into a trance. Catalepsy and spontaneous amnesia have been signs of hypnosis, but only among people who believed that these were to be expected. Many people believe that hypnosis enhances memory, and this belief leads them to accept more of their confabulation as memory. It would be interesting to see the extent to which the provision of accurate information might inoculate people against the impact of hypnosis on the confidence with which memories are held.

The data on hypnosis and memory have led to an a priori disqualification of witnesses in many jurisdictions. This is probably an overreaction. Although the effects are real, they are relatively small—much smaller than the effects of the nonhypnotic methods commonly used by attorneys to prepare witnesses for their appearance in court (see Spanos et al., 1991).

The clinical use of hypnosis to uncover repressed memories is particularly dangerous. Without obtaining independent corroboration, there is no way to know whether or not the memory is accurate. Neither the vividness nor the emotional intensity of the experience is a reliable guide. During hypnosis, one is urged to make use of one's ability to fantasize, and mistaken beliefs about hypnosis can make people more likely to accept their fantasies as reality. Once again, the effect of hypnosis is relatively small. False memories can be created without hypnosis as well (Lynn & Nash, 1994; Loftus, 1993). But hypnosis makes this problem worse, rather than better.

It is sometimes argued that the actual truth of a memory may be unimportant. What matters is its narrative truth. According to this view, if the recovery of a memory is therapeutic, it does not matter if it is true. The idea that the recovery of a memory is therapeutic is an untested and questionable assumption. But the proposition that a false memory can have negative effects is unquestionable. Among other things, it can lead to the disruption of family bonds.

## WHAT WE NEED TO KNOW

There is much about hypnosis that we still do not know. Among the unanswered question that Lynn and I identified are the following (Kirsch & Lynn, 1995). Is there a uniquely hypnotic state that serves as a background or gives rise to the altered subjective experiences produced by suggestion? What makes suggestibility so stable? To what extent can suggestibility be modified? What is the role of cognitive strategies in hypnotic involuntariness and responding? How can we better understand the unique subjective experience of the participant? Is the structure of hypnotic communications (e.g., the use of direct versus indirect suggestions) an important determinant of responsiveness? To what extent does hypnotic behavior result from intentional compliance with the perceived demands of the situation?

What are the physiological substrates of hypnotic experiences? Are there physiological correlates of differences in suggestibility?

McConkey, in his commentary, adds the task of establishing the parameters of self-hypnosis. This is especially important because many of us hold that self-hypnosis is paradigmatic (e.g., Hilgard, 1986), in that heterohypnosis is really guided self-hypnosis. One reason for testing this assumption is that interactional theories and some altered state theories (e.g., Woody & Bowers, 1994) imply that the term "self-hypnosis" is an oxymoron. Another reason is that self-hypnosis may be an especially important concept in clinical applications.

In furthering our understanding of the subjective experience of hypnosis, McConkey urges us to study people's beliefs about the reality of their suggested experiences. This is indeed an important task, because hypnotic responses have been characterized as believed-in imaginings (Perry, 1992; Sarbin & Coe, 1972). As a start, one of my students and I have been looking at the frequency with which people report believing that suggested states of affairs are real (Comey & Kirsch, 1995). We did so by asking them whether they believed their arm had actually become lighter during an arm levitation suggestion, whether they believed music was actually playing during a suggested auditory hallucination, and so on. We found that about two-thirds of responders to ideomotor and challenge suggestions reported believing in the reality of the suggested state of affairs. However, only 46% of people who reported seeing a suggested cat also reported believing that the cat was real, only 32% of successful responders to the hallucinated music suggestion thought the music was real, and only 17% of participants who displayed amnesia for suggestions thought they actually had forgotten them.

This raises an interesting question. Are there two types of responders, believers and nonbelievers? Or does this reflect a difference in the way questions are interpreted? Only further research will tell.

## REFERENCES

Comey, G., & Kirsch, I. (1995, November). *Intentional and spontaneous imagery in hypnosis.* Paper presented at the annual meeting of the Society for Clinical and Experimental Hypnosis, San Antonio, TX.

Hilgard, E. R. (1986). *Divided consciousness: Multiple controls in human thought and action* (expanded ed.). New York: Wiley.

Holroyd, J. (1996). Hypnosis treatment of clinical pain: Understanding why hypnosis is useful. *International Journal of Clinical and Experimental Hypnosis, 44,* 33–51.

Kirsch, I. (1994). Defining hypnosis for the public. *Contemporary hypnosis, 11,* 142–143.

Kirsch, I. (in press). Hypnotic enhancement of cognitive-behavioral weight loss treatments: Another meta-reanalysis. *Journal of Consulting and Clinical Psychology,*

Kirsch, I., & Lynn, S. J. (1995). The altered state of hypnosis: Changes in the theoretical landscape. *American Psychologist, 50,* 846–858.

Kirsch, I., Montgomery, G., & Sapirstein, G. (1995). Hypnosis as an adjunct to cognitive behavioral psychotherapy: A meta-analysis. *Journal of Consulting and Clinical Psychology, 63,* 214–220.

Kuhn, T. (1970). *The structure of scientific revolutions* (2nd ed.). Chicago: University of Chicago Press.

Loftus, E. R. (1993). The reality of repressed memories. *American Psychologist, 48,* 518–537.

Lynn, S. J., & Nash, M. R. (1994). Truth in memory: Ramifications for psychotherapy and hypnotherapy. *American Journal of Clinical Hypnosis, 36,* 194–208.

McConkey, K. M. (1992). The effects of hypnotic procedures on remembering: The experimental findings and their implications for forensic hypnosis. In E. Fromm & M. Nash (Eds.), *Contemporary hypnosis research* (pp. 405–426). New York: Guilford.

Perry, C. (1992). Theorizing about hypnosis in either/or terms. *International Journal of Clinical and Experimental Hypnosis, 50,* 238–252.

Sarbin, T. R., & Coe, W. C. (1972). *Hypnosis: A social psychological analysis of influence communication.* New York: Holt, Rinehart & Winston.

Spanos, N. P., Quigley, C. A., Gwynn, M. I., Glatt, R. L., et al. (1991). Hypnotic interrogation, pretrial preparation, and witness testimony during direct and cross-examination. *Law and Human Behavior, 15,* 639–653.

Woody, E. Z., & Bowers, K. S. (1994). A frontal assault on dissociated control. In S. J. Lynn & J. W. Rhue (Eds.), *Dissociation: Clinical, theoretical and research perspectives* (pp. 52–79). New York: Guilford.

# Behavioral Medicine

# 6

# Hypnosis in the Treatment of AIDS

*Myer Stratton Reed*

In 1985, a mother whose son died of the acquired immune deficiency syndrome (AIDS) in my city predicted that "this disease will test our humanity like few things in this generation." After more than a decade of dealing with the illness, most professionals would add that AIDS has tested the limits of our clinical skills as well. It combines our culture's most forbidden subjects—death, sex, homophobia, and racism—and asks that we maintain our creativity and caring despite fear, sadness, and haunting hopelessness.

Here we consider how hypnosis can be helpful in this effort. First, we review existing evidence for the effectiveness of hypnosis in directly influencing the disease and modulating its physical effects, and then the evidence concerning the role of emotional factors in the progression of the human immunodeficiency virus (HIV). At that point we question whether hypnosis might indirectly affect the illness by reducing the psychological pains of AIDS. Next, we offer suggestions for using hypnotherapy to improve the quality of life for those

The author wishes to acknowledge the very important assistance of Rodger Kessler, Ph.D., and the helpful suggestions of Mickey Skidmore, L.C.S.W.

with HIV. The final focus is on the effects of social and cultural variables on those experiencing AIDS and recommendations are made for hypnotic intervention at the broadest possible level.

## HYPNOSIS AND THE PHYSIOLOGY OF AIDS

The first question concerning the usefulness of hypnosis is a deceptively simple one. Can it directly alter a patient's physiology and meaningfully affect the course of HIV? Some believe that hypnosis can have an effect at the cellular-genetic level and that the scientific documentation of this potential is not far away (Rossi, 1994). But that evidence does not now exist. Nor does specific evidence exist that hypnosis can alter the course of HIV.

The focus of most AIDS research is on CD4+ cells, the major regulatory units in the immune system. Their decline is the principal indicator of the advance of HIV. In the first year of infection, the CD4+ cell count typically drops from over 1,000 cells per microliter to around 650. In subsequent years, the decline is nonlinear and more gradual. If the CD4+ cell count falls below 200, the patient's immune system becomes very vulnerable to the opportunistic infections associated with full-blown AIDS.

Hypnosis would have to be shown to raise the CD4+ count and the effect would have to be more than temporary to establish direct benefits on the immune systems of those with HIV. But even if this stringent test were met, these changes might prove to be insignificant compared with lethal variations in strains of the virus itself. Or it might be that any positive benefits of hypnosis are outweighed by the effects of interacting opportunistic infections on the immune system (for a fuller discussion, see Kertzner, 1991; O'Leary, 1990; Saah et al., 1992). Furthermore, one must establish whether or not the benefits of hypnosis can be accomplished at any and every stage of the infection.

If hypnosis produces positive physiological benefits, research must ascertain which aspects of the hypnotic intervention are responsible. Is it deep relaxation that produces desired consequences, or is it imagery of some form with direct and indirect suggestions that influences the disease process? Can these benefits be shown to be more than an artifact of the positive social support involved in the experimentation (Hall & O'Grady, 1991)?

After decades of exploring the potential impact of hypnosis and other approaches to relaxation and imagery on cancer, these questions still remain to be answered. It is unlikely that they will be resolved soon for AIDS. Only one study to date has employed hypnosis with HIV seropositives (Auerbach, Oleson, & Soloman, 1992), and this was done in combination with thermal biofeedback and guided imagery. The 13 male subjects, as compared with controls, showed increased hardiness, decreased reporting of HIV-related symptoms, and increased perceived vigor. No changes occurred, however, in the number of CD4 cells, in tension, or in depression levels. With multiple interventions, a small number of subjects, and mixed results, it is impossible to draw meaningful conclusions about the role of hypnosis.

Although it cannot be claimed that hypnosis can alter the progression of HIV, it can affect some physiological symptoms associated with the accompanying opportunistic infections. Hypnosis has long been used to reduce nausea, vomiting, and pain (Gennuis, 1995), as well as for a variety of other discomforting symptoms, including ashma, itching, and loss of appetite. Erickson (1980) suggested numerous hypnotic strategies for alleviating discomfort, among them the interspersal of suggestions in metaphors, the formation of suggestions for negative and positive hallucinations, and use of dissociation and amnesia. Others, as well, have written about hypnosis for pain control and for maintaining general physical comfort (Barber & Adrian, 1982; Rossi & Cheek, 1988; Poncelet, 1988; Hammond, 1990; Edgette & Edgette, 1995).

Hypnotherapy may help in relieving some opportunistic infections. Herpes simplex, for example, appears more responsive to psychological distress than cytomegalovirus or Epstein-Barr (Robertson, Wilkins, Handy, & van-der-Horst, 1993) and may be amenable to suggestion and relaxation (Kiecolt-Glaser et al., 1985; Surman & Crumpacher, 1987). No research has been reported on the use of hypnosis to control the fungal infections commonly associated with AIDS, such as thrush. But, again, hypnosis should at least be helpful with the discomforts associated with oral infection, as well as to relieve various dermatologic irritations. The extent to which these and other opportunistic infections associated with AIDS may be responsive to hypnotic intervention should be the subject of future research.

## HYPNOSIS AND THE PSYCHOIMMUNOLOGY OF AIDS

If hypnosis cannot be proved to have a direct impact on an immune system under attack from HIV, is it possible that an indirect effect can be realized through the alleviation of psychological distress? Previous research in psychoimmunology has shown health consequences of anxiety, depression, loneliness, and passivity. Would a reduction of these prolong the life of people with HIV?

Again, there is trouble in answering a seemingly simple question. The most challenging task is to separate the effects of confounding variables. Most important of these are access to and willingness to use current medical treatments, preexisting immune status, ongoing substance abuse, chronic mood disorders, and nutritional status. All are intertwined with emotional states and, as will be discussed later, are intricately related to socioeconomic status and to the social consequences of HIV (Kertzner, 1991; Lyketsos et al., 1993).

In addition, in psychoimmunology there are unresolved questions of particular import to AIDS. First, which psychological variables affect which parts of the immune system? Second, is previous immune system impairment a precondition for these effects? Third, are the effects of emotional factors simply temporary modulations that homeostatic mechanisms in the immune system will correct?

Early in the epidemic, there was promising evidence for the role of psychological factors in AIDS (Soloman, 1989; O'Leary, 1990; Burack, Stall, Barret, & Coates, 1992; Goodkin, Fuchs, Feaster, & Leeka, 1992). Recent analyses of longitudinal data, however, have suggested a conservative stance (Rabkin, Williams, Goetz, & Gorman, 1991; Perry, Fishman, Jacobsberg, & Frances, 1992; Kertzner, 1993). The largest and latest of these studies (Lyketsos et al., 1993) in an eight-year follow-up failed to establish an independent effect of depression on the progression of HIV. The sample consisted of 1,809 HIV-positive gay men without AIDS who entered the Multicenter AIDS Cohort Study in 1984 and 1985.

Studies assessing the impact of various psychotherapies on the immune functioning of persons with HIV are few and inconclusive.

LaPerriere et al. (1992) reported stress management training outcomes with a sample of HIV-positive gay men and a control group of matched seronegatives. Their interventions included progressive relaxation, cognitive skills and assertiveness training, and the provision of a social support group.

The frequency with which both groups practiced relaxation exercises positively affected their CD4+ cells. After a 10-week training period, seronegatives showed significant immune system benefits, including increases in CD4+ cell counts. Seropositive men showed immune system improvement, too, but no significant increase in the number of CD4+ cells. Here, and in a similar study (Antoni et al., 1992), there was no demonstration of a link between any immune system changes and illness progression. The subjects also were in an asymptomatic stage of HIV infection, leaving unresolved the question of the robustness of psychosocial interventions at later stages.

Mind/body questions about the development and progression of disease are similar to nature/nurture issues in educational and career success. Both are so broad and involve such complexities that one gets lost in the entangling dimensions. The ensuing confusion produces a moral dilemma for those practicing hypnotherapy: Do you practice good hypnotherapy by encouraging positive outcomes or do you exercise professional restraint and acknowledge the scientific uncertainties?

There is considerable room here for conscientious disagreement among therapists. And in noting some of these complexities with AIDS, the intent of this review is not to discourage responsible therapists from seeking to have a positive influence on the course of their clients' illnesses. It intends only to suggest caution and humility.

People with AIDS are subjected to many moralistic assertions about their role in acquiring the illness. One danger in overselling psychoimmunology is the potential for further self-blame for "failing to maintain correct attitudes" as the illness progresses. There is also a risk of clients' avoiding effective medical treatments under the illusion that positive thinking will suffice (Kertzner, 1991). Furthermore, our contemporary culture rigidly prescribes "being positive" and denies the reality of sadness, tragedy, and irreversible loss. Therapists, therefore, must be alert to the possibilities of magical thinking and collective avoidance.

If therapists address these dangers, though, they should be free to use whatever helpful therapeutic skills they have. Again, there are those who believe that research will soon confirm that hypnotic interventions can have physiological effects (Rossi, 1994). Others would see little reason to wait for the rigorous demands of scientific proof to be satisfied before attempting to prolong lives through whatever tools they have. AIDS taught the medical/governmental bureaucracy to take more risks with experimental drugs for those with terminal diseases. Hypnotherapists should be free to take responsible risks as well.

Whatever his or her conservatism, the skilled therapist will recognize many opportunities for hypnosis with HIV clients. Psychotherapists may not be able to forestall death, but they can improve the quality of life. Those factors that psychoimmunology has suggested as important in mortality are the same issues one would address anyway—a reduction in anxiety and depression, the maintenance of good social relationships, and the encouragement of spirit. The concern of the remainder of this chapter is with using hypnotherapy to accomplish these ends.

## HYPNOTHERAPY FOR HIV-INFECTED CLIENTS

There are many issues that confront therapists working with HIV clients and these change as the client goes through the various stages of the illness. Central concerns persist, however, throughout the course of the illness. These are the reduction of anxiety, the alleviation of loneliness and isolation, and the acceptance of loss.

Recently diagnosed HIV-positive clients often are most in need of basic education and reassurance. Frequently, they assume that they have only weeks or months to live, and they may have haunting fears of imminent disfigurement and pain. Suicide is a serious risk, as are slower forms of self-destruction. Substance abuse, obviously, is a central therapeutic concern for intravenous drug users. Yet all gay men, as well as members of most racial minorities, are at a higher-than-average risk of substance abuse (Finnegan & McNally, 1987). The anxiety brought on by an HIV diagnosis often increases addictive patterns; it may result also in hyperactivity as a way of avoiding overwhelming emotions (Thome, 1990).

dropped dramatically to seven. As his health deteriorated, he began to lose the sobriety he had maintained throughout his infection. He became very agitated. Relationships he had been slowly building with his estranged parents and those with ASO volunteers began to deteriorate as his anger escalated. Suggestions during hypnosis to receive an inner gift yielded the realization that his life needed "stillness" now. He concluded that he had resisted it to avoid experiencing sadness. To help with this, his emotions were framed as children in need of containment, and yet each was entitled to recognition and attention.

Hypnosis can assist with unfinished business as well. Gordon's mother had abused him physically as a child and verbally demeaned him as an adult. His alcoholic father, the last of six brothers who had committed suicide or had died of various alcohol-related diseases, also suffered her abuse. Gordon feared that his illness would render him dependent on his parents and unable to resist their demands that he move back home. His dream, even before contracting HIV, was to live in another city across the state. Now receiving disability income and in contact with an ASO and an experienced therapist there, it only remained for Gordon to tell his parents of the decision.

He mentally rehearsed assertiveness in hypnotic sessions. Confidence and courage were elicited by reviewing times when he had experienced these qualities. Then he was asked to have a positive hallucination of previously elicited models of strength (such as Superman). They were to be sensed standing behind him, placing their hands on his shoulders and magically passing on fortitude. When these qualities could be felt inside and perceived in his dissociated image on an imaginary movie screen, he was to picture a split screen developing. On one side was to be a review of experience with confidence and courage. On the other side, he was to imagine future conversations with his parents. This was repeated several times, with care taken to maintain the positive feelings. The attacks he had suggested they would make were read back to him in an attempt to further desensitize and steel him. Within the month, Gordon told his parents of the impending move, appropriately expressed anger when his mother became disrespectful, and resisted attempts by both to undermine his resolve.

As a further aid in helping clients prepare for death, Levitan (1990) has suggested future projection to reduce the fears of dying. He asks clients to imagine their own death, noting who is present, what it is like to die, and how others are reacting. Clients are reassured that they will be kept comfortable and suggestions are offered to frame the events described in the most positive light. For further discussion of future projection and a broader consideration of time distortion in hypnotherapy, see Kessler and Miller (1995) and Edgette and Edgette's *The Handbook of Hypnotic Phenomena in Psychotherapy* (1995).

For those dying of AIDS, the fear of aloneness and abandonment can be the most frightening prospect. It is important, therefore, to be reassuring in this regard. In the author's experience, family members and friends who avoided contact and appeared disengaged before often reappear in the final days. Furthermore, seemingly isolated individuals often tend to acquire professional and volunteer caregivers in the final stage of the illness who provide crucial support at death. It is reassuring for those estranged from family, as well, to realize that imminent death puts many disagreements into proper perspective. Reconciliation can be envisioned in a future projection.

## AIDS AND THE SOCIAL INDUCTION OF DIS-EASE

Individual hypnotherapy with persons with AIDS sometimes seems as Sisyphean an enterprise as psychotherapy in a war zone. Although there is no question but that individuals are better off with the help, one is striving against great countervailing forces. The factors that play the clearest role in complicating the lives of those with AIDS are not individually based attitudes and issues, but are social/cultural ones. Current research does not provide conclusive evidence that anxiety, depression, and passivity speed the progression of HIV, but they undoubtedly undermine the quality of life. All are greatly influenced by the sociopolitical meaning of AIDS and by the inferiorized status of most who have carried this illness.

The most unexplored part of the genius of Milton Erickson was his understanding that hypnosis is not an esoteric phenomenon. Rather, it is a pervasive part of everyday communication coexisting tervention as an adjunctive treatment for HIV-related illness. *Psychology and Health, 6,* 325–334.

Barber, J. & Adrian, C. (Eds.) (1982). *Psychological approaches to the management of pain.* New York: Brunner/Mazel.

Burack, J., Stall, R., Barret, D., & Coates , T. (1992). Depression predicts accelerated CD4 decline among gay men in San Francisco. In *Eighth International Conference on AIDS abstract book.* Amsterdam: International AIDS Society.

Cohen, S. (1988). Voodoo death, the stress response, and AIDS. *Advances in Biochemical Psychopharmacology, 44,* 95–109.

Della Fave, R. (1980). The meek shall not inherit the earth: Self evaluation and the legitimacy of stratification. *American Sociological Review, 45,* 955–971.

Edgette, J., & Edgette J. (1995). *The handbook of hypnotic phenomena in psychotherapy.* New York: Brunner/Mazel.

Erickson, M. (1980). Hypnotherapeutic treatment of pain. In E. Rossi (Ed.), *The collected papers of Milton H. Erickson on hypnosis* (Vol. 4, pp. 235–236). New York: Irvington.

Finnegan, D., & McNally, E. (1987). *Dual identities: Counseling chemically dependent gay men and lesbians.* Center City, MN: Hazelden.

Gennuis, M. L. (1995). The use of hypnosis in helping patients control anxiety, pain, and emesis: A review of recent empirical studies. *American Journal of Clinical Hypnosis, 37,* 316–325.

Goodkin, K., Fuchs, I., Feaster, D., & Leeka, J. (1992). Life stressors and coping style are associated with immune measures in HIV infection—a preliminary report. *Psychiatry in Medicine, 22,* 155–172.

Gorman, J., Kertzner, R., & Todak, G. (1991). Multidisciplinary baseline assessment of homosexual men with and without human immunodeficiency virus infection. *Archives of General Psychiatry, 480,* 120–123.

Hall, N., & O'Grady, M. (1991). Psychosocial interventions and immune function. In *Psychoneuroimmunology* (2nd ed.). New York: Academic.

Hammond, D. C. (Ed.) (1990). *Handbook of hypnoptic suggestions and metaphors.* New York: Norton.

Hilgard, E. R., Morgan, A. H., & Macdonald, H. (1975). Pain and dissociation in the cold pressor test: A study of hypnotic analgesia with "hidden reports" through automatic key pressing and automatic talking. *Journal of Abnormal Psychology, 84,* 280–289.

Kessler, R. S., & Miller, S. D. (1995). The use of a future time frame in psychotherapy with and without hypnosis. *American Journal of Hypnosis, 38,* 39–46.

Kershaw, C. (1992). *The couple's hypnotic dance: Creating Ericksonian strategies in marital therapy.* New York: Brunner/Mazel.

Kertzner, R. (1991). Future directions for psychoimmunology: HIV infection and beyond. In J. Gorman & R. Kertzner (Eds.), *Progress in psychiatry. Number 35: Psychoimmunological update* (pp. 153–163). Washington, DC: American Psychiatric Press.

Kiecolt-Glaser, J., Glaser, R., Williger, D., Stout, J., Messick, G., Sheppard, S., Ricker, D., Romisher, S. C., Briner, W., Bonnell, G., & Donnerberg, R. (1985). Psychosocial enhancement of immunocompetence suppression in a geriatric population. *Health Psychology, 4,* 25–41.

Lankton, S., & Lankton, C. (1983). *The answer within: Clinical framework of Ericksonian hypnotherapy.* New York: Brunner/Mazel.

Lankton, S., & Lankton, C. (1986). *Enchantment and intervention in family therapy: Training in Ericksonian approaches.* New York: Brunner/Mazel.

LaPerriere, A., Antoni, M., Klimas, N., Ironside, G., Schneiderman, N., & Fletcher, M. (1991). Psychoimmunology and stress management in HIV-1 infection. In J. Gorman & R. Kertzner (Eds.), *Progress in psychiatry. Number 35: Psychoimmunological update* (pp. 81–112). Washington, DC: American Psychiatric Press.

Levitan, A. (1990). Hypnotic death rehearsal. In D. C. Hammond (Ed.), *Handbook of hypnotic suggestion and metaphor* (pp.215–216). New York: Norton.

Lyketsos, C., Hoover, D., Guccione, M., Senterfitt, M., Dew, M., Wesch, J., VanRaden, M., Treisman, M., & Morgenstein, H. (1993). Depressive symptoms as predictors of medical outcomes in HIV infection. *Journal of the American Medical Association, 270,* 2563–2567.

Minuchin, S., Rosman, B., & Baker, L. (1978). *Psychosomatic families.* Cambridge, MA: Harvard University Press.

O'Leary, A. (1990). Stress, emotion, and human immune function. *Psychological Bulletin, 108,* 363–382.

Perry, S., Fishman, B., Jacobsberg, L., & Frances, A. (1992). Relationships over a one year period between lymphocyte subsets and psychosocial variables among adults with infection by HIV. *Archives of General Psychiatry, 49,* 396–401.

Poncelet, N. (1988). Pain and pleasure: Awareness and trust In S. Lankton & J. Zeig (Eds.), *Ericksonian monographs no. 3: Treatment of special populations with Eriksonian approaches.* (pp. 25–43). New York: Brunner/Mazel.

Rabkin, J., Williams, J., Remien, R., Goetz, R., & Gorman, J. (1991). Depression, distress, lymphocyte subsets and HIV symptoms on two occasions in HIV positive men. *Archives of General Psychiatry, 48,* 111–119.

Remien, R., Rabkin, J., Williams, J., & Katoff, L. (1992). Coping strategies and health beliefs of AIDS longterm survivors. *Psychology and Health, 6,* 335–345.

Ritterman, M. (1983). *Using hypnosis in family therapy.* San Francisco: Jossey-Bass.

Ritterman, M. (1991). *Hope under siege: Terror and family support in Chile.* Norwood, NJ: Ablex.

Ritterman, M. (1992). Notes from a psychology watcher: Words that harm, words that heal. *Erickson Newsletter, 12,* 11.

Ritterman, M. (1994). *Decency induction* (videotape). Oakland, CA: Tele-Video Production Services.

Robertson, K., Wilkins, J., Handy, J., & van-der-Horst, C. (1993). Psychoimmunology and AIDS: Psychological distress and herpes simplex virus in human immunodeficiency virus infected individuals. *Psychology and Health, 8,* 317–327.

Rossi, E. (1986). *The psychobiology of mind–body healing: New concepts of therapeutic healing.* New York: Norton.

Rossi, E. (1994, April). New theories of healing and hypnosis: The emergence of mind–gene communication. *European Journal of Clinical Hypnosis,* 1–14.

Rossi, E., & Cheek, D. (1988). *Mind–body therapy: Methods of ideodynamic healing in hypnosis.* New York: Norton.

Saah, A., Munoz, A., Kuo, V., Fox, R., Kaslow, R., Phair, J., Rinaldo, C., Jr., Detels, R., & Polk, F. (1992). Predictors of the risk of AIDS within 24 months among gay men seropositive for HIV—a report from the MACS. *American Journal of Epidemiology, 135,* 1147–1155.

Soloman, G. (1989). Psychoneuroimmunology and HIV infection. *Psychiatric Medicine, 7,* 47–57.

Surman, O., & Crumpacher, C. (1987). Psychological aspects of herpes simplex infection: Report of six cases. *American Journal of Clinical Hypnosis, 30,* 125–131.

Thome, A. (1990). Alexithymia and acquired immune deficiency syndrome. *Psychotherapy and Psychosomatics, 54,* 40–43.

# 7

# Rehabilitation of Chronic Pain Patients: Expanding an Ericksonian Approach to Interdisciplinary Team Treatment

*Jeffrey B. Feldman*

Pain is the symptom that most frequently causes people to seek medical treatment, generating over 35 million new office visits to physicians each year in the United States (Turk & Melzac, 1992, p. 3). Some of these individuals will develop chronic, persisting pain, either accompanying a disease process or associated with an injury that does not resolve within an expected length of time. Such condi-

A significant portion of this chapter was initially presented at a workshop at the Fifth International Congress on Ericksonian Hypnosis and Psychotherapy, December 1992. I wish to thank the Erickson Foundation for the impetus to formulate these ideas and the opportunity to present them at a professional forum of such high caliber. I would also like to thank Dr. Meg Gwynne for her patient and painstaking editorial assistance, which, as usual, makes me look better than I am. Finally, I would like to express my appreciation to Kathy Sims and Gail Taylor for their assistance with the preparation of the various drafts of this manuscript.

tions include back pain, headaches, fibromyalgia, arthritis, pelvic pain, and reflex sympathetic dystrophy. Among those suffering chronic pain, a subset will become increasingly disabled and exhibit a constellation of symptoms termed chronic pain syndrome. The annual cost of compensation and medical payments in the United States for just one of its diagnoses, occupationally related back disorders, has been estimated at $7.2 billion, with the rate of resulting disability increasing four times faster than did the U.S. population between 1957 and 1976 (Waddell & Turk, 1992, p. 15).

This chapter briefly reviews the concept of chronic pain syndrome, describing the multiple interacting reactions and perpetuating factors that make it so difficult to treat. The treatment goals from a multisystems perspective are also reviewed, and the members of an interdisciplinary team needed to implement such goals enumerated. The application of Ericksonian principles to both the treatment of chronic pain patients and the management of an interdisciplinary team is discussed. Finally, the consistency between Ericksonian and mind–body healing approaches is mentioned, with particular emphasis on the implications of such principles for health care policy.

## WHAT IS CHRONIC PAIN SYNDROME?

A number of definitions and distinctions are helpful to note when discussing chronic pain syndrome. When referring to chronic pain, professionals are generally referring to chronic benign pain to distinguish it from the pain accompanying cancer. Cancer pain is embedded in a network of issues associated with terminal illness, death, and loss. It usually is primarily treated through drug or interventional approaches that provide comfort to persons in their final days of life. Hypnosis can be a useful adjunct in the management of cancer pain, affording patients a sense of control and a means to reduce medication use if they choose. Chronic pain is also differentiated from acute pain, which is pain that bears a straightforward relationship to peripheral stimulus and tissue damage. Acute pain tends to be time limited (hours, days, or perhaps weeks) and to be relieved by appropriate treatment directed at the underlying physical problem (Turk & Melzac, 1992, p. 4; Waddell & Turk, 1992, p. 20). In contrast, chronic pain is defined as pain that lasts three months or longer or as pain that lasts beyond the length of time in which one might expect normal healing to take place. Chronic pain encompasses a number of painful conditions that are progressive in nature (e.g., multiple sclerosis, diabetic neuropathy), or involve recurrent acute episodes (migraine, arthritis) (Turk & Melzac, 1992, p. 5). The presence of a chronically painful condition can lead to a wealth of interacting disabling responses and reactions, which have been termed chronic pain syndrome.

The distinction between individuals experiencing chronic pain and those exhibiting chronic pain syndrome has been made largely on the basis of behavior and functioning. Individuals suffering from chronic pain syndrome generally exhibit pain behaviors, as well as a marked restriction in functional activities (Rucker, 1990). Pain behavior is a form of what Waddell and his associates termed abnormal illness behavior. Such behaviors include persistent audible and body language displays, such as grimacing, bracing, or guarding movements; preoccupation with pain in the form of persistent and repeated complaints; overutilization of the health care system, including visits to physicians and emergency rooms or repeated surgeries; and persistent or excessive use of analgesics and/or sedative drugs (Waddell, Pilowksi, & Bond, 1989, pp. 49–50). Waddell has developed a number of nonorganic signs or behavioral responses to examination by which the clinician can evaluate abnormal illness behavior (Waddell, Bricker, Finlayson, & Main, 1984). It is important to emphasize that these pain or abnormal illness behaviors are best interpreted as communications of distress by the patient, rather than as indications of malingering or psychogenic pain (Waddell et al., 1989).

To better understand chronic pain syndrome and its marked features of functional restriction, disability, and pain behavior, it is helpful first to discuss the nature of pain, and second to take a systems view of the syndrome. A conceptual tool frequently used in the pain field is Loeser's (1982, p. 18) concept that pain has four components: nociception, the pain itself, suffering, and pain behavior. Nociception is the biomechanical or physiological processes by which a nerve impulse is generated as a result of tissue impingement or damage and then conducted through the central nervous system to the brain. Pain is the perceptual experience of this nerve impulse. This perception is affected by numerous factors, including one's beliefs or cognitions concerning the meaning of the painful message, as well as emotions associated with these cognitions. Suffering involves the emotional or affective response to this painful perception. Finally, pain behaviors are the physical and verbal expressions of distress and the functional limitations just discussed. These restrictions on functioning follow from an individual's cognitive beliefs about pain and his or her affective response to it.

The classic example illustrating the distinctions among nociception, pain, suffering, and pain behavior is Beecher's observations of soldiers wounded in World War II. These soldiers were suffering from wounds severe enough to require them to be removed from the battlefield. It was noted that they appeared to be in far less distress and required far less pain medication than did individuals who might suffer comparable injuries in a civilian setting. The major difference appeared to be that by allowing the wounded soldiers to be removed from the battle site, the injuries were, in a sense, lifesaving. Thus, rather then being a source of distress and pain amplification, they provided relief from the threat of death in further battle (Beecher, 1959, as quoted by Melzack & Wall, 1982, p. 35).

On a contemporary note, one might think in terms of two individuals, both with sore throats. One individual, viewing it as the first sign of a cold, will not be in acute distress, will not experience a great degree of pain or symptom preoccupation, and most likely will not be significantly impaired in his or her occupational or social life. In contrast, a person with the same degree of nociceptive stimulation who views this mild sore throat as the first signs of infection by the human immunodeficiency virus (HIV), due to some prior at-risk behavior, most likely will suffer acute distress, becoming preoccupied with every nuance of the pain, with the pain magnified by the preoccupation as well as by anxiety. Repeated outpatient visits, requests for blood testing, and difficulty functioning at work would be probable consequences based on the attributions associated with this sore throat. Cognitive factors thus can play a large role in the perception of pain and the affective and behavioral responses it generates. One can imagine how pain behavior becomes magnified or exacerbated in patients who see multiple physicians, all of whom state that they cannot find anything really wrong, and convey the attitude, "You're just going to have to live with the pain." The implicit or, at times, explicit message that this pain is "all in your head" further causes patients to magnify symptoms as a means of communicating, "I truly am suffering! I have something physically wrong with me!"

A number of other factors come into play in the development of chronic pain syndrome. These factors, illustrated in Figure 7.1, exacerbate and perpetuate pain, leading to long-term multisystem dysfunction. In this diagram, arrows point in both directions to indicate that the factors are both cause and causative. For instance, muscles tense as part of the fight-or-flight reaction that prepares the body to run or fight. Unfortunately, this muscle tension is not useful for individuals in chronic pain and tends to generate more pain. Muscle tension constricts blood flow and can create biomechanical factors, which increase pain. Individuals enter a vicious cycle of pain, generating muscle tension that generates more pain, which, in turn, generates increased muscle tension.

The second factor exacerbating chronic pain is physical deterioration (Figure 7.1). Injured persons are typically told to rest in bed to allow for healing. While this is good advice for a recent or acute injury, over time it leads to physical deterioration. Physical deterioration, in turn, exacerbates pain symptoms and leads to overall decreased functioning and health. Specifically, in the case of back pain, weakening of the supporting musculature in the back and abdominal regions results in less support for the spine and thus increases the force of gravity and movement on the spinal vertebra. Increased pain leads to less activity, increasing weakness and dysfunction.

Individuals in chronic pain, unable to work, sleep, or enjoy activities, are often depressed and anxious (Figure 7.1). They tend to feel as if they have lost control of their lives and are controlled by the pain. They often limit or discontinue social activities due to the discomfort of traveling or sitting and being questioned about their health. Social withdrawal, financial difficulties, changes in role responsibilities, and the general irritability associated with chronic pain place great stress on the entire family, and family conflict can ensue. Alternatively, in an attempt to "take care of the patient," some family members restrict the patient's activities more than is warranted by his or her physical condition. Well-intentioned efforts to assist the patient tend to foster disability.

In their search for relief, many patients turn to medication. Unfor-

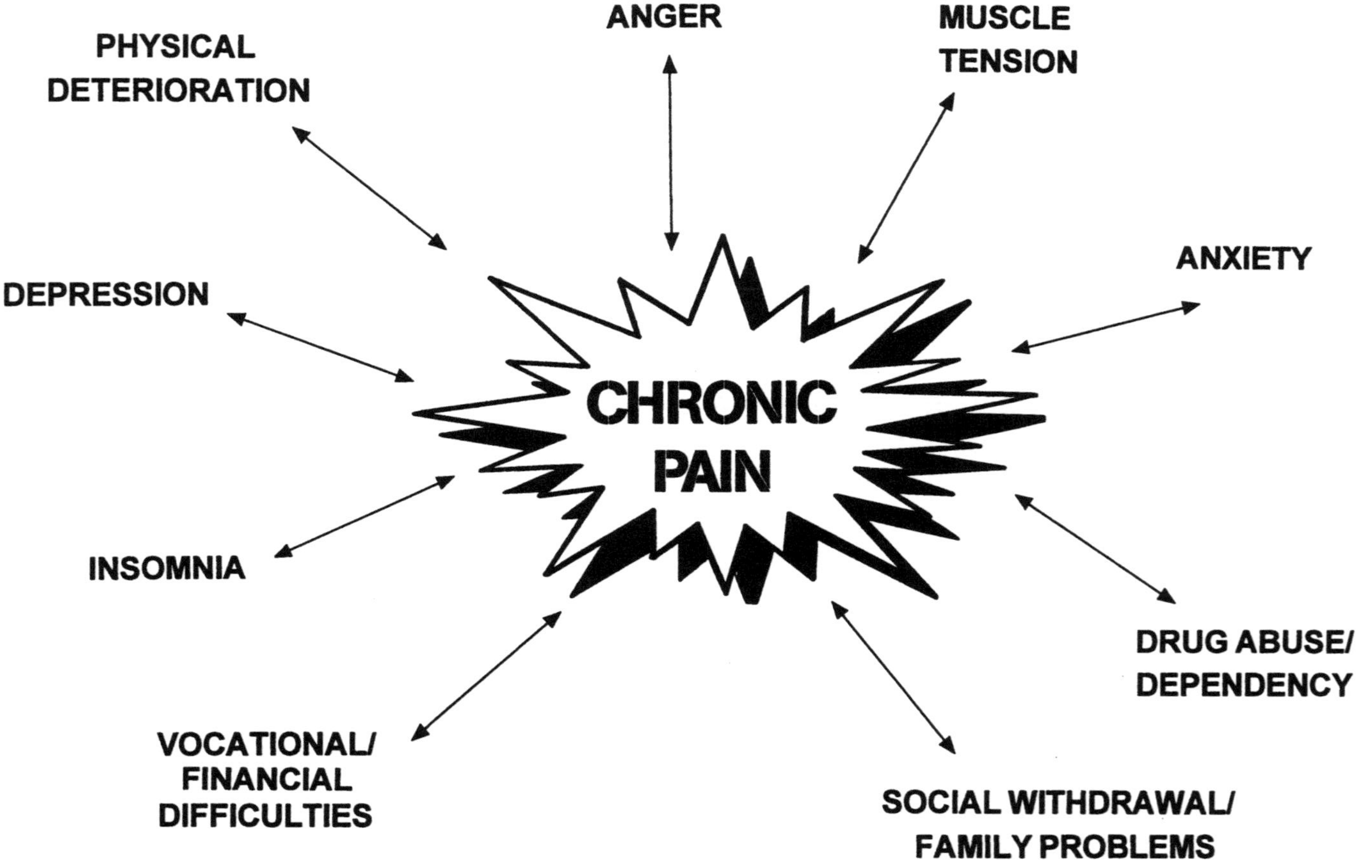


FIGURE 7.1. Factors in the Development of Chronic Pain Syndrome.

tunately, narcotic medication, highly useful on a short-term basis often becomes problematic with long-term use (Figure 7.1). Individuals generally develop a tolerance to narcotic medication that results in a progressive need for stronger medication. Narcotic medications depress cognitive, affective, and behavioral functioning. They also bind with the brain's endogenous opiate receptor sites, reducing the brain's ability to produce pain-controlling neurochemicals.

Patients can develop a conditioned anxiety reaction to pain, especially if their pain is intermittently severe (Figure 7.1). They often respond to the initial feelings of worsening pain with a panic reaction that tenses muscles and sensitizes the body, thereby increasing the pain symptoms. The pain conditions may be exacerbated either by the panic reaction in response to pain or by a chronically tense state that is related to anxiety. This anxiety response or heightened sympathetic arousal can also be generated by the patient's life history. While estimates vary, the literature indicates that 30 to 70% of women suffering chronic pain report having been sexually or physically abused (Wortele, Caplan, & Kearins, 1990, p. 110; Walker, et al., 1992, p. 658). While these abuse rates are similar to those in the general psychotherapy population, they are notable because these patients rarely initially seek treatment through psychotherapy. Pain patients with a history of sexual and physical abuse feel further traumatized by any suggestion that their pain is "all in their head." Currently experienced pain seems to trigger emotional and physiological responses conditioned by earlier painful abuse. The concept of state-dependent learning, as extensively described by Rossi (1986, pp. 36–56), and Kardiner's notion of physioneurosis (as cited in Herman, 1992, pp. 35–36) are relevant descriptions of this conditioned psychophysiological process. Chronic pain syndrome can be in part the physical expression of the distress of prior abuse. The patient is communicating, often without awareness, "I have been hurt and remain hurt."

Pain can also trigger other symptoms of posttraumatic stress disorder, including flashbacks, generalized anxiety, and feelings of rage. A 45-year-old male patient suffering from a low back injury told me that the pain was less difficult to handle than the horrible scenes that flooded back to him like "movies in my mind." For many years, he was able to numb with alcohol and drugs the emotional pain of periodically emerging memories, but the ongoing chronic physical pain had overwhelmed his capacity to manage symptoms in these unproductive ways. While few patients can so directly recognize a link between prior traumatic abuse and current chronic pain, individuals often present with a degree of emotional sensitivity and intensity of affect that is perplexing and distressing to both themselves and the professionals working with them. Seemingly irrational expressions of anger and hypersensitivity to issues of control often do not make sense until the patient's life history is understood.

Anger is a further source of sympathetic nervous system arousal that exacerbates pain and generalized muscle tension (Figure 7.1). Patients are often angry for various reasons related to their pain. Some are injured at work due to unsafe conditions, which they had reported or attempted to change. Others report being instructed to perform unsafe duties. Physicians or insurance company personnel can generate anger through an attitude of disbelief in the pain, or a belief that the patient is malingering. The resulting inability to obtain authorization for appropriate treatment is a further source of distress. Patients are often angry because their injury might result in their dismissal in spite of 20 or 30 years of dedicated work. This situation can evoke feelings related to a history of neglect or abandonment. Simply having to ask others for help may trigger painful dependency issues and anger.

From a systems perspective, Figure 7.1 would be more accurate, although overly complicated visually, if there were bidirectional lines connecting all of the above-discussed reactions. Patients' generalized anger and irritability can generate family problems, which can increase overall stress. The stress then generates a sense of loss of control, fueling feelings of anger and depression. The patient's anxiety disrupts sleep, and consequently increases muscle tension, symptoms of depression, and physical deconditioning. Chronic pain patients' increased dependency on narcotic drugs typically increases symptoms of depression, hastens physical deterioration, and creates biochemical and physical reasons for behavioral inactivity.

Additionally, there often are financial realities affecting the patient. Perceiving themselves as unable to return to their jobs, patients with limited education often conclude that there is no meaningful work they can do. While it is rare that individuals are consciously malingering, pain can be generated, in part, by the Ericksonian principle that people make the best choices available to them based on their perception of the alternatives (Lankton & Lankton, 1983, p. 13).

## CHRONIC PAIN PROGRAM TREATMENT GOALS

Treatment goals follow from the multiple interacting sources of dysfunction and disability characteristic of chronic pain syndrome (see Table 7.1). Withdrawal from problematic medications, usually narcotics, is a primary goal, often requiring hospitalization. Hospitalization, in turn, may pose a threat to those who have come to rely on medication. Careful and repeated explanations on the part of the physician and other team members are needed to emphasize that narcotic medication blocks the body's ability to produce natural painkillers and that there are more effective ways to manage pain.

Aerobic exercise is one way the body produces endorphins and therefore is a natural way to combat pain and depression. Physical conditioning thus is a major focus of most chronic pain programs (Table 7.1). Goals involve increasing strength, stamina, flexibility, and aerobic capacity. Spinal stabilization exercises are taught along with appropriate physical therapy interventions to help the patient correct dysfunctional neuromuscular activity. Another goal is, when possible, to increase the patient's endurance such that he or she can be active for eight hours a day.

Alternative methods of pain management are taught to facilitate withdrawal from medication and to enable patients to become more active. These methods include the use of ice, heat, massage, relaxation, and self-hypnotic techniques. Most patients respond better to the term "relaxation training" than to "hypnosis." Patients generally accept the notion that they can ease pain through muscle relaxation and "quieting" of the nervous system. This is the fundamental concept underlying psychophysiological self-regulation whereby patients shift from sympathetic arousal associated with the fight-or-flight reaction to activation of the calming parasympathetic branch of the nervous system. This significantly reduces the neurological and neurochemical reactions generating hyperalgesia, which is a sensitizing component of an alarm reaction (Maier, Watkins, & Fleshner, 1994, pp. 10–11).

**TABLE 7.1**
**Program Goals**

| | |
|---|---|
| I. Medication | Eliminate excessive medication. |
| II. Physical Conditioning | Increase strength, stamina, flexibility, and aerobic capacity. |
| III. General Activity Level | Increase general activity endurance level to eight hours a day. |
| IV. Pain Management | Develop nonmedication pain management skills such as relaxation, ice, and massage. |
| V. Functional Living | Improve body mechanics, pacing, work simplification, activities of daily living, and assertive communication. |
| VI. Nutrition | Improve nutritional habits in terms of a balanced diet, and caloric and cholesterol intake. |
| VII. General Health Care | Eliminate nicotine, reduce caffeine, and regulate blood sugar levels (to name a few examples). |
| VIII. Vocational | Develop and implement alternative vocational plans (when appropriate). |
| IX. Psychological/Spiritual | Shift from a pain-focused lifestyle to one involving personal meaning and fulfillment. |
| X. Relationship/Family Life | Improve/renew relationships with family and friends. |
| XI. Leisure | Develop satisfying leisure activities and have them become a regular part of life. |

It has been my experience that relaxation techniques are most efficiently taught in daily group sessions, with individual hypnosis and biofeedback selectively used to enhance patients' pain management capabilities. I have found that many patients appear to do as well, if not better, using relatively simple relaxation techniques rather than sophisticated hypnotic techniques. This appears to be in accord with Large's (1994) review of the literature on hypnosis for chronic pain in which he concluded that while hypnosis may be a useful modality in chronic pain management, there is little evidence that it is any more effective than simple relaxation techniques. It should be noted, though, that the number of studies using experimental controls is very limited. Further, there is little comparability from study to study concerning the nature of the patients, their pain symptoms, the type of hypnosis done, or the skill or training of the hypnotists. Quite simply, there has not been sufficient, well-controlled research to enable us to state with scientific certainty the relative value of hypnosis in the treatment of chronic pain. The lack of credible studies is underlined by Large, who pointed out that hypnosis was "virtually invisible" at the World Pain Meeting in 1993, which featured 16,043 abstracts. Nevertheless, I have found clinically that while many patients respond best to simple techniques, such as deep breathing or progressive muscle relaxation, other patients can significantly improve their pain management capability by using hypnotic techniques. Furthermore, it is my general practice to enhance relaxation techniques through the interspersal of suggestions for comfort, confidence, and self-control, and for patients to practice these techniques on their own. For example, I tell them:

> You can make the changes you need to make within yourself to get as comfortable as you can with yourself, and each and every time you practice this or whatever techniques you choose, you can become more and more comfortable with getting comfortable in this way. You therefore can develop a greater and greater confidence in your abilities to get comfortable, which can make you more and more confident to do more and more, always knowing that you can get comfortable in this way whenever you choose.

The use of psychophysiologically oriented techniques to modify pain provides a means of approaching psychological issues. Patients are generally initially resistant to seeing a psychologist and are highly sensitive to any implication that their pain might be "all in my head." Patients typically strongly agree with the questionnaire statement, "My pain is purely physical and has nothing to do with my emotions." On the other hand, patients often will acknowledge, "Stress in my life can increase my pain." In other words, patients start with the conceptual notion that their pain symptoms are purely physical, although they acknowledge that stress can increase the symptoms of this "purely physical" condition. Stress management concepts are, therefore, effectively introduced as a means of managing pain. Group sessions begin with a discussion of the ways in which stress increases pain. Patients gradually become more comfortable, acknowledging other stressors in their lives and their difficulties in coping. No distinction is made between the psychological and spiritual aspects of a person's life. Religious beliefs are a primary source of meaning for many people and, therefore, an essential coping resource. Spirituality is an area in which most mental health professionals are neither trained nor comfortable with. Nevertheless, spiritual beliefs and practices are essential to the inner lives of many patients (Jones, 1994, 184–199). Accordingly, a chaplain coleads the stress management group once a week.

To increase activity in a safe manner, the patient is taught correct body mechanics, work simplification techniques, and pacing to balance physically demanding and sedentary activities. Developing an awareness of one's body and the preliminary signs of overload, as well as assertively expressing limitations to significant others, is necessary. Patients are frequently in chronic pain because over the years their bodies have been communicating to them, " You have taken too much on your back."

Teaching people to attend to their bodies and care for themselves is part of a general wellness orientation that includes changes in diet and decreased use of nicotine and caffeine. As part of taking responsibility for themselves and their future, patients often need to accept the fact that they cannot return to a job that requires frequent heavy lifting, and so must begin to develop alternative vocational plans. Finally, many patients need to be taught how to enjoy themselves. Most have long lost the ability to laugh and play and many have never had leisure activities as a part of their lives. To truly care for themselves, patients need to find and permit themselves activities they enjoy, and not take "more on their backs" than is reasonable.

## THE INTERDISCIPLINARY TREATMENT TEAM

The complexity of interacting multisystem factors involved in chronic pain syndrome and the goals that follow, generally make effective treatment beyond the capability of any one professional. Table 7.2 presents a general picture of the large number of disciplines and professionals represented on the interdisciplinary treatment team and involved the healing process.

The first group of professionals noted in Table 7.2, comprising a nurse, physician, physical therapist, occupational therapist, and psychologist, is defined by the Committee on Accreditation for Rehabilitation Facilities (CARF) as the core team (*Standards Manual,* 1993, p. 58). In other words, these disciplines are viewed as essential to the provision of chronic pain rehabilitation services. In brief, the physician is necessary for the phased elimination of narcotic medication and the medical management of complicating conditions, such as hypertension, diabetes, or cardiac or gastrointestinal difficulties. The nurse generally functions as case manager, coordinating the medical, physical, and psychological aspects of treatment, and providing liaison among various professionals, the insurance company, and the patient. The physical therapist designs and monitors the exercise program and provides therapy to increase strength, stamina, flexibility and aerobic capacity. While the physical therapist might work with patients concerning appropriate body mechanics and work simplification, this is more commonly done by the occupational therapist, who teaches patients how best to perform specific activities of daily living. The psychologist is responsible for issues related to coping, and facilitates changing the patient's perspective from one of learned helplessness and hopelessness in the face of pain to one of taking control.

The case manager usually has primary responsibility for the management of the individual case; however, management of the team is also required. Although the team may have well intentioned and motivated professionals, a leader with the authority to manage is

**TABLE 7.2**
**Interdisciplinary Team: Chronic Pain Rehabilitation**

| Core Team: | Core Team members can be: |
|---|---|
| Nurse | Case Manager |
| Physician | Medical Director |
| Physical Therapist | Program Director |
| Occupational Therapist | |
| Psychologist | |
| **Other Therapy Staff:** | |
| Social Worker | |
| Vocational Specialist | |
| Exercise Physiologist | |
| Physical Therapy Assistant | |
| Biofeedback Specialist | |
| Chaplain | |
| **Support Staff:** | |
| Receptionist | |
| Secretary | |
| Transcriptionist | |
| **Outside Participants:** | |
| Rehabilitation Specialist | |
| Insurance Case Manager | |
| Attorney | |
| Referring Physician | |
| **Other Participants:** | |
| Family Members | |

needed. Although in some programs the medical director is also the program director, primarily more often the medical director is responsible solely for the medical care of patients, whereas the program director manages the staff and the program.

The next group of professionals listed in Table 7.2 may or may not be involved in treatment, depending on the needs of the patient and the program. Social workers are well suited as program directors, family therapists, and case managers because of their training and skills in organizational work, group dynamics, and systems. A vocational specialist, exercise physiologist, physical therapy assistant, chaplain, biofeedback specialist, and dietician are regular members of our treatment team.

Ancillary staff are also important. As is well known by anyone who works in an office or on a ward, the receptionist or secretary usually has the initial contact with the patients by telephone and subsequently in person. Also, front office staff members are the first people patients see each day during the program. Finally, the transcriptionist does not have direct contact with the patient, but will be transcribing personal information about the patient and, therefore, needs to maintain confidentiality.

Individuals outside the treatment facility who are involved in the case further complicate patient care. These include a rehabilitation specialist, often hired by the insurance company in Worker's Compensation cases to direct the case and help return the patient to work. The rehabilitation specialist, often a nurse, coordinates communication among the patient, the treatment facility, the referring physician, the insurance adjustor, and the employer. In many cases an adversarial relationship arises between the patient and the insurance company, resulting in attorney involvement. It is not uncommon for a patient to listen politely to whatever is said by the treatment team and the treating physician and then ask the attorney for advice. Similarly, it is not uncommon for the patient to view the referring physician as "the doctor." In such a situations the patient listens to the treatment team's recommendations and then goes back to the referring physician, believing that he or she will have the final say concerning the patient's standing. Consequently, one must be aware of these "outside" individuals, their importance to the patient, and the contingencies under which they operate. The inclusion of these ancillary professionals in the treatment process whenever possible is advantageous.

Finally, readers who are knowledgeable about family systems might argue that members of the family system are of primary importance. Frequently, the patient will improve considerably during inpatient care, subsequently return to the family system, and quite rapidly decline to a pretreatment level of functioning. Lasting improvement necessarily involves family members in treatment, educates them about chronic pain and the changes in the beliefs and views of the patient that are essential to improved functioning, and deals with problematic aspects of family interaction. Patterns of family dysfunction often replicate or are fueled by patterns in the family of origin.

The interdisciplinary team has been presented in part to convey the complex number of individuals and systems involved in the treatment process. Adequate treatment of chronic pain patients thus requires not only treatment of the patient and the patient's family, but management of a complex group of individuals, within and outside the facility, to enhance team functioning. The importance of Ericksonian principles in both the treatment of chronic pain patients and in working with treatment teams will be reviewed next.

## ERICKSONIAN PRINCIPLES IN THE TREATMENT OF CHRONIC PAIN PATIENTS

It is argued in this chapter that principles concerning attitudes toward the individual and modes of relating are more central and important in Ericksonian work than are specific hypnotic or therapeutic techniques. The Ericksonian principles enumerated in Table 7.3 are generalizable not only to chronic pain patients but to all medical patients, particularly those with chronic conditions. These principles will be reviewed briefly as they apply to chronic pain syndrome.

First, as discussed above, a multisystems view is necessary. One must shift from a biomedical perspective to a biopsychosocial view of the patient's condition (Lipkin, Quill, & Napodano, 1984, p. 277). This multisystems viewpoint (principle 1) requires evaluation of the cognitive and affective components of pain. Developmental issues, including psychophysiological patterns of response generated by a history of trauma, should be one component of the evaluation.

The clinician must build upon a foundation of trust and caring to surmount the multisystem and historical factors that may appear overwhelming to both the patient and treater (principle 2). This has been well documented as being critical not only for abuse survivors (Herman, 1992, p. 133), but also for all psychotherapy patients. Expanding this principle to medical patients is a logical extension of the fact that the mind and body are essential to healing. In the context of Worker's Compensation or accident situations, patients commonly encounter professionals in an atmosphere of distrust and suspicion.

**TABLE 7.3**
**Ericksonian Principles**

1. Take a multisystems viewpoint.
2. Build upon a foundation of trust and caring.
3. Meet individuals at their model of the world.
4. Approach therapy as a process of cocreation (pacing and leading).
5. Utilize:
   a. Belief systems
   b. Strengths
   c. Patterns of happiness
   d. Yourself
6. Reduce tasks to components.

They often have experienced suspicion on the part of the employer from the moment the injury was reported, and typically this attitude is further expressed by physicians ("company doctors") or rehabilitation case managers who question the validity of the patients' complaints. Even when the person appears to be somatizing or exhibiting pain behavior, it is essential that the clinician accept the person as someone who is suffering. Individuals who are somatizing, exhibiting pain behavior or magnifying symptoms are usually doing so to communicate distress (Waddell et al. 1989, pp. 50–53). For anyone familiar with the medical and legal systems, there are numerous systemic reasons for somatizing. The best explanation for this was given by an astute and compassionate coworker of mine, Maddy Fillman, who stated, "Physical despair legitimizes care; emotional despair confuses care."

To build this foundation of trust and caring, one first needs to meet individuals at their model of the world (principle 3). Fundamentally, this means that one needs to understand and accept the patient's pain as experienced by that person. One must assess the patient's understanding of the pain and the meaning it holds. This extremely important process is generally overlooked by most professionals. The patient must have the following three cognitions in place in order to cope with and manage chronic pain: (1) an explanation of the cause of pain in understandable terms, (2) a belief that everything that should be done medically has been done to address the condition, and (3) an understanding that the pain being experienced is not causing harm to the body. Patients who have these beliefs can begin to shut off the alarm reaction naturally generated by pain and begin to involve themselves in activities and exercises that might lead to increased pain in the short term but long-term improvement in functioning. These understandings are essential as one works with the patient because, as in psychotherapy, rehabilitation is a process of cocreating a new reality with the patient (principle 4). This involves the process, familiar to Ericksonian therapists, of pacing and leading. In other words, rehabilitation, like psychotherapy, is not something you do to the person. One needs to work with the person starting from where he or she is (pacing) and provide a structure and process for change (leading). The clinician starts where the patient is in terms of understanding, empathizes with suffering, and provides (or has appropriate professionals provide) the explanations that alleviate the patient's suffering. Subsequently, the treater guides the patient toward a process of rehabilitation that leads to a sense of hope and improved functioning.

Patient beliefs are utilized to cocreate an individualized approach so that the principles of rehabilitation are relevant and meaningful. For instance, if the patient believes that the pain is being caused by a nerve's being irritated by a "bulging disk", then one works with the patient on ways to soothe that nerve by quieting the nervous system (relaxation or trance) as well as through hypnotic suggestions to "shut off the nerve flow" or numb that specific nerve. One also works toward helping the patient understand that through exercise and increased strength, one's spine becomes stabilized, with the muscles providing the support that keeps the spine in place so that the bulge presses less on the nerve. It is important to recognize the patient's beliefs about the self and the world, and his or her religious beliefs. For instance, the clinician should know whether the patient believes that the pain is a form of penance or punishment for wrong doings, that it is the person's "cross to bear," or that God is testing the individual with this pain (Oates & Oates, 1985, pp. 12–19). One generally wants to utilize the patient's religious belief system, leading to the notion that, "God helps those who help themselves."

Patients' strengths should be utilized in the process of rehabilitation or therapy. Patients tend to feel that the pain controls them. They increasingly isolate themselves from others as well as from previous sources of enjoyment and satisfaction. They feel helpless and powerless, as if stuck in a "black hole" in which they and the world increasingly contract into an intense focus on pain. Patients are cut off from their resources and strengths. As has probably most cogently been argued by Gilligan (1987, pp. 16–17), therapy is a cooperative process for helping individuals access resources within themselves and apply them to their current situation. This idea was implicitly stated by Erickson when he exhorted therapists in their work with patients to "discover their patterns of happiness" (Erickson, as quoted by Parsons-Fein from a workshop in Dr. Erickson's home/office in 1979, personal communication, 1993). These patterns of happiness involve prior experiences of productive and meaningful work, leisure activities, and experiences involving laughter and loving. Accessing patterns of happiness or sources of strength activates via state-dependent learning the psychophysiological processes associated with these positive experiences (Rossi, 1986, pp. 36–56). The wealth of physical, cognitive, and affective associations tied to experiences of strength, coping, and happiness are thereby evoked as an antidote to the feelings of helplessness and hopelessness associated with chronic pain.

The issues and difficulties facing patients and staff members can appear to be overwhelming. For this reason, it is important to follow the Ericksonian principle of reducing tasks to their components (Lankton & Lankton, 1983, pp. 23–25). The clinician must break down these overwhelming tasks into specific long-range objectives and the step-by-step goals needed to meet these objectives. Long-term goals are goals that realistically can be accomplished within the four weeks of the program. These long-term goals are then broken down into specific weekly short-term goals.

For instance, a long-range objective might be for a person to lose 50 pounds. Within the time frame of a four-week program, it might be realistic for the patient to lose 8 to 10 pounds. This might be broken down to a weekly short-term goal of following a low-fat, high-carbohydrate diet such that two pounds per week are lost. It is important that the patient feel involved in the goal-setting process and not as if the goals are being externally imposed. This is part of the process of cocreation described earlier. Similarly, one must ascertain that both patient and team goals are congruent. A considerable amount of time discussing goals with patients typically is required, because goal setting is a novel experience for many. Goals should be realistic and built upon whatever successes are achieved, no matter how minimal they might seem. Goal setting also tends to generate a future orientation, which, as emphasized by Yapko (1992, p. 18), can be an important antidote to the sense of hopelessness associated with depression and dysfunction.

Goal attainment is a synergistic process in that improvement in one area facilitates improvement in other areas as well. For instance, an improved ability to use relaxation techniques may help a patient to sleep better, which will then increase the person's ability to attain physical conditioning goals. Better physical conditioning, in turn, increases self-esteem and improves affect and outlook, possibly furthering the capacity to relax. Staff members working on goals in these different areas, therefore, must work together to engender this multisystem change process. But how can team effectiveness be facilitated?

## ERICKSONIAN PRINCIPLES OF TEAM MANAGEMENT

While each team member may follow Ericksonian principles to improve his or her work with patients, the agent of therapeutic change is not any one professional or the sum of professionals involved. The agent of therapeutic change is the treatment team. Thus, from a systems perspective, as one might treat a child by working with the family, one treats a patient with chronic pain syndrome by working with or managing the treatment team. The term "management" is meant here to be a far different process than is typified by current business or health care practice. Management is meant to indicate the facilitation of a collaborative process between the team and patients that enables rehabilitation goals to be met. The principles that can best guide professionals in such a management endeavor, once again, are the Ericksonian principles delineated in Table 7.3.

The importance of a multisystems viewpoint (principle 1) has been emphasized and is implicit in the team concept. Understanding and effectively intervening on the appropriate systems levels are essential for team management and patient care. A more fundamental role of a team leader, though, is to create among team members an atmosphere of trust and caring (principle 2). This atmosphere of trust and caring is readily sensed by the patient and becomes a primary therapeutic factor in rehabilitation. The reader need only review his or her professional experience to recall the effects of working in agencies or institutions in which dealing with one's supervisor or other staff members was more stressful than working with the patients.

To function as a team in an atmosphere of trust and caring, each team member must have certain presumptions regarding other team members (see Table 7.4). In the following, I briefly discuss assumptions readily agreed on by most individuals, yet rarely experienced in the workplace. First, one needs to presume that all team members are competent (team principle 1). One has to trust the professional judgment of one's coworkers and assume that the interventions they are providing are of the best professional quality.

Second, one needs to assume that everyone on the team has something valuable to contribute (team principle 2). This refers to both the professional expertise and personal experience of team members. To avoid conflict, this has to be done within the context of clearly defined roles and responsibilities. One must assume that everyone is in this for the patient's welfare and not for their own personal aggrandizement or advancement (team principle 3). In other words, when a team member describes or recommends an intervention, one must believe that the recommendation is based on a competent professional assessment of the best interests of the patient.

To be able to contribute fully and openly to a team, one must believe that "no one is out to get you" (team principle 4). In other words, one must feel it is possible to express oneself freely without fear of distortion by someone else. A realistic viewpoint is that there will indeed be differences of opinion (team principle 5) because team members come from different personal and professional backgrounds. The team obviously functions best if differences can be expressed without becoming personalized, and without individuals' lobbying for their viewpoint as a means of becoming "one up" on another team member. Additionally, a true atmosphere of caring and trust acknowledges the fact that chronic pain patients are inherently difficult and that at times everyone needs help (team principle 6). To be able to

**TABLE 7.4**
**Presumptions for Optimal Team Functioning**

1. Everyone is competent.
2. Everyone has something valuable to contribute.
3. Everyone's primary interest is the patients' welfare.
4. No one is out to get you.
5. There will be differences of opinion.
6. Everyone needs help sometime.
7. Everyone falls if one team member falls.
8. "Things" happen (often phrased differently).
9. Roles and responsibilities are clear and agreed upon.

ask for help without fear of negative judgment by fellow team members requires trust. Similarly, to be able to offer help without fear that it will be perceived in a negative way is also necessary. The acceptance of the necessity for mutual help and support comes from the conviction that everyone falls if one team member falls (team principle 7); that is, if any one aspect of treatment fails in this multisystem model, the patient tends not to get better. If the patient's medical condition is not properly addressed, then progress in other areas is stymied. Similarly, if the family situation to which the patient is returning is not changed, then the work of the team often is of little value, as the patient goes back to the same environment that fostered illness and disability.

While it is often phrased differently, a realistic knowledge that things happen is necessary for working with both team members and patients (team principle 8). Unexpected illness, problems with authorization of treatment, budget cutbacks, and staff members' having to move on for personal and professional reasons are simple facts of life. The realization that things rarely (if ever) go smoothly is important to keep in mind in facilitating team functioning, so that finger pointing and blame do not occur.

A significant source of friction can be lessened, though, if the roles and responsibilities of staff members are clear and agreed upon (team principle 9). While this is desirable in any work situation, it is particularly important when team members work with the same patients every day and where clinical competencies often overlap. Hostilities can arise when individuals feel their self-worth is threatened by their perception that someone else is doing what should be in their professional domain. Team discussion of areas of overlap and collaborative determination of responsibilities can prevent distress.

Parallel to the patient model, one manages team members by meeting individuals at their model of the world (Ericksonian principle 3). One has to be aware of the different orientations, viewpoints, and models, which vary from profession to profession, as well as the different disciplines within professions. For instance, in pain management, there are significant differences in orientation and practice among an orthopedist, an anesthesiologist, a physiatrist, a psychiatrist, a neurologist, and a rheumatologist. Similarly, there are personal differences among different members of a team. One would expect, for instance, a different perspective on the part of a staff member who has raised children and has grandchildren than of a young, single person who recently completed school.

The process of team treatment, as well as of team building, is a collaborative process of cocreation (Ericksonian principle 4). To involve all team members fully in an interdisciplinary process entails valuing and utilizing the uniqueness and importance of each team member. In other words, utilizing each staff member's "patterns of happiness" is crucial, and involves determining what each enjoys doing and creating an environment where this can happen. For instance, a nurse colleague derives particular satisfaction from helping patients bridge the gap between mind and body. Her development of skills in the area of biofeedback has helped in our mutual development.

Finally, as with patients, the treatment team can reduce tasks to components by setting long- and short-term goals. Frank discussion of the problems facing the team and facility is a first step. After problem identification, the setting of long-term and short-term goals and specific task assignments with clear time frames are essential. In addition to setting team goals, the team as a whole moves ahead if each individual feels movement toward personal goals. In contrast to some of the antiquated ways in which performance is appraised, I suggest that staff members, in consultation with supervisors, set personal goals in the areas of professional growth, personal growth, and productivity. Having individuals conduct their own performance appraisals in these areas with input from other team members tends to be far more useful than the traditional top-down management approach. One of the most important roles of the team leader or supervisor is to temper self-criticism with genuine appreciation for the staff member's contributions. Finally, appraisal should be a two-way process in which the team manager or leader is also evaluated by fellow team members or supervisees. In this way, team functioning and team building can be a far more collaborative process.

## CASE EXAMPLES

While prior sections of this chapter might have implied a lock-step approach to the treatment of patients with chronic pain syndrome, the following three case examples will demonstrate that the Ericksonian principle of tailoring one's approach to the individual remains fundamental.

In the first case, a 68-year-old woman was seen approximately four months following a traumatic back injury. While delivering x-rays and radiology reports, the patient was hit by a laundry cart that sent her airborne, and she landed on her back on a concrete floor. She presented at evaluation with midback pain that ran down her right side. Physical therapy had not helped significantly and the pain prevented her from sleeping through the night. She had been prescribed, as is common practice, a nonsteroidal anti-inflammatory medication, which, in her case, led to gastric irritation and loss of appetite. This resulted in a 13-pound weight loss. It was her perception that the weight loss, poor sleep, and pain had led to greatly reduced strength so that she was unable to be on her feet more than half an hour at a time. This perception prevented her from doing relatively simple homemaking tasks or shopping. She also felt that weakness and stiffness in her neck (due to her pain) prevented her from driving safely, which greatly reduced her independent functioning.

The woman was highly active prior to her injury and had always been the "can do" or "take charge" person in her family. Similarly, in the radiology department, she was the person one would go to if no one else could find records or if something needed to be done quickly. The patient presented as a proper, well-mannered woman, who interacted in an endearingly traditional southern manner. Prior to her injury, she had been actively involved in volunteer work at her church and in the choir, in which she performed frequently as a soloist. She described her symptoms as also affecting her intimate relationship with her husband, saying that due to her pain her husband was "afraid to hug me and murmur sweet nothings."

When asked about symptoms of depression she replied, "You bet." She reasonably believed that her depression was secondary to her decreased activity level and inability to do things she enjoyed because she was "too weak." Utilizing her beliefs, treatment was framed as a process whereby she would be working to regain her strength. We agreed that she had always been an active person and that her injury threw her off track ("like a Mack truck hit me"). Therefore, through exercise and improved eating, she would regain weight, regain strength, and actively work to get herself back on track.

Prior physical therapy alone had not been able to accomplish these goals. In my judgment, individual psychotherapy alone similarly would not effect recovery. As a psychologist, I would not have been able to provide the guided progressive exercises and strengthening activities that were essential to recovery. Although the patient received antidepressant medication, it seemed doubtful that her central depressogenic belief of being too weak to undertake enjoyable activities would have changed unless supportive professionals guided her to actually experience increased strength.

Formal hypnosis was not used. Instead, we discussed her prior life experience and the inner strength that had enabled her in the past to persevere and could now be accessed and utilized. Counseling and teaching of relatively simple deep-breathing relaxation techniques provided a framework for treatment. Relaxation techniques were framed as periods in which the patient could recover from exercise and physical activity and regain her strength. These techniques were also presented as a means of muscle relaxation, allowing for increased blood flow and, therefore, nourishment of the muscles to rebuild them. The relaxation was further presented as a way of relaxing the abdomen, allowing for the increased flow of gastric juices and thus facilitating increased appetite and renourishment.

After four weeks of treatment, the patient was walking 2.7 miles per hour on the treadmill for 30 minutes, had a sitting tolerance of two hours, and had a work tolerance of four hours. She was able to lift ten pounds and to push a cart similar to one she used at work. She reported feeling “much stronger,” her depression lifted, and her appetite had improved significantly. With the help of physical therapy, she was able to turn her head so that she could check the blind spot while driving. She returned to church and the choir, but did not take on soloist responsibilities, feeling that she was not yet strong enough. The initial plan was for her to return to work part-time and gradually increase her hours as her strength and work tolerance increased, but she decided not to do so. She and I discussed different ways of relating to her husband such that there was significant improvement in their intimate relationship. She reported being able to enjoy being at home with him for the first time in many years and decided to retire.

The second case involved a 27-year-old man from a small southern town who had suffered chronic daily headaches with periodic migraines for about two years prior to being seen for evaluation. These symptoms followed an electrocution accident. Surgery eliminated back pain caused by the fall, but he still suffered from general low-level pain in his neck and shoulders, as well as chronic headaches. He was married and had two children, three and five years of age. He continued to work at a light-duty position with the same employer, but was unhappy with his work assignment.

At the initial interview, the patient described himself as “one ill son of a gun.” He indicated that he was extremely irritable, stating, “I don’t even have a short fuse, I have no fuse at all.” In addition, he described a moderate degree of depression and general anxiety, saying that his “nerves are always on edge.” He described himself prior to his injury as being highly active physically. Competitive sports were a primary outlet for him; in particular, he enjoyed playing basketball, during which he would “talk a lot of trash.” He stated that he had previously enjoyed fishing, but was unable to sit still in a boat since the accident.

The initial plan was to focus on the patient’s symptoms of anxiety and the degree of tension in his neck and shoulders using biofeedback, relaxation training, and the stress management group. The patient did not respond well to this. He appeared uncomfortable in the group and described it as "too stressful." He explained that he was from a small town, was comfortable only with people he knew, and became anxious in the group situation. He also reported feeling very uncomfortable in a one-on-one meeting with myself or the biofeedback therapist, and found it difficult either to sit still and relax or to talk.

The primary focus of therapy, therefore, shifted to physical exercise and reconditioning. The patient was emotionally comfortable while using the treadmill and weight-training machines. This was congruent with his self-perception of being athletically oriented and his belief that the way to make oneself well is to "work out." I discontinued formal individual and group sessions with him and would casually discuss sports while he was doing his exercises. Eventually, we would lightheartedly disagree about upcoming or previously played basketball games. This evolved into some mild "trash talking" in which I would playfully tease him about the mismatch in his exercise outfit, calling him a "country boy," while he would make fun of my tie or some other aspect of my attire, calling me a "city boy." In this way, his natural means of coping with stress and releasing tension in terms both of physically oriented activity and "trash talking" was utilized.

While this patient presented with symptoms typically viewed as amenable to psychophysiological self-control techniques, such as hypnosis or biofeedback, it was primarily the guided exercise program that led to a reduction in his overall tension, irritability, anxiety, and depression. The patient's self-esteem improved as he felt himself "get in shape" with a resumption of his premorbid "cocky" manner. A dramatic reduction in the frequency of his headaches ensued and the patient was able to return to full-time light-duty work in a more responsible supervisory capacity. Treatment, therefore, involved the evocation and utilization of positive state-dependent learning (Rossi, 1986, pp. 36–56) without formal hypnosis, individual sessions, or a multidisciplinary team approach.

In the third case, hypnosis played a central role in individual treatment without the use of an interdisciplinary team. This 44-year-old man was first seen bedside at the general medical hospital to which he had been admitted by his orthopedic physician for tests to determine the nature of his back and leg pain. The patient had fallen in a twisting motion while carrying a moderately heavy mail sack. Psychological consultation was requested because of what the physicians termed the patient's "hypersensitivity" to pain, and his demanding and agitated manner. The patient had great difficulty tolerating traction due to his pain and "hyper manner." Although a computerized tomography (CT) scan identified definite pathology, the physician stated that he would not perform surgery until the patient was able to better manage his pain and explosive personality. The surgeon also stipulated that he wanted the patient to lose weight, quit drinking, reduce the use of narcotics, and stop smoking. Fully expecting him not to be able to accomplish these goals, the surgeon nonetheless agreed that the patient should consult with a psychologist for approximately six months to aid him in this endeavor.

The patient had an idiosyncratic personal style that combined a sophisticated vocabulary with a rough-hewn manner. He described himself as a self-made man who had come out of the orange groves of Florida and worked his way through college. According to the patient, he had been accepted at Oxford for postgraduate studies but became a seaman to support his wife and child. After working as a cook on ships, he became a chef in various restaurants, but eventually took a job with the post office because he wanted the accompanying benefits. Due to the nature of his injury and his need for surgery, physical therapy was not appropriate for him, nor were the progressive physical reconditioning exercises characteristic of the pain rehabilitation program. He was instructed by his physician simply to walk as much as possible.

Our first priority in treatment was better control of his pain and anxiety. When anxious, the patient would become overactive ideationally and lose control of rational thinking, which he termed "being hyper." A hypnotic technique was used to enable the patient to slow his thinking and clear his mind, leading to relaxation and reduced pain. It involved focusing on his hands and warming them to "discharge excess nerve energy." It was suggested that nerve energy would be drawn from his legs and lower back until they were numb, and then released from his warm, tingling hands. To facilitate this numbness, the patient visualized himself wading in water. Self-hypnosis, as well as thought-stopping techniques and psychotropic medication, were used to help the patient develop the capability to manage pain and to quiet his mind.

Hypnotic techniques were used, in conjunction with attendance at Alcoholics Anonymous (AA), to develop abstinence from alcohol and cigarettes and to maintain a weight-loss diet. As a therapeutic relationship developed, the patient revealed that the pain itself was not so overwhelming. Rather, the memories of the abuse he had suffered as a child, which came flooding back to him when he hurt, were most troubling. In other words, his current pain triggered prior painful memories. Similarly, his prior experience made him hyperalgesic or hypersensitized to the experience of pain, resulting in what others perceived to be his emotional overreaction to pain. Hypnotic techniques were used to help the patient deal with these traumatic memories and to take care of the "child within." Over time, we discussed the way in which his former lifestyle, including alcohol and drug use, provided a means of numbing his previously painful experiences.

Much to the surgeon's surprise, the patient was able to fulfill the conditions for surgery by maintaining his abstinence from alcohol, nonprescription drugs, and tobacco, and by losing a significant amount of weight. Hypnotic techniques were used to help the patient prepare for surgery and to cope with the exacerbation of pain following the surgery. After his recovery from surgery, the patient separated from his wife, thereby changing what had been a long-term dysfunctional relationship. The patient moved to another state and worked with me by telephone as he developed a new supportive social network. This included involvement in AA and other recovery groups and membership in a church, where he increasingly took a leadership role. He also developed a relationship with a supportive significant other. I continue to maintain contact with him by telephone, encouraging him in his inner work, a part of which he reports to me in letters.

The case histories are presented to illustrate that various approaches are needed with different individuals. In the first case, the patient needed a supportive team to guide her in a progressive physical reconditioning program so that she could experience regaining her strength. Although psychological treatment provided a useful component of a team approach, individual treatment with or without the use of hypnosis would have been insufficient and inappropriate.

In the second case, following the lead of the patient, treatment was effectively conducted for a psychophysiological condition through a physical reconditioning program without a team approach or formal psychotherapy intervention. Finally, in the third case, a patient physically unsuitable for a physical rehabilitation approach was effectively treated on an individual basis, largely with hypnosis. Hypnosis provided an initial means of managing pain, as well as an avenue for helping to heal prior traumatic experiences and a means of changing dysfunctional behaviors.

These cases were also presented to demonstrate how Ericksonian principles transcend issues of therapeutic technique or of specific agents of change. Whether or not hypnosis is used, treatment begins with the patient's beliefs and proceeds with the accessing and activation of patterns of positive state-dependent learning. Individualizing one's approach by meeting patients at their model of the world, building on a foundation of trust and caring, and taking a multisystems viewpoint is essential whether one is in a treatment dyad or is part of an interdisciplinary team.

## SUMMARY AND IMPLICATIONS

This chapter has focused on the following areas: (1) the complex interacting symptoms of chronic pain syndrome, (2) the treatment goals that follow from these symptoms, (3) the interdisciplinary team often needed to provide treatment to meet these goals, (4) the application of Ericksonian principles in the treatment of chronic pain patients, and (5) the application of Ericksonian principles in team management and the facilitation of team functioning.

Ericksonian principles are fully consistent with mind–body healing approaches that educate and empower people to heal themselves (Zawecky, in Moyers, 1993, p. 151). Healing involves the active participation of the patient (Kabat-Zinn, in Moyers, 1993, p. 134) in accessing and activating inner resources and experiences. Erickson advocated this orientation when he advised practitioners to discover patients' patterns of happiness. Rossi elaborated on and applied the concept to the field of mind–body medicine when he described the process as activating positive state-dependent learning (Rossi, 1986, p. 55). Traditionally, when this was done at all in health care, it was done within the context of the doctor–patient relationship. For this reason, Delbanco has stated, "The doctor/patient relationship is the core of mind–body healing" (in Moyers, 1993, p. 16).

This chapter has argued that the coordinated efforts of a treatment team are required for an increasing number of complex biopsychosocial health care problems, including chronic pain syndrome. A single practitioner, whether doing hypnosis or any modality in the office, may not be able to provide adequate treatment. Ericksonian principles have been shown to be a useful guide not only in the dyadic relationship between patient and healer, but also in the facilitation of a multisystem team process.

The implication of applying Ericksonian principles to team treatment is that professionals must be empowered to develop caring teams that can flexibly and creatively adapt to individual patient needs in order to help patients heal and care for themselves. This goal cannot be attained when treatment decisions are made on a formula basis by faceless individuals uninvolved in the team–patient process. In other words, the direction toward managed care increasingly taken by our health care system stands in opposition to what we are learning from mind–body medicine and multisystem approaches to healing. A health care system that disempowers professionals and patients, thereby removing a sense of control and choice, runs counter to the components that facilitate healing. Policies that ignore the multisystem nature of health and disallow team treatment as too costly may lead to ineffective and ultimately more costly piecemeal approaches. An Ericksonian perspective, therefore, can guide us not only in effective interventions and team treatment approaches, but also in advocating for a caring and more effective health care system. An effective health care system empowers clinicians to create treatment teams that function as communities of caring. Only within such a context can we truly facilitate healing.

## REFERENCES

Gilligan, S. (1987). *Therapeutic trances: The cooperation principle in Ericksonian hypnotherapy.* New York: Brunner/Mazel.

Herman, J. L. (1992). *Trauma and recovery.* New York: Basic Books.

Jensen, N. P., Turner, J. A., & Romano, J. N. (1994). Correlates of improvement in multi disciplinary treatment of chronic pain. *Journal of Consulting and Clinical Psychology, 62,* 172–179.

Jones, J. L. (1994). A constructive relationship for religion with the science and profession of psychology. *American Psychologist, 49,* 184–199.

Lankton, S. R., & Lankton, C. H. (1983). *The answer within: A clinical framework of Ericksonian hypnotherapy.* New York: Bruner/Mazel.

Large, R. G., (1994). Hypnosis for chronic pain: A critical review, *Hypnos, 21,* 234–237.

Lipkin, M., Quill, T., & Napodano, R. (1984). The medical interview: A core curriculum for residencies in internal medicine. *Journal of Internal Medicine, 100,* 277–284.

Loeser, J. D. (1982). Concepts of pain. In M. Stanton-Hicks & R. Boss (Ed.), *Chronic low back pain.* New York: Raven.

Maier, S. F., Watkins, L. R., & Fleshner, M., (1994). Psychoneuroimmunology: The interface between behavior, brain, and immunity. *American Psychologist, 49,* 1004–1017.

Melzack, R., & Wall, P. (1982). *The challenge of pain.* New York: Basic Books.

Moyers, B. (1993). *Healing and the mind.* New York: Doubleday.

Oates, W. E., & Oates, C. E. (1985). *People in pain. Guidelines for pastoral care.* Philadelphia, PA: Westminster.

Rossi, E. (1986). *The psychobiology of mind–body healing. New concepts of therapeutic hypnosis.* New York: Norton.

Rucker, K. (1990). *The future of pain and disability.* Paper presented at the annual meeting of the Academy of Physical Medicine and Rehabilitation.

Seligman, M. (1991). *Learned optimism.* New York: Knopf.

*Standards manual for organizations serving people with disabilities (1993).* Tucson, AZ.: Commission on Accreditation of Rehabilitation Facilities.

Toomey, J. C., Hernadez, J. T., Gettleman, D. F., & Hullsa, J. F. (1993). Relationships of sexual and physical abuse to pain and psychological assessment variables in chronic pain patients. *Pain, 53,* 105–109.

Turk, D., & Melzack, R. (1992). The measurement of pain and the assessment of people experiencing pain. In D. Turk & R. Melzack (Ed.), *Handbook of pain assessment.* New York: Guilford.

Waddell, G., Bricker, M., Finlayson, D., & Main, C. J., (1984). Symptoms and signs: Physical disease or illness behavior? *British Medical Journal, 2,* 739–741.

Waddell, G., Pilowski, I., & Bond, M. (1989). Clinical assessment and interpretation of abnormal illness Behavior in low back pain. *Pain, 39,* 41–53.

Waddell, G., & Turk. D. (1992). Clinical assessment of low back pain. In D. Turk & R. Melzack (Eds.), *Handbook of pain assessment.* New York: Guilford.

Walker, E. A., Katon, W. J., Hamson, J., Harrop-Griffith, J., Holm, L., Jones, M. L., Hickok, L., & Jemelka, R. P. (1992). Medical and psychiatric symptoms in women with childhood sexual abuse. *Psychosomatic Medicine, 54,* 658–64.

Wortele, S. K., Caplan, G. N., Kearins, M. (1990). Childhood sexual abuse among chronic pain patients. *Clinical Journal of Pain, 6,* 110–113.

Yapko, M. D. (1992). *Hypnosis and the treatment of depression. Strategies for change.* New York: Brunner/Mazel.

# 8

# Teaching Children with Asthma to Help Themselves with Relaxation/Mental Imagery

*Daniel P. Kohen*

Asthma is one of the most common chronic illnesses of childhood, affecting 6.9% of children from 3 to 17 years of age (Gevgen, Mullally, & Evans, 1988). An estimated 10 million persons in the United States have asthma, and asthma prevalence rates in the country increased by 29% from 1980 to 1987 (Sheffer, 1991). Well-known morbidities include economic stress (physician and hospital visits, medications, laboratory studies) (Marion, Creer, & Reynolds, 1985), time missed from school (Konig, 1978) and play (Oseid & Edwards, 1983; Leffert, 1980), and negative effects on healthy, normal development, such as maladaptive lifestyles (Leffert, 1980; Mattson, 1975). Nationally, 20 to 25% of school absenteeism is due to asthma, and an estimated 12 million days are spent in bed rest and 28 million days in restricted activities (Gevgen et al., 1988).

While the specific definitions of asthma may vary, a clinical working definition with which most agree acknowledges that "asthma is a lung disease with (1) airway obstruction that is usually (although not always completely) reversible, either spontaneously or in response to treatment; (2) airway inflammation; and (3) increased airway responsivity or reactivity to a variety of stimuli" (Sheffer, 1991). The airway obstruction is responsible for the clinical manifestations of asthma, such as wheezing, shortness of breath, and cough. It is thought to be initiated by inflammation of the airway, but can be influenced by swelling of the lining of the bronchial tree, production of mucus, and airway smooth-muscle contraction (bronchospasm). One of many initial triggers may cause the release of inflammatory mediators from bronchial mast cells, macrophages, and epithelial cells, and these substances then cause the propagation of the inflammatory response. Airway hyperresponsivity is an exaggerated bronchoconstrictor response to many physical, chemical, and pharmacological agents (such as inhalant allergens like pollens and animal danders; environmental irritants, such as air pollutants; and viral respiratory infections, cold air, or exercise). Some believe that this hyperreactivty of the airways is present from birth in a genetic predisposition, and others believe it is acquired, such as through occupational or other exposures. "Airway inflammation is thought to be a key factor in airway hyperresponsiveness" (Sheffer, 1991).

It is recommended (Sheffer, 1991; Marion et al., 1985) that appropriate and effective management of asthma include four carefully integrated components: (1) objective measures of lung function, for assessment and monitoring of progress; (2) pharmacological therapy; (3) environmental measures to control irritants and allergens; and (4) patient education. Goals of therapeutic intervention are to maintain normal pulmonary function; maintain normal activity levels, including exercise; prevent chronic and troublesome symptoms, such as nighttime cough or exertional difficulties; prevent recurrent exacerbations (acute episodes); and avoid adverse effects of medications. The National Asthma Education Program definitively notes: "Asthma is not an emotional or psychological disease, although strong emotions can sometimes make asthma worse" (Sheffer, 1991).

## HYPNOSIS FOR ASTHMA: HISTORICAL PERSPECTIVES

Recent reports have focused on education-based self-management programs. At least 11 such programs have been developed in the

United States since 1977 (Creer, 1991; Plaut, 1988; Taggert et al., 1991; Rachelefsky, 1987; Hindi-Alexander, 1987; Bauchner, Howland, & Adair, 1988; Kohen, M. D., 1985; Rakos, Grodek, & Mack, 1985).

A review of the clinical and research literature reveals that a variety of different hypnotherapeutic approaches and techniques result in similar and sometimes dramatic improvements in asthma. The mechanisms for these changes remain as yet elusive, and more study clearly is needed. Possible mechanisms may include direct (physiological) effects in relaxing bronchial smooth muscle, reduction of anxiety with some form of resultant physiological smooth-muscle relaxation, enhancement of mastery, and/or changes in parental attitudes and behaviors (Collison, 1975; Barbour, 1980; Carson, Council, & Schauer, 1991; Lehrer, Sarguanaraj, & Hochron, 1992).

Relaxation training, with and without systematic desensitization (Alexander, Miklich, & Hershkoff, 1972; Phillip, Wilde, & Day, 1972; Luparello et al., 1968; Moore, 1965; Yorkston et al., 1974), has been shown to produce statistically significant improvement in pulmonary function. Biofeedback, with and without relaxation, has also been described to be effective as an adjunct therapeutic strategy in asthma. Kotses and colleagues (Kotses & Miller, 1987; Kotses et al., 1991) suggest that biofeedback as a method of producing relaxation in facial muscles improves some measures of pulmonary function in children with asthma. Spevack and associates (Spevack, Vost, Maheux, & Bestercezy, 1978) reported that children with asthma responded well to training in "passive relaxation."

Self-hypnosis has also been successful in the interruption of the vicious cycle (anxiety → wheezing → increased anxiety → increased wheezing) of asthma symptoms (Kohen, Olness, Colwell, & Heimel, 1984; Kohen, D. P., 1986a, 1995; Kinsman et al., 1980; Neinstein & Dash,1982; Maher-Longhman, 1970, 1978; Zeltzer et al., 1980; Aronoff, Aronoff, & Peck,1975)

The response of children with asthma to training in self-regulation techniques, such as relaxation/mental imagery (RMI), has not been adequately studied. While most studies attempted to evaluate clinical improvement, none (Khan, 1977; Feldman, 1976, Scherr & Crawford, 1978) included any controls for attention. Previous studies have not addressed the issue of long-term maintenance of pulmonary function changes in children with the use of self-hypnosis or other self-regulation techniques. Prior studies also lacked appropriate controls, and failed to determine clinical improvement or to assess clinical correlation with pulmonary function changes. In a controlled study, we developed a protocol designed to investigate the effectiveness of a personal, mastery-based self-management technique, RMI (self-hypnosis), as an adjunct therapeutic tool in the management of childhood asthma. In this study, children with asthma were randomly assigned to either an experimental group learning hypnosis, a "waking suggestion" control group whose members were given similar suggestions without learning hypnosis, an attention control group whose members were given no suggestions but received the same time and attention, and a traditional control group that received neither attention nor suggestion (Kohen, 1995). We are unaware of any previous published studies that have attempted to assess the so-called placebo effects of positive suggestion or of attention on the outcome of intervention with hypnosis or other self-regulation techniques. We incorporated these concerns in an effort to better understand the effects of RMI on childhood asthma.

This study (Kohen, 1995) demonstrated (1) a reported reduction in anxiety during wheezing episodes, (2) a reduction in the frequency of wheezing episodes, and (3) a reduction of functional morbidity, including a decrease in emergency room visits, a decrease in school absenteeism, a reduction in (self-rated) severity, an increase in (subjective) exercise tolerance, and, in some individuals, a decrease in the need for medication and improved pulmonary function. Perhaps most important, children learning RMI reported improved self-confidence and a sense of personal mastery (over asthma symptoms).

In a recent study, we described and reviewed the effectiveness of a revised form of the original work of Dr. Beata Jencks with the Utah Lung Association. (Jencks et al., 1982) In four different offerings of the Preschool Family Asthma Program, families reported no decrease in the frequency of episodes of asthma. However, management of those episodes reportedly changed dramatically, with a significant decrease in symptom severity, an improved sense of comfort and control in managing acute episodes, and a corresponding decrease in the frequency of physician visits (for acute exacerbations). After their participation in the program, and in the context of their increased self-confidence, parents also reported an increase in positive expectations regarding the future of their child's asthma. While the individual effects of imagery, storytelling, and relaxation were not differentially assessed, it was clear that these techniques, as integrated into the overall family asthma program, were easily incorporated, easily learned, enjoyed, and "taken home" by parents who reported their continued use with their children at home (Kohen & Wynne, 1997, in press).

## THEORETICAL BASIS: VALUE OF RMI FOR ASTHMA

The common and sometimes relentless cycle operative during an acute episode of asthma is well recognized (Kohen, 1986). Regardless of which trigger initiates the cycle, the trigger acts on the hyperresponsive airway of the child with asthma, and the process of wheezing begins, accompanied by inflammation and bronchoconstriction. Anxiety follows, driven by the discomfort of the tightness, shortness of breath, cough, and the need to stop or slow down if involved in exercise. Anxiety and fear are also driven, perhaps unconsciously, by the memory of multiple prior unpleasant episodes, and perhaps by prior relentless deterioration preceding ultimate improvement.

Often the very thought of going to the physician's office or the emergency room may worsen the anxiety and fear, which, in turn, worsen the wheezing. In fact, this cycle may turn negative many times before being interrupted by some intervention(s) that work, from rest, to fluids, to medications. Ultimately, improvement is accompanied at some level by an expectation for that improvement to at least "begin to work."

In the alternative cycle (Kohen, 1986b), the triggers and their initial response of initiating an acute exacerbation of wheezing are the same. For many children, a positive cycle may occur, of course, through the appropriate use of immediate medications (such as inhaled beta$_2$-agonists), cessation of vigorous exercise, and notification of an appropriate helping adult. For those children who experience the negative cycle described, the teaching of an RMI exercise (self-hypnosis) may be sufficient to shift the negative cycle to a positive one. In the critical context of understanding their asthma, children can be taught a self-hypnosis exercise that helps to interrupt the negative cycle and to create a positive one, that is, one in which the child feels a sense of empowerment over the asthma and its effects rather than vice versa, and one in which the child can take a measure of personal internal control in addition to using medication, making environmental changes, and modulating behaviors to improve.

Once a child has learned and begins to believe in a self-hypnosis exercise to help their asthma, the cycle changes to one in which the first sign of any wheezing is a signal to the child to *do* self-hypnosis. In so doing, the child interrupts the relentless cycle of bronchospasm → anxiety → fear → increased wheezing → increased fear, and instead *perpetuates a cycle of self-control* in which relaxation and imagery are accompanied by slowing of the respiratory rate, decreased wheezing, decreased bronchospasm, increased ease of breathing, and an increased expectation for resolution of the problem. Clinical experiences repeatedly describe this positive cycle, even in the emergency room environment, where the effectiveness of hypnotic techniques in allaying anxiety and empowering the patient to be in control help to reverse the negative cycle.

While it is clear that hypnosis is not a panacea for, or is recommended as a singular treatment for, the management of asthma, it also seems apparent that hypnotic techniques can do more to help the child with asthma than we yet know how to measure effectively. It is critical, therefore, that the application of hypnotic techniques and strategies to the management of asthma be understood and presented properly to families. It is a mistake to consider asthma in a theoretical framework that characterizes it as a psychological disorder. Those involved in the care of children with asthma understand the psychoemotional component as one of the many aspects of a child's experience that, like other triggers, can stimulate an acute episode of wheezing and that can be modulated—as through the use of self-hypnosis training—to help the child help himself or herself.

## PRESENTING HYPNOSIS TO THE CHILD PATIENT/FAMILY

As with all interactions with children, approaches to children with asthma are most effective when they greet children where they are. In this sense, naturalistic, Ericksonian strategies of positive expectations, disruption of negative mind-sets, creation and purposeful evocation of curiosity, and reframing are the first and, by definition, informal hypnotic interventions that can and should be utilized.

**TABLE 8.1**
**Value of Relaxation/Mental Imagery (Self-Hypnosis) for Children with Asthma**

1. Reduced anxiety during acute episodes.*
2. Reduced frequency of episodes of asthma.†
3. Reduced functional morbidity.†
   a. Decreased emergency room visits.†
   b. Decreased school absenteeism.†
   c. Increased exercise tolerance.*
   d. Decreased medication needs.*
   e. Improved self-esteem, sense of personal mastery.‡
   f. Improved pulmonary function.‡
   g. Improved long-term functional morbidity.‡

*From Kohen, 1995. Clinical observation.
†Research (Kohen, 1995).
‡Anecdotal, speculation.

In an initial (and subsequent) visit with a child with asthma (and family), the clinician should assess the history of the child's asthma with regard to its onset, the nature of the triggers, and the past as well as current components of management. In this context, one should naturally learn about and explore the child's and parents' expectations, positive and negative, and the child's (and family's) belief model about the asthma; that is, whether they believe they can (and do) help it, and how they do so and at what (financial, emotional, energy) costs. Reframing is easily accomplished in the context of such natural education and rapport building. For example, as patients speak about their negative expectations of limitations of their asthma, this presents a natural opportunity to speculate with them how things will change *when* (not *if*) the asthma is better (not worse), acute episodes are less often and less severe, less medication is needed, and less school is missed. For some, of course, this will mean an expectation for more freedom to play, including sports, and not to miss out on activities, whereas for others, it will also mean more family activity. It may mean vacations, or it may mean being less restricted by a schedule (of nebulized or other medications). This process of helping the child to identify "what's in it for me?" begins to provide a positive expectancy mind-set for the child and family. It also sets the tone that for the clinician, the family's views and ideas are important and expected, and provides salient information about what the child enjoys doing and what goals are identified. These goals and favorite activities should be utilized later in the development of personalized imagery to be incorporated as part of the hypnotic therapy.

Even when a child has had asthma for a long time and has been cared for by good clinicians, it is often astonishing how little the child seems to know about the asthma. One reason might be that in the constraints of a busy clinical office practice, no one took time to ask. Simply asking what the child knows and believes will usually reveal misconceptions and fears, realistic and otherwise. It will also begin to identify the clinician as someone who is interested in the child's opinions and ideas. This spontaneous but important validation of the value of the child's attitudes and beliefs will facilitate the therapeutic communication by stimulating the child to pay increased, careful attention to the clinician, who has, in fact, been paying careful attention to the child.

Clarifying misunderstandings about the disease, the medications, the limitations on activity, and expectations for the future can often go a long way toward shifting a negative cycle to a positive one. In turn, this sets the tone for the introduction of more formal hypnotic technique training. Part of a thorough history for a child with asthma should, of course, identify the circumstances—place, activity—in which the child has had problems with asthma before, as well as those circumstances in which he or she has been wheeze-free. Having this information allows for the more creative development of positive imagery during this phase of the hypnotic work.

## WHAT DOES THE PATIENT KNOW ABOUT HYPNOSIS?

The introduction of hypnotic strategies requires an understanding of the patient's and family's beliefs about hypnosis and related techniques. If they have been referred to the clinician for hypnosis or self-management or biofeedback, then the fact that they kept the appointment may well mean that they have a beginning belief that at least it is possible that this might be useful. If, however, the patient and family have no information in advance about hypnosis, then the introduction of these strategies may meet with quite different results.

While issues of personal style certainly dictate the manner in which educational and therapeutic relationships unfold, the clinician must be particularly clear with children with asthma and their families to reflect himself or herself as one who is competent, confident, and experienced in what is proposed to be taught and how it is proposed to help.

## TALKING ABOUT HYPNOSIS

When a family indicates that they have come for hypnosis or biofeedback or relaxation or imagery, I almost invariably respond by first asking the child, and then the parents, what those techniques are: "What is hypnosis, anyway?" While the response, "I don't know," usually follows immediately, I am not inclined to accept that response, and instead say, "Well, tell me what you've heard, what you've seen, maybe on TV, or what you wondered about it." Misconceptions are thus easily communicated, with the child frequently making a gesture as though swinging a watch back and forth in front of his or her (or my!) eyes. As we explore this popular myth, children (and parents) may further indicate that what happens next is that the subject "falls asleep" and "then does whatever you tell the person to do," recalling little or nothing of the process when he or she "wakes up." With therapeutic intent, I usually respond with humor-focused incredulity, "You don't believe that, do you?"—clearly implying that perhaps there is a more appropriate alternative. I reinforce this by explaining, "That would be someone else controlling what you do, but that's not really possible, is it? Who *is* the boss of your body anyway?" This shift is purposeful, moving from a discussion about hypnosis generally to personal beliefs about control. Invariably, the child's response, even with some hesitation, is "I am."

This is the beginning of planting the seeds, the use of so-called waking suggestions and naturalistic hypnotic-like language to set the tone for change that can and, it is hoped, will occur later. After all, if a child is willing to say that he or she is the boss of his or her body, then talking about the mind effecting changes in the lungs and the breathing process is not such a big leap. Such a discussion naturally allows for clarification about what hypnosis is or is not, that is, that all hypnosis is self-hypnosis and no one else can be in charge of another's body. The discussion naturally leads to an introduction of my role as a good coach and teacher of hypnosis to help children learn how to deal with their asthma. Dispelling other myths at this time is both easy and critical. Clarification that hypnosis is not sleep, and that the clinician doesn't have any particular investment in its being called "hypnosis," aids in removing the shroud of mysticism that commonly cloaks the popular mythology about the technique. It also helps to take the fantasy of "magic" away, while providing a series of positive expectations and laying the groundwork for the more formal hypnotic work to follow. Thus, I may say something like, "You know, some people call this imagery or visualization, some call it hypnosis, some call it imagination or daydreaming, some call it biofeedback, and I don't really care what you call it, because what is really important is that you can learn how to do it pretty fast and that you can use it to help your asthma. Isn't it good to know that?" The embedded hypnotic suggestions offered are "really important," which focuses attention; "you can learn ... pretty fast," which is ego strengthening and positively future oriented; and "help your asthma," which is a positive suggestion, and which is why they have come in the first place.

## TEACHING EXPECTATIONS HONESTLY

To move forward in teaching hypnotic strategies, it is important to clarify reasonable expectations, and to remind the family about the importance of a comprehensive clinical approach to asthma. Thus, while the clinician may believe strongly in the clinical efficacy of hypnotic techniques to the exclusion of other methods, in the face of current knowledge, it is a disservice to portray hypnotic intervention as anything other than an adjunct to therapy, albeit a potentially potent one.

I commonly tell families, "Everyone I have ever met who has asthma has learned hypnosis techniques fairly quickly and easily, and everyone has benefited. No one has ever told me they wished they hadn't learned hypnosis, or that it didn't help. Some have said it helped more than others, but most have said it helped a lot. Most have said they have reduced their need for medications, and some have said they have eliminated all of them. Most have missed less school, and most seem to be able to play and do stuff more easily than before. I don't know how well you will learn [an obvious embedded hypnotic suggestion, this should be viewed as having multiple layers of meaning, that is, as a kind of positively expectant and friendly challenge, and as a direct suggestion that the child *will* learn well]. I'll be glad to be your teacher and coach and help you however I can. Would you like to see a video of how other kids have used this technique for their asthma?"

## THERAPEUTIC STRATEGIES AND SUGGESTIONS

### INDUCTION

Induction, or the formal beginning, of hypnosis is relatively easy, particularly when the clinician has developed the kind of comfortable rapport with the patient described above. In one sense, the hypnotic relationship has already begun, with the offering of positive expectancies and the creation of a context in which suggestions can be easily offered and accepted. In a more concrete sense, the parents and child have learned at a first or second visit that at the next visit the child can expect to "learn hypnosis" and thus "do" something differently.

Like anything we do with children, the manner in which we develop rapport, the induction strategies, the language utilized, and the content and expectations embodied in the hypnotic suggestions must all derive from a developmental context. Just as four-year-olds are different from seven-year-olds and both are different from 10- and 13-year-olds, as they all are in different stages of development, so they think differently and have different needs, and hypnotic inductions, language, and suggestions must be tailored to their level of psychoemotional and cognitive development (Olness & Kohen, 1996; Kohen & Olness, 1993). The hypnotic process may be portrayed to a four-year-old as similar to "pretending," and such children may comfortably slip in and out of hypnotic states as fantasy plays such an integral role in their daily lives. For example, "Let's pretend that we are riding bikes together in a park" or "You're cozy in your room with your kitty or stuffed animals" or "I'll bet you can really smell your grandma's cookies when you pretend you're at her house having fun!" A "young" seven-year-old may be similarly approached, whereas an "older" seven-year-old may, along with a 10-year-old, most easily understand hypnosis when it is suggested that "it's really the same as daydreaming, only you do it on purpose to help yourself, like to learn how to help yourself with asthma while daydreaming." And then, "So, just go ahead and daydream about something you really enjoy, like playing baseball.... have it be a wonderful game.... it helps to close your eyes and just daydream that you're really there, because you really are there in your mind, aren't you?"

For adolescents, an appeal to their more sophisticated developing ego and their intellects is much more likely to be effective. Accordingly, one might suggest, "You know, this hypnosis is just like what you already do when you use your imagination to focus on something you enjoy, rather than listening to your parents when you are getting reprimanded, or really focusing in on something, like your favorite music." It is frequently useful to add, "Most kids discover when they do this that they really have done it before, kind of on their own, only they didn't know they were doing it ... or didn't until now know that it was the same as what you now know is a kind of self-hypnosis." An induction can be as matter-of-fact as, "Just go ahead and close your eyes and imagine that you're not here. I don't know where you'll imagine you are, perhaps with your girlfriend/boyfriend, perhaps at the beach, or out partying, but wherever it is, make it fun, because it's your imagination and you are the boss of it. Some people like to do it by closing their eyes and just being there. Some like to do it by imagining a blank screen—either white or black—and then watching their imagination come onto the screen like a movie beginning. I don't know which you'll do" (The message is that they *will do* something.) (Olness & Kohen, 1996; Kohen & Olness, 1993).

## DEEPENING/INTENSIFICATION

As with any hypnotic work, deepening or intensification and enhancement of the trance experience are easily accomplished by enhancing the imagery with suggestions for a multisensory focus. For example, "Notice who is there with you, or maybe you are alone. Notice what you see there. Notice the weather just the way you like it ... and the more you notice, the more comfortable you get ... and you can get very comfortable. Then notice the sounds there in your imagination, maybe the sounds of the weather, or voices, or music, or maybe it's quiet and you can listen to the quiet." (Note: permissive, choice-focused options within a context are very empowering and remind patients implicitly that they are in charge of the experience, which in itself enhances the experience.)

Particularly with children with asthma, it is very effective as a deepening strategy, as an ego-strengthening suggestion, and as a positive therapeutic suggestion to point out to patients the physiological changes that have taken place since they began the hypnotic experience a few moments earlier. In using the relaxation response, therefore, it is useful to say something like, "It's nice to know that you are doing this *just right*. You probably have already noticed [this is experienced by patients as a compliment as well as an invitation to notice now, if they hadn't already noted] that even though we didn't even mention it, you are sitting very still ... and that means that your body and mind are communicating very effectively while you are in this different state of mind we call imagination or hypnosis. Also, I'm sure you noticed that your face muscles have become very relaxed. That's really good because it's sometimes pretty automatic that when the mind relaxes doing imagination, the body automatically begins to listen and go along and relax too. You probably also noticed that you are breathing more slowly now than you were before we began ... and that's really great to feel ... because it's usual and common that when the mind relaxes, the body responds by breathing more slowly."

This kind of personal biofeedback is invariably affirming, anchors the trance behavior, and typically allows the child patient to become increasingly comfortable and confident. From these observations, there is a natural flow into teaching progressive relaxation by "noticing" with them that "now you can just extend that natural relaxation downwards from your face muscles that are already relaxed, into the other muscles of your body because you may wish to be more relaxed and it's a nice feeling." (Remembering to include the "because" in suggestions is important as it both is motivating and gives the patient a reason to do the suggestion that is offered.) In reinforcing progressive relaxation, what is done should depend on the child's developmental level. To a very young child, one might simply say, "Let your shoulders and arms get all loose and floppy just like a rag doll.... oh, that's great!" With a teenager, one might aim to evoke curiosity by saying something like, "Did you ever notice the body's natural tendency to relax when we breathe out? Test that now ... just take a deep breath in and when you breathe out, just notice your shoulders and what they do.... that's right ... they go down, don't they? That relaxing is natural and you can kind of extend that now, maybe just by thinking the word 'relax' when you breathe out, and kind of send the relaxing down your body."

Observation of other physiological changes, such as eyelid flutter or rapid eye movements under closed lids, can be similarly "fed back" to the patient. Such trance ratification is very important for children, especially for those with asthma, as such ratification sets the tone for the link between mind and body that follows.

## THERAPEUTIC SUGGESTIONS FOR MODULATION OF WHEEZING

The nature and formulation of additional therapeutic suggestions depend on the individual patient's needs. In general, they should refer directly to the previously taught understanding of asthma, that is, an inflammation of the bronchial tree and narrowing of the airway due to accumulation of mucus, and the spasm of muscles around airways. To personalize and increase the value of the therapeutic suggestions, the clinician should aim to incorporate specific words, language, and phraseology used by the child/parent.

It is natural to flow from a focus on progressive relaxation for deepening of hypnosis to therapeutic suggestions directly related to asthma. Thus, as suggestions for progressive relaxation extend to the feet and toes, one might simply provide a link that begins, "Now that all of your *outside* muscles are as comfortable as you want them to be for *this* self-hypnosis practice time." There are several suggestions by implication here: (1) by saying "now," the patient is encouraged to get to this point of comfort if he or she wasn't already there;

(2) by using the word "comfortable" rather than relaxed, one avoids being demanding or expecting that muscles *must* be droopy and floppy in order to be comfortable, and avoids evoking an internal conflict in this regard for the patient; and (3) by reference to *this* practice time, one implies not only the idea and value of future practice, but also that future experiences with self-hypnosis might be somewhat different.

The link would then continue, "It might be good to *turn your attention to the tension of any inside muscles....* take your time.... and when you're ready, just imagine those muscles around your air tubes like we discussed. Maybe you'll see them in your mind's eye, or maybe you'll sense them, or perhaps you'll notice them some other way ... but just notice them ... and perhaps their color ... and how tight or loose they were (past tense) ... and now, as you breathe out [pacing the suggestion to the patient's respiratory cycle], *let those muscles get loose and soft too ... because when* they are, *then* the breathing tubes are wide open and all the air that you need can get in ... and out ... so easily ... that's right ... and you can *enjoy breathing easily.*"

Stories might be constructed that are consistent with the child's level of development and that describe others' success with analogous techniques: For example, "You know, I knew a kid once who told me that she used to have a problem with breathing." (The "used to" is a purposeful embedded suggestion to imply that it's no longer there, and to stimulate the patient to be curious to listen and find out how that child in the story did it.) "After she learned to do her self-hypnosis, she imagined that she was tiny enough to actually go inside her own body, and in her imagination she could take a trip around the body ... to visit and check out all the organs, and eventually to make it to the main breathing tube, where she kind of slid down into the lungs and their breathing tubes, saw the lung muscles around the airways, and when they were tighter than they should be, she would just give them a kind of a push and shove and they would relax and then the air could get in and out more easily." I might go on, "Then there was this boy I knew who, whenever he was having his asthma and was having a lot and mucus and coughing, would do his self-hypnotizing and pretend that Pacman was in his breathing tubes going all around gobbling up all of the mucus like a vacuum cleaner, and the more he got, the more room there was for the air to get through ... nice ... and easily ... in and out ... and the more he thought and pictured that, the better he got, so that pretty soon he just had to *think of it* this way in his inside mind for a few moments and he'd begin to feel better very soon."

Or, for an older child, one might say, "This other guy I knew decided that whenever there was trouble with asthma, he would just imagine that he was somewhere where he never had any trouble with wheezing. The more he pictured himself being there, the more he began to feel better." It is often useful to conclude this area of therapeutic suggestion with an Ericksonian empowerment and curiosity-evoking suggestion to the effect that, for example, "I don't know which way you will use to give instructions to those muscles around your airways, but the more you do it, the better you'll get." This sort of suggestion implies quite directly that the child can indeed give instructions to the airways, and offers a kind of posthypnotic suggestion and challenge to be sure to practice the strategies at home.

Ego-strengthening suggestions should be interspersed with other suggestions throughout the hypnotic experience, to encourage patients, compliment them on doing it right, and tell them to be proud of themselves so that parents, and even doctors and nurses, "might be surprised at how very well you are learning to help yourself."

To foster the belief that all hypnosis is self-hypnosis, and to reinforce what is being experienced, it is advisable to teach self-hypnosis during the first hypnotic session. Thus, toward the end of a first trance experience, it is useful to offer something like: "Now that you have learned so well and are beginning to discover how neat it is to be able to help yourself this way, I'm sure that you want to know what's next. When [not if] you do this at home, it will probably be *easier than you thought* it would be, and every time you do it, it will be easier and easier. Just as you have learned so well today, you will find it easy at home to begin by being in a quiet place where no one will bother or disturb you, and maybe you will even have some of your favorite music on. Then, when you're ready, you can close your eyes and imagine something you enjoy, just like you are doing so easily. Then, notice your body relaxing as much as you need it to, and send the relaxing throughout your body's muscles, inside and out. You can start at your shoulders and relax down your body just like now, or you can start at your feet and relax up. One kid I know starts at her belly button and relaxes in both directions! Then do whatever you want to do to imagine about your breathing tube muscles relaxing, so that you can get all of the air you need. Tell yourself that from now on, each time you have a wheeze or cough, it is an *automatic* reminder [embedded suggestion] to go into this good feeling of hypnosis, of your mind and body working together and create the comfort you deserve [ego strengthening]. Then stay in that good feeling for a while. The last thing that you really need to learn today and for at-home practicing is how to finish ... and that's just as easy. If you are practicing in the daytime, then tell yourself that when you're done, you'll feel just as though you just had a refreshing relaxing one- or two-hour nap, and then you can open your eyes and feel great. Of course, be sure to bring your relaxed body and good feelings with you! *Or,* if you are practicing at night, like before bed, you can just let your self-hypnosis imagination drift into a wonderful and comfortable night's sleep. So, for these last few moments, just give your mind and body any instructions you want them to have, and when you're done, you'll be finished." (Note: Some people like to count, or suggest one or two or three deep breaths, to facilitate a formal ending of the hypnosis. I have never found that necessary or useful and am content to rely on patients' own resources. They always complete the trance on their own.)

## AFTER HYPNOSIS

After a first hypnotic session, it is important to "debrief" and review the experience with the child. Commonly, children will talk about what they imagined and how they felt. Rarely, a child might protest or complain, noting something like, "But I don't feel any different, I still have my wheezing." One of many calm, reassuring responses might be, "Well, this was only the first time. Remember, it took a while to learn the alphabet, and now you can write whole sentences without even thinking much about it. I'm glad you're learning this." And then one might shift to reinforce again the importance of practice and clarify the child's understanding of how to practice self-hypnosis at home.

## FOLLOW-UP VISITS

Commonly, I will see a patient for a second hypnosis visit within a week or two of the initial session. Typically, the first half of such a half-hour visit is spent reviewing patients' experiences of practicing self-hypnosis in the interim, their excitement and their dilemmas. Often they note that it was "really cool how it worked" as well as noticing that it was "different" or "hard" when they *did* it themselves as compared with doing it with me in the office. Although they seem to be complaining when I ask what they did when it was "hard," they invariably say that they figured out what to do. It is natural, then, to validate that experience and to compliment their ingenuity in having figured out what to do. I frequently universalize this by pointing out, "That's what a lot of kids tell me, but they also tell me, as you did, that they figure out how to do it without the coach, because they know that I can't come to their house and help them anyway!" This not only allays the common childhood anxiety that they were the only ones who had to struggle with it, but also reinforces their success.

Before practicing hypnosis, it is important to clarify with the patient which parts of the first session they liked or didn't like, and perhaps offer the opportunity for this particular session to be audiotaped. This allows the option to "have the coach at home" in case they are feeling lazy one day or "in case you sort of know you should practice, but don't feel like it." In the interest of promoting autonomy and self-confidence, it is not recommended that audiotapes be made until one is assured that the patient knows how to practice at home on his or her own, has been doing so, and has experienced at least a modicum of success in feeling good with self-hypnosis.

Common follow-up questions and concerns relate mostly to implementation and integration of the self-hypnotic, RMI strategies. Children and families often wonder what they might do if the child develops wheezing in the middle of class or during a basketball game. In these or other situations, it is important to be sure that the child and family know the appropriate medical steps to take in addition to whatever they have learned to do hypnotically to help their asthma. All involved should be assured that the child and parents understand the medications (if any) and their appropriate use. It is very reassuring to most families when the clinician offers to write a note to the teacher or school nurse indicating, for example, "This student has learned a self-relaxing technique to use to help himself (or herself) with asthma. If he (or she) is having difficulty, with a lot of wheezing, in the classroom or on the playground, it would be good to have a private, quiet place to rest, to use the inhaler or other medication, and then to go through the self-relaxation routine. A personal audiotape can be used to help with this and earphones keep it from disturbing others. If you have any questions, please give me a call."

## SUPPORT GROUPS

As with any other chronic illness, children with asthma and their families may benefit from the opportunity to talk with others who have the same problem. Such asthma support groups commonly provide resources for education and discussion of medication use, clarify the understanding of decision making concerning clinical problems, and can serve as a reinforcement of the value of RMI self-hypnosis exercises. In such settings, we have also noted the value of teaching the parents RMI self-hypnosis strategies (Kohen & Wynne, 1997, in press; Kohen, 1990). For preschool and younger children, the fact that their parents participate in learning RMI often serves as an incentive for them to participate and learn for themselves. For their part, the parents learn self-hypnosis for personal relaxation, and also come to understand the process so that they can then be more comfortable and capable in facilitating their children's use of RMI. For older children, learning or reinforcing RMI self-hypnosis in a group is reinforcing both of the RMI itself and of the demystification of the self-hypnosis. Thus, seeing others doing it and using it makes it even more "okay" for them to do it, while also reinforcing the process itself (Kohen & Wynne, 1997, in press; Kohen, 1990).

## CONCLUSION

For children and adolescents with asthma, self-hypnosis is a very effective self-management strategy that is easily integrated into a comprehensive management approach. An adjunct easily learned by most children, self-hypnosis can be utilized to help reduce discomfort and anxiety, and perhaps abate an acute episode of wheezing. It can help to promote a child's sense of personal control and mastery over symptoms that otherwise might have been disabling, and in ways as yet poorly understood, it can help the patient to reduce the intensity and duration of episodes by increasing body awareness and noticing and intervening with episodes earlier in their evolution. Self-hypnosis can help to reduce the potential morbidity of asthma through reduction of the need for emergency department visits and days missed from school, and may, in some cases help reduce the need for medications (Kohen, 1995).

## REFERENCES

Alexander, A. B., Miklich, D. R., & Hershkoff, H. (1972). The immediate effects of systematic relaxation training on peak expiratory flow rates in asthmatic children. *Psychosomatic Medicine, 34*(5), 388–394.

Aronoff, G. M., Aronoff, S., & Peck, L. W. (1975). Hypnotherapy in the treatment of bronchial asthma. *Annals of Allergy, 34,* 356–362.

Barbour, J. (1980). Medigrams: Self-hypnosis and asthma. *American Family Physician, 21,* 173.

Bauchner, H. C., Howland, J., & Adair, R. (1988). The impact of pediatric asthma education on morbidity: Assessing the evidence (abstract). *American Journal of Diseases of Childhood, 142*(4), 398–399.

Carson, D. K., Council, J. R., & Schauer, R. W. (1991). The effectiveness of a family asthma program for children and parents. *Children Health Care, 20*(2), 114–119.

Collison, D. R. (1975). Which asthmatic patients should be treated by hypnotherapy? *Medical Journal of Australia, 1,* 776–781.

Creer, T. L. (1991). The application of behavioral procedures to childhood asthma: Current and future perspectives. *Patient Education and Counseling, 17,* 9–22.

Feldman, G. M. (1976). Effect of biofeedback training on respiratory resistance of asthmatic children. *Psychosomatic Medicine, 38,* 27–37.

Francis, P. W. J., Krastins, I. R. B., & Levison, H. (1980). Oral and inhaled salbutamol in the prevention of exercise induced bronchospasm. *Pediatrics, 66*(1), 103–108.

Gevgen, P. J., Mullally, D. I., & Evans, R. III (1988). National survey of prevalence of asthma among children in the United States 1976–1980. *Pediatrics, 81*(1), 1–7.

Hindi-Alexander, M. C. (1987). Asthma education programs: Their role in asthma morbidity and mortality. *Journal of Allergy and Clinical Immunology, 80*(3), part 2, 492–494.

Jencks, B., et al. (1982) *Preschool asthma program: Self-care training for asthmatic children ages two to five—teacher's manual.* Salt Lake City: Utah Lung Association.

Khan, A. U. (1977). Effectiveness of biofeedback and counter-conditioning in the treatment of bronchial asthma. *Journal of Psychosomatic Research, 21,* 97–104.

Kinsman, R. A., Dirks, J. F., Jones, N. F., et al. (1980). Anxiety reduction in asthma: Four catches to general application. *Psychosomatic Medicine, 42*(4), 397–405.

Kohen, D. P. (1986a). Applications of relaxation/mental imagery (self-hypnosis) in pediatric emergencies. *International Journal of Clinical and Experimental Hypnosis, 34*(4), 283–294.

Kohen, D. P. (1986b). The value of relaxation/mental imagery (self-hypnosis) to the management of children with asthma: A cyberphysiologic approach. *Topics in Pediatrics, 4*(1), 11–18.

Kohen, D. P. (1990). *Group hypnotherapy for children with asthma and for their parents* (videotape). St Paul, MN: Children's Hospital of St. Paul Asthma Support Group.

Kohen, D. P. (1995). Relaxation/mental imagery (self-hypnosis) for childhood asthma: Behavioral outcomes in a prospective, controlled study. *HYPNOS, The Swedish Journal of Hypnosis in Psychotherapy and Psychosomatic Medicine, 22*(3), 133–144.

Kohen, D. P., & Olness, K. N. (1993). Hypnosis with children. In J. Rhue, S. J. Lynn, & L. Kirsch (Eds.), *Handbook of clinical hypnosis.* Washington, DC: American Psychological Association.

Kohen, D. P., Olness, K. N., Colwell, S. O., & Heimel, A. (1984). The use of relaxation mental imagery (self-hypnosis) in the management of 505 pediatric behavioral encounters. *Journal of Developmental and Behavioral Pediatrics, 5*(1), 21–25.

Kohen, D. P., & Wynne, E. (1997, in press). A preschool family asthma education program: Uses of storytelling, imagery, and relaxation. *American Journal of Clinical Hypnosis.*

Kohen, M. D. (1985). Educational and exercise programs for asthmatic children. *Southern Medical Journal, 78*(8), 948–950, 953.

Konig, P. (1978). Pharmacologic management of childhood asthma. *Advances in Asthma and Allergy, 5*(3), 58–65.

Kotses, H., Harver, A., Segreto, J., Glaus, K. D., Creer, T. L., & Young, G. A. (1991). Long term effects of biofeedback-induced facial relaxation on measures of asthma severity in children. *Biofeedback and Self-Regulation, 16,* 1–22.

Kotses, H., & Miller, D. J. (1987). The effects of changes in facial muscle tension on respiratory resistance. *Biological Psychology, 25,* 211–219.

Leffert, F. (1980). The management of acute severe asthma. *Journal of Pediatrics, 96*(1), 1–12.

Lehrer, P. M., Sarguanaraj, D., & Hochron, S. (1992). Psychological approaches to the treatment of asthma. *Journal of Consulting and Clinical Psychology, 60*(4), 639–643.

Luparello, T., et al. (1968). Influences of suggestion on airway reading in asthmatic subjects. *Psychosomatic Medicine, 30*(6).

Maher-Longhman, G. P. (1970). Hypnosis and autohypnosis for the treatment of asthma. *International Journal of Clinical and Experimental Hypnosis, 18,* 1–14.

Maher-Longhman, G. P. (1978). Hypnosis in bronchial asthma. In E. B. Weiss, & M. S. Segal, (Eds.), *Bronchial asthma in mechanisms and therapeutics* (pp. 1041–1054). Boston: Little Brown.

Marion, R. J., Creer, T. L., & Reynolds, R. V. C. (1985). Direct and indirect costs associated with the management of childhood asthma. *Annals of Allergy, 54,* 31–34.

Mattson, A. (1975). Psychologic aspects of childhood asthma. *Pediatric Clinics of North America, 22*(1), 77–89.

Moore, N. (1965). Behavior therapy in bronchial asthma: A controlled study. *Journal of Psychosomatic Research, 9,* 257–267.

Neinstein, L. S., & Dash, J. (1982). Hypnosis as an adjunct therapy for asthma: Case report. *Journal of Psychosomatic Research, 9,* 257–276.

Olness, K. N., & Kohen, D. P. (1996). *Hypnosis and hypnotherapy with children* (3rd ed.). New York: Guilford.

Oseid, S., & Edwards, A. M. (Eds.) (1983). *The asthmatic child in play and sport* (proceedings of an international symposium, Oslo, Norway). London: Pitman.

Phillip, R. L., Wilde, G. J., & Day, J. H. (1972). Suggestion and relaxation in asthmatics. *Journal of Psychosomatic Research, 6*(3), 193–204.

Plaut, T. (1988). *Children with asthma: A manual for parents* (2nd ed.). Amherst, MA: Pedipress.

Rachelefsky, G. S. (1987). Review of asthma self-management programs. *Journal of Allergy and Clinical Immunology, 80*(3, part 2), 506–511.

Rakos, R. F., Grodek, M. V., & Mack, K. K. (1985). The impact of a self-administered behavioral intervention program in pediatric asthma. *Journal of Psychosomatic Research, 29*(1), 101–108.

Scherr, M. S., & Crawford, P. L. (1978). Three-year evaluation of biofeedback techniques in the treatment of children with chronic asthma in a summer camp environment. *Annals of Allergy, 41,* 288–292.

Sheffer, A. L., et al. (Eds.) (1991a). *Guidelines for the diagnosis and man-*

*agement of asthma: National asthma education program and expert panel report.* Office of Prevention, Education, and Control, National Heart, Lung and Blood Institute, National Institutes of Health, Bethesda, MD, Publication no. 91-3042 (U.S. Department of Health and Human Services).

Sheffer, A. L., et al. (Eds.) (1991b). *Executive summary: Guidelines for the diagnosis and management of asthma.* Office of Prevention, Education, and Control, National Heart, Lung and Blood Institute, National Institutes of Health, Bethesda, Md, Publication no. 91-3042A (U.S. Department of Health and Human Services).

Spevack, M., Vost, M., Maheux, V., & Bestercezy, A. (1978). Group passive relaxation exercises in asthma. *Pediatric News, 12,* 14.

Taggert, V. S., Zuckerman, A. E., Sly, R. M., Steinmueller, C., Newman, G., O'Brien, R. W., Schneider, S., & Bellanti, J. A. (1991). You can control asthma: Evaluation of an asthma education program for hospitalized inner-city children. *Patient Education and Counseling, 17,* 35–47.

Yorkston, N. J., McHugh, R. B., Brady, R., et al. (1974). Verbal desensitization in bronchial asthma. *Journal of Psychosomatic Research, 18,* 371–376.

Zeltzer, L., LeBaron, S., Barbour, J., et al. (!980). Self-hypnosis for poorly controlled adolescent asthmatics. *Clinical Research, 28*(5), 862A.

# 9

# Consulting About Insomnia: Hypnotherapy, Sleep Hygiene, and Stimulus-Control Instructions

*Gary R. Elkins*

Insomnia refers to a patient's complaint and perception that his or her sleep is inadequate in terms of quantity or quality. Generally, insomnia is seen as a symptom rather than as a disease. Among its symptoms are that the patient has difficulty in initiating sleep, is able to initiate sleep but awakens after a short time, has frequent awakenings from sleep, or sleeps but the sleep is nonrestorative (Kales & Kales, 1984). In addition, insomnia is the most common disorder of sleep reported by patients (Bixler, Kales, & Soldatos, 1979). A consensus conference held by the National Institute of Mental Health (1984) reported that 35% of a nationally representative sample reported "trouble sleeping in the past." Of this group, half described it as a serious problem. Fully 47% of these individuals exhibited elevated anxiety, depression, or medical or psychiatric illness as compared with only 11% of those who denied having difficulty with their sleep. These findings suggest that insomnia not only is common, but is also frequently related to other problems.

With regard to diagnosis, the symptom of insomnia can be related to depression, alcohol or drug abuse, medical disorders, or specific sleep disorders (Gillin & Byerly, 1990). Therefore, accurate differential diagnosis is essential for the effective management of this problem. The treatment of chronic insomnia can be difficult, and it is not uncommon for it to take weeks or even several months. This may include a clinical interview, taking a sleep history, sleep laboratory studies, and psychological assessment, as well as other procedures (Becker & Jamieson, 1990). In spite of this, clinicians are often called on to provide once-only consultations or very brief focused therapy in the treatment of insomnia (Hauri, 1993).

Psychological approaches have been found to be useful in the treatment of psychophysiological insomnia and insomnia associated with stress (Borkovec, 1982). Persistent psychophysiological insomnia involves behavioral issues that are thought to play a predominant role in the maintenance of the patient's disturbed sleep. Several studies attest to the effectiveness of behavioral therapy and relaxation therapy in the treatment of insomnia (Turner & DiTomasso, 1980; Lacks, Bertelson, Gans, & Kunkel, 1983). As an example, Bootzin, Epstein, and Wood (1991) described the use of stimulus-control instructions. These are direct instructions to the patient to associate the bed and bedroom with sleep as opposed to other activities, such as reading or watching television. Glovinsky and Spielman (1991) have reported on a somewhat similar behavioral treatment involving sleep restriction therapy in which the patient is instructed to limit the time in bed so that sleep curtailment also results in improved sleep as the cues in the bedroom are associated with tiredness and sleep. Also, almost all clinical treatment programs involve recommendations for good sleep hygiene, such as avoiding caffeine products before bedtime, exercising regularly, and not taking naps during the day (Lacks & Rotert, 1986; Hauri & Linde, 1990).

There have been a limited number of studies regarding the use of hypnotherapeutic approaches to the treatment of insomnia. Graham, Wright, Toman, and Mark (1975) compared the effectiveness of hypnosis and relaxation training in the treatment of insomnia among 22 student volunteers. The subjective ratings obtained showed substantial improvement for both the hypnosis and relaxation conditions. However, only subjects in the relaxation condition achieved a significant reduction in the frequency of nights of insomnia on objective measurement. There was a higher attrition rate with regard to the hypnosis condition, which may have been a reflection of lower motivation or lower expectation of success on the part of the hypnosis subjects. Borkovec and Fowles (1973) compared progressive muscle relaxation, hypnotic relaxation, and a no-treatment control condition. The study was well designed and randomized. Results indicated that both hypnotic relaxation and progressive muscle relaxation resulted in significant decreases in the latency of sleep onset in comparison with the no-treatment condition. Although there were no measures of hypnotizability, these results do suggest that relaxation may be an important component of effective treatment.

More recently, Stanton (1989) conducted a study in which subjects were assigned to one of three treatment conditions: hypnotherapy, stimulus control, or placebo. Subjects in the treatment groups received four weekly 30-minute sessions. Hypnosis involved mental imagery and ego-strengthening suggestions. The members of the placebo group were instructed in imagining neutral presleep images. A significant reduction in sleep-onset latency was found only for the hypnotherapy group, with subjects in that group achieving a reduction of over 50%. While the results obtained by Stanton demonstrated a superiority of hypnosis over the behavioral treatment, both are likely to be important considerations in clinical practice.

The present study sought to investigate a brief intervention for the treatment of insomnia in a clinical population. This study involved consecutive patients referred to an insomnia clinic in a medical setting as opposed to student volunteers. Specifically, the combined treatments of hypnotherapy, stimulus-control instructions, and recommendations for sleep hygiene were investigated.

## METHOD

### SUBJECTS

The subjects were eight consecutive patients who were referred for the treatment of insomnia. Each patient completed a detailed sleep history questionnaire and a clinical interview that indicated a diagnosis of either psychophysiological insomnia (according to the *Diag-*

*nostic and Statistical Manual of Mental Disorders* [DSM-IV], 307.42, Primary Insomnia) or insomnia associated with stress (DSM-IV 307.42, Insomnia Related to Adjustment Reaction with Mixed Emotions). Patients who received other diagnoses were excluded from this study. Six of the patients received the diagnosis of insomnia associated with stress. To be included, each patient had to meet the criteria of insomnia with sleep-onset latency of more than 30 minutes or awake time during the night totaling more than 30 minutes or less than 6 1/2 hours of total sleep at night, with a duration of symptoms for at least three months. The age range of subjects was 27 to 66 years old with a mean age of 42. Three of the subjects were men and five were women.

## PROCEDURES

During the initial consultation, the sleep history was reviewed, a clinical interview was completed, and the patient was rated, on a 1–10 scale, the seriousness of the sleep problem for the past week, the average number of hours and minutes he or she slept each night during the past week, and an estimate of how many times the patient awoke each night during the past week prior to consultation.

The patient's sleep-related behaviors and sleep hygiene were reviewed. Each patient was given recommendations with regard to sleep hygiene that included:

1. Do not go to bed until you are drowsy.
2. Get up at approximately the same time each morning including weekends.
3. Do not take naps during the day.
4. Do not drink alcohol prior to bedtime.
5. Do not consume caffeine within six hours prior to bedtime.
6. Do not smoke for several hours prior to bedtime.
7. Exercise regularly but avoid strenuous physical exertion after 6 P.M.
8. Arrange for a comfortable sleep environment that is darkened, cool, and free of distracting noise.
9. You may have a light snack prior to bedtime.

In addition, patients were also given stimulus-control instructions, both verbally and in written form. The specific recommendations for stimulus-control instructions included:

1. Use your bed and bedroom only for sleep. Do not read, eat, or watch television in bed.
2. Establish a regular presleep routine prior to going to bed.
3. If you do not fall asleep within 30 minutes, get up and go into another room. Engage in a boring activity. Do not eat, listen to the radio, or watch television. You may read if it is material that you find boring.
4. Return to bed when you feel sleepy. If you do not fall asleep within 30 minutes, repeat the step 3.

The session ended with a discussion of the use of hypnosis to facilitate sleep. In addition, the patient was provided with information regarding the use of hypnosis and dispelling any myths regarding hypnosis. The next session was scheduled within seven days.

At the second session, the sleep hygiene rules and the stimulus-control instructions were reviewed with the patient and any questions were answered. The importance of these recommendations were emphasized to the patient. A hypnotic induction was then completed, which was tape recorded for the patient's home practice.

The hypnotic induction utilized an eye focus induction with suggestions to focus on breathing and direct suggestions for relaxation. Suggestions were then given for dissociation and pleasant imagery of being in a peaceful and safe place. Suggestions were also given for "letting go" and deeper relaxation. Suggestions for peace and tranquility were interspersed, as well as suggestions for setting aside any worries by placing them inside a box and closing the lid. As an example, the verbalization included: "These things are set aside the way one might put things into an old trunk or box and put them on a shelf so that after a time one could hardly even remember what things were in the box." The specific goals and steps for the hypnotic induction are outlined in Table 9.1.

Suggestions were given in a monotone with frequent repetitions and were interspersed with very permissive suggestions emphasizing

**TABLE 9.1**
**Tape-Assisted Self-Hypnosis**

1. Eye focus induction.
2. Focus on breathing and suggested relaxation.
3. Suggestions for dissociation and pleasant imagery.
4. Suggestion for "letting go" and deep relaxation.
5. Suggestion for peace and tranquility.
6. Imagery for setting aside any worries.
7. Verbalization given in monotone, boring repetition.
8. Permissive suggestions.
9. Relaxation emphasized—physical, mental, emotional.
10. Suggestions for restful sleep.

choice. Relaxation was emphasized in terms of physical relaxation, mental relaxation, and emotional relaxation. Suggestions were also given for a positive expectation for restful sleep. At the end of the session, each patient was provided with an audiocassette tape of the hypnotic induction, utilizing suggestions that were given during the session.

## RESULTS

Follow-up was completed at three months' posttreatment. Each patient was contacted by telephone to answer a series of questions with regard to he or her consultation and sleep. Patients were asked to provide an overall assessment regarding the question: "To what degree do you feel that your sleep has changed?" A rating of -10 represented much worse, 0 represented no change, and +10 represented much better than utilized. The average rating was +5.25 (range, 3.5 to 8.0), reflecting at least a moderate degree of positive improvement.

Next, patients were asked about what aspect of their consultation they found to be most helpful. They all rated the instruction in self-hypnosis and the use of the tape recording for self-hypnosis as the most helpful aspect of the consultations. In terms of the next most helpful aspects of treatment, six patients rated the recommendations for sleep hygiene as most helpful followed by the recommendations for stimulus-control instructions.

With regard to the recommendations for sleep hygiene, the results indicated that patients utilized at least some of these recommendations, with all patients reporting that they had used at least one of them. They then were asked to rate the recommendations for sleep hygiene on a 1 to 10, with 1 representing "not helpful at all" and 10 representing "very helpful." There was an average rating of 4.8 (range, 3.0 to 6.0), again suggesting at least a moderate positive response to these recommendations.

As a measure of compliance, the patients were also asked whether they had actually used the treatment and recommendations after they returned home. The majority of the patients reported that they did not use the stimulus-control instructions, with many describing the instructions as inconvenient to follow or not practical. The percentage of 37% represents three of the eight patients in the present study who indicated that they actually did utilize the stimulus-control instructions for at least one night.

Those three patients who used the instructions were asked to rate their helpfulness on the 1 to 10 scale, with 1 representing "not helpful at all" and 10 representing "very helpful." There was an average rating of 4.3 (range, 2.0 to 7.0), which is slightly lower than the ratings of the other recommendations.

With regard to the use of hypnotherapy, patients were asked to rate on a 1 to 10 scale how helpful they found the tape-assisted hypnosis practice. Again, 1 represented "not helpful at all" and 10 represented "very helpful." The results were positive, with the majority of patients rating this aspect of the therapy as helpful, with an average of 9.0 (range, 8.0 to 10.0). The patients were also asked whether they would recommend hypnosis to a friend or relative who was suffering from insomnia. All of the patients indicated that they would recommend hypnosis to others.

The last series of questions were aimed at gathering data regarding the patient's change in sleep along several dimensions. The first question asked was: "During the week, on the average, how long did it take you to fall asleep?" In comparing the average pre- and postnumber of minutes, the average was an improvement from about 88 minutes (range, 60 minutes to 120 minutes) to an average of 28 minutes (range, 15 minutes to 40 minutes). The patients were then asked: "During the past week, on average, how many times did you awaken each night?" Again, an improvement was indicated, from an average of about five awakenings per night to three awakenings per night.

Patients were also asked: "During the past week, how long did you sleep each night in total number of hours and minutes?" The length of sleep improved in the patient's subjective ratings from an average of about four hours to an average of six hours of sleep per night.

## DISCUSSION

The present study reports on the successful use of hypnosis in a brief multimodal intervention for insomnia. The data suggest that hypnosis was well accepted by patients and was perceived as a useful component of the treatment and consultations. Hypnosis may be particularly useful in the treatment of psychophysiological insomnia or where stress may be an important component of difficulty with sleep. The data in general support the conclusions of Stanton (1989), which found hypnosis to be superior to a behavioral treatment in a clinical population. The study suggests that one reason for the relative superiority of hypnosis may lie in the greater degree of patient acceptance of and compliance with the hypnotic intervention in comparison with the stimulus-control instructions. Hypnosis in the treatment of insomnia is pleasant, goal directed, and usually results in some early validation as the patient is able to achieve physiological relaxation. While stimulus-control instructions have been shown to be effective, the requirement that the patient get out of bed may lead to resistance.

Also, the data indicate that hypnosis was seen as a credible intervention. In fact, all of the participants in the study said that they would recommend hypnosis to a friend or relative who was suffering from insomnia. Graham et al. (1975) have suggested that the expectation of success is an important determinant of the treatment outcome of approaches to insomnia. From a clinical perspective, it may be important to precede any treatment for insomnia, whether hypnosis or a nonhypnotic intervention, by suggestions that build a positive expectation for success.

While clinically relevant, the present data are preliminary. Further research is needed comparing patients of high and low hypnotizability, as are research designs in which a no-treatment control group is included. Also, since the experimenter delivered all treatments, the influence of experimenter bias is impossible to determine. Further, inasmuch as the present study utilized a multimodal approach, it is impossible to determine the exact components that most contributed to the outcome. Hypnosis may be a very valuable component of the treatment of insomnia, particularly that utilizing brief interventions. It is hoped that this study will stimulate controlled experimental outcome research on this important and frequently encountered sleep disorder.

## REFERENCES

Becker, P. M., & Jamieson, A. O. (1990, December). Insomnia: Practical assessment and management. *Dallas Medical Journal,* 281–283.

Bixler, E. O., Kales, A., & Soldatos, C. R. (1979) Sleep disorders encountered in medical practice: A national survey of physicians. *Behavioral Medicine, 6,* 1–6.

Bootzin, R. R., Epstein, D., & Wood, J. M. (1991). Stimulus-control Instructions. In P. J. Hauri, (Ed.), *Case studies in insomnia.* New York: Plenum.

Borkovec, T. D. (1982). Insomnia. *Journal of Consulting and Clinical Psychology, 50,* 880–895.

Borkovec, T. O., & Fowles, D. C. (1973). Controlled investigation of the effects of progressive and hypnotic relaxation on insomnia. *Journal of Abnormal Psychology, 82,* 153–158.

Gillin, J. C., & Byerly, W. F. (1990). The diagnosis and management of insomnia. *New England Journal of Medicine, 322,* 239–248.

Glovinsky, P. R., & Spielman, A. J. (1991). Sleep restriction therapy. In P. J. Hauri, (Ed.), *Case studies in insomnia* (pp. 49–63). New York: Plenum.

Graham, K. R., Wright, G. W., Toman, W. J., & Mark, C. R. (1975). Relaxation and hypnosis in treatment of insomnia. *American Journal of Clinical Hypnosis, 18,* 39–42.

Hauri, P. J. (1993). Consulting about insomnia: A method and some preliminary data. *Sleep, 16*(4), 344–350.

Hauri, P. J. & Linde, S. (1990). *No more sleepless nights.* New York: Wiley.

Kales, A., & Kales, J. D. (1984). *Evaluation and treatment of insomnia,* New York: Oxford University Press.

Lacks, P., Bertelson, A. D., Gans, L., & Kunkel, J. (1983). The effectiveness of three behavioral treatments for different degrees of sleep onset insomnia. *Behavior Therapy, 14,* 593–605.

Lacks, P., & Rotert, M. (1986). Knowledge and practice of sleep hygiene techniques in insomniacs and good sleepers. *Behavior Research and Therapy, 24,* 365–368.

National Institute of Mental Health (1984). Consensus Development Conference: Drugs and insomnia: The use of medications to promote sleep. *Journal of the American Medical Association,* 251, 2410–2414.

Stanton, H. E. (1989). Hypnotic relaxation and the reduction of sleep onset insomnia. *International Journal of Psychosomatics, 36,* (1–4), 64–68.

Turner, R. M. & DiTomasso, R. A. (1980). The Behavioral treatment of insomnia: A review and methodological analysis of the evidence. *International Journal of Mental Health, 9,* 129–148.

# 10

# Diminishing Skin Test Reactivity to Allergens with a Hypnotic Intervention

*Tannis M. Laidlaw, Robert G. Large, and Roger J. Booth*

Hypnosis is a powerful intervention widely used in clinical psychology for treating a range of psychosomatic and other conditions. Our interest focuses particularly on the relationship between psychological processes and immune system behavior. Given that hypnosis has been effectively used in the treatment of asthma (Collison, 1975; Aronoff, Aronoff, & Peck, 1975; Wilkinson, 1981; Ewer & Stewart, 1986) and allergies (Kershaw, 1987), we have explored the use of hypnotic-type interventions in laboratory-based, allergy-related responses. We used skin-prick testing as a method of assessing a person's reaction to a particular allergen. In this method, small drops of allergen solution are placed on a person's arm and pricked into the top layer of skin. An immediate hypersensitivity reaction (a raised weal and reddened flare) is produced within a few minutes if the person is allergic to the substance. All of us exhibit a similar reaction to solutions of histamine, which is one of the substances produced by the body that mediate the weal and flare reaction to allergens.

Our initial studies centered on the extent and magnitude of the day-to-day variation in such skin responses (Laidlaw, Richardson, Booth, & Large, 1994). Although we could find no evidence of systematic changes in skin reactivity due to repeated allergic skin testing, we did find that much of the variation in the size of weals could be explained by changes in a person's moods (Laidlaw, Booth, & Large, 1994). Other investigators have reported that hypnosis could be used to alter responses to allergic provocation, especially Black in the 1960s (e.g., Black, 1963a, 1963b; Black, Humphrey, & Niven, 1963; Black & Friedman, 1965; Black, 1969) and, later, Zachariae (Zachariae, Bjerring, & Arendt-Nielsen, 1989; Zachariae & Bjerring, 1993). The question then arises as to how much these effects could be due to hypnotically induced mood changes and also how important hypnotizability might be as a contributory factor. We set out to test this by using a hypnotic visualization procedure to assess whether normal people could deliberately decrease their reactivity to histamine skin-prick testing. That study (Laidlaw, Booth, & Large, 1996) illustrated that a hypnotic technique, using visualization of self-generated images, was an effective intervention for reducing the magnitude of the histamine weals. The study included 38 subjects, 18 of whom also gave positive skin tests in response to at least one of six common allergens. A further question, therefore, is whether the allergen weals in those 18 allergic subjects responded during the hypnotic intervention in a manner similar to those reactions generated in response to histamine. This chapter reports the results of that comparison and discusses the character of the hypnotic procedure used in the study.

## METHODS

The study design is described fully elsewhere (Laidlaw et al., 1996) and so only a brief summary of the experimental procedure is presented here, although we will describe the hypnotic intervention in more detail. Out of 38 volunteers (13 men and 25 women ages 18 to 65 years; mean ages 39.2 years), 18 exhibited positive skin tests with one or more of six common allergens (dust mite [*D. pteronyssimus*] and dust mite [*D. farinae*], cat hair epithelium, dog hair dander, plantain, and grass pollen mix from Miles-Hollister-Steir, Elkart, IN) and it is the responses of these 18 people that provide the focus of this chapter. The subjects were not selected by their hypnotizability scores, although all had participated in a general hypnotizability testing program (Harvard Scale of Hypnotic Susceptibility: A (HGSHS:A) some months earlier. The unpaid volunteers were drawn from within and around the University of Auckland School of Medicine. They were given a relaxation tape at the completion of the study.

## SKIN TESTS AND PSYCHOLOGICAL TESTS

Sessions were conducted with each subject individually in a small, quiet, pleasantly furnished laboratory in the School of Medicine. The methodology for administering skin test reagents and photographing the weals, and determining their areas was described in detail in our previous work (Laidlaw et al., 1994). In brief, droplets of the histamine solution (consisting of six serial fivefold dilutions of histamine beginning at a concentration of 10 mg/mL) or allergen solutions (similarly diluted in a series of six fivefold steps) were placed on the anterior surface of the forearm (allergen on the left arm, histamine on the right) and then the skin was pricked through the droplets with a Hollister-Stier Prick Lancetter.

The resulting weals were photographed on slide film after 10 minutes using oblique illumination to create light and shade highlighting of the weals. The slides were later projected onto paper at a magnification greater than 100-fold, so that outlines of weals could be drawn and then read into an image analyzer computer program to calculate the weal areas. Mean weal size represents the average of all six areas in each titration series.

Two mood tests were administered, the Profile of Mood Scale (POMS) (McNair, Lorr, & Droppleman, 1971) and the Brief Mood Rating (BMR), which is based on the Stress Scale of Naliboff et al., (1991), to measure emotions on the day of prick testing with the allergen. The POMS has six subscales measuring depression, fatigue, vigor, confusion, tension, and anger. The BMR has two subscales, irritability/peacefulness and liveliness/listlessness. These factors were used as variables in predicting the proportional change in the size of weals from the nonintervention (baseline) session to the session that included the hypnotic intervention (see below).

## BASELINE AND INTERVENTION SESSIONS

All experimenters were experienced in hypnotic procedures, the one who conducted the sessions (T.L.) was kept blind to the subjects' HGSHS:A hypnotizability ratings throughout the study.

After prick testing all 38 subjects with the allergen solutions to determine groupings and the appropriate allergens to titrate, all subjects were seen again individually for two more sessions about a week apart. The first experimental session (the baseline session) for the 18 subjects who tested positively to an allergen was held to determine each person's reaction to a sixfold titration series of the allergen. Mood was measured with the POMS and the BMR immediately before skin testing.

The second session was identical to the first except for the addition of a hypnotic intervention, which was described to the subjects as an attempt to use their imagination to alter their skin responses. They were advised that they would be having some fun using their "imagination" or "the power of your mind" or "visualization" to decrease their skin-test responses in this session. The subjects had no prior knowledge of what was to be involved in the intervention session and the term "hypnosis" was never used in the study in order to avoid carryover effects related to expectations of hypnosis (Spanos & Chaves, 1970). Again, mood was measured with the POMS and the BMR before hypnosis and skin testing.

The subjects were induced by a progressive muscular relaxation procedure and a countdown deepening. They were then requested to use their imaginations creatively by pretending that they were at the point of awakening on the first day of a vacation. They were invited to plan a nice day for themselves. It was suggested that the vacation spot could be one they knew or remembered, or one they would like to visit, or somewhere totally imaginary. One minute of silence was provided for this internal activity.

The vacation activity was chosen for two reasons. First, it would act as a deepener in itself. Second, such an activity (planning) is a normal sort of cognitive activity that is not classified as being creative or using visualization or requiring any special skills, so that all participants could feel that it was within their reach. As it happened, all 18 subjects could and did participate in this activity easily.

After the vacation visualization, the experimenter commented that she hoped that they had enjoyed it, and that now she was going to ask them to continue to use their imagination in the same way: having some fun, casually, effortlessly. This instruction was based on Bowers' (1978) effortless experiencing to help prevent people from "trying too hard." It was emphasized that this was all to be fun and that they should approach it just like planning their nice day while on vacation. This preliminary activity was included to lighten the proceedings and to foster the effortlessness of decreasing the reactivity of the skin-prick testing.

After warning the subject that the skin testing was about to begin, the experimenter proceeded to perform the test in silence, which ended with her suggestion that the skin did not have to react to the skin-prick testing as it did the last time. She pointed out that the patient could use his or her imagination, just as in the vacation activity, only this time to imagine a situation that would calm any reaction on the skin. "Perhaps you can imagine your skin cooling down somehow so it is no longer so reactive ... or maybe you can imagine that the solutions contain only sterile water ... or perhaps today you can feel yourself so strong and healthy, so full of vitality, that your arm does not react. You can think of your own ways to keep your skin smooth and unresponsive."

The suggestions were purposely lacking in detail so that to use them, the subjects would have to make them their own, filling in details from previous experiences or imagination. This was primarily for those people not proficient in hypnosis or those lacking confidence in their own creativity. It was felt that the highly hypnotizable could make use of anything from direct suggestion to this loosest of suggestion styles (Kirsch, Mobayed, Council, & Kenny, 1992).

The experimenter then included several emphatic suggestions for success, particularly for those people who prefer that type of emphasis. She requested that the person listen to her closely for a moment. She then said firmly, "You don't have to react to the skin testing; you really don't," but with no direst suggestion as to how it would be accomplished. This type of suggestion was included because of the preference by some people for very clear instructions on what to do. No suggestions for imagination were made, just for clarity of outcome.

These instructions took about three or four minutes of the 10 minutes between skin testing and photographing the resultant weals and flares. The remaining six or seven minutes were silent to allow maximum opportunity for the internal task. Once the weals had been photographed, the subjects were realerted using a count-up procedure, along with suggestions of vitality and well-being. Antihistamine cream was provided for the few who needed it.

## RESULTS

As a group, the 18 allergen-responsive subjects exhibited a reduction in their allergen mean weal sizes from the baseline to the hypnosis session ($t = 1.9$, $P = 0.08$). Individually, 13 subjects showed a decrease in mean weal size between the two sessions (see Figure 10.1). All subjects were also tested for responses to histamine in the other arm and these weal responses were similarly decreased ($t = 5.6$, $P < .0001$) from the baseline to the intervention session. Further, when the proportional changes in weal sizes for allergen and histamine tests were subjected to a pairwise comparison, a significant correlation was seen between the responses in each arm ($r = .626$, $P < .007$).

Of the psychological variables, stress scores at the second session (as assessed by the BMR) were significantly higher ($t = -2.7$, $P < .01$) for the five unsuccessful subjects (mean = 47.2) than for the 13 subjects who successfully reduced their weal sizes (mean = 22.9). For the group as a whole ($n = 18$), the proportional change in allergen weal sizes between the baseline and intervention sessions was correlated with several of the mood variables measured during the inter-

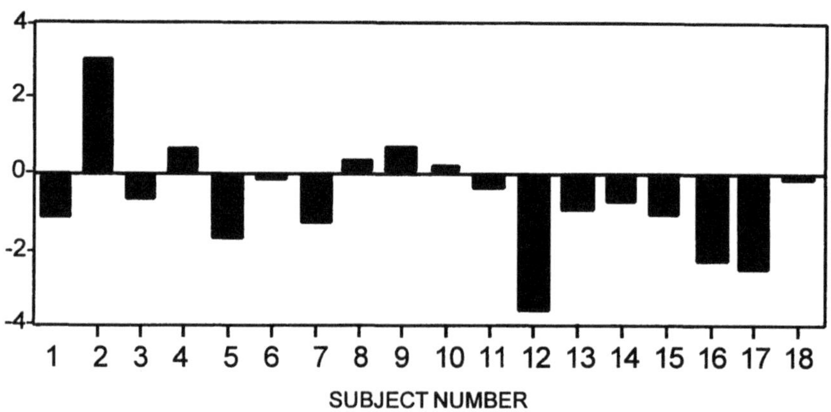


**FIGURE 10.1.** Difference in weal areas from baseline to intervention session for all subjects.

vention session. These were the POMS anger score ($r = .60, P = .008$), the POMS depression score ($r = .46, P < .05$), and the BMR irritability score ($r = .45, P < .06$).

In a stepwise analysis of variance, 60% of the variance in proportional change in allergen weal size was accounted for by three psychological variables: the POMS depression score, the POMS confusion score, and the BMR irritability score. These same variables were all significant in predicting proportional change in the mean weals in a multiple regression analysis (see Table 10.1).

The 13 successful subjects had slightly higher HGSHS:A scores ($n = 13$, mean = 8.8) than the unsuccessful group ($n = 5$, mean = 6.5), the difference was not statistically significant, and for the group as a whole ($n = 18$; mean HGSHS:A = 7.1, ranges 1–11), there was no correlation between HGSHS:A scores and proportional changes in mean weal size between the baseline and intervention sessions.

Although it was not part of the paradigm, many people commented on less weal itchiness during the hypnosis session as compared with the baseline session.

## DISCUSSION

Subjects were able to decrease their reactivity to allergen just as they were able to do with their histamine reactions (Laidlaw et al., 1996),

**TABLE 10.1**
**Predictors of proportional change in weal areas**

| | *Stepwise Regression* | | *Multiple Regression* | |
|---|---|---|---|---|
| Variable | Variance accounted for: | Pr > F | F value | Pr > F |
| POMS anger | 36% | 0.008 | 8.37 | 0.003 |
| POMS confusion | 14% | 0.05 | 8.20 | 0.01 |
| BMR irritability | 10% | 0.08 | 3.44 | 0.08 |

suggesting that the effect is not specific for allergen but rather may be on the inflammatory pathways of weal production that are shared by the responses to both allergen and histamine. There were clear differences between those people who could use the intervention to reduce the sizes of their skin test reactions to allergen or histamine when compared with those who could not do so. Those who were unsuccessful in decreasing their reactions rated themselves more negatively on all psychological negative mood variables and less positively on all positive mood variables. These ratings were consistent for both sessions, with the implication that those in the unsuccessful group were unhappier, negative-feeling people.

Hypnotizability, as measured by the HGSHS:A, was not a factor in the ability to use the hypnotic intervention in this group and there was no difference in scores between those who were successful and those who were not. There was no correlation between hypnotizability and the proportional weal change or between hypnotizability and any of the other variables. This indicates that the HGSHS:A test did not assess the talent displayed by the successful people, and neither did it predict who would be unsuccessful. Either irrelevant aspects of hypnotizability were being assessed in the test or other factors, such as day-to-day variations in mood or motivation, eclipsed the hypnotizability rating. Perhaps the mood variables were strong enough to render the hypnotizability rating meaningless.

Erickson once said that the therapist must give considerable consideration to the "functional capacities and abilities and the experiential and acquisitional learnings of the patient" (Erickson, 1965). By using the free-flowing techniques of the subjects' own imagination, which, of course, draws on unique life experiences and is perceived through individualized perceptual filters, such significant results as reported here from people with a variety of hypnotizability levels becomes possible. Letting subjects (or clients/patients) produce their own stories does not have the immediate sense of gratification for experimenters/therapists that weaving elegant stories for them does. Yet as therapists, we have learned, sometimes painfully, that taking control of people's lives is counterproductive even though, in the use of hypnosis and of other psychological techniques, we are encouraged to utilize our own creativity in therapeutic circumstances. It is not easy to realize that our brilliance and artistic efforts are perhaps best kept for our own uses of self-hypnosis and that our task in hypnotherapy is to encourage the creative efforts of our clients/subjects in the most appropriate and effective manner.

In this study, because all subjects underwent an intervention session following the baseline session, it is conceivable that the results were attributable to order effects as a consequence of repeated testing, or to the well-known problem of one's expectation of hypnosis (Spanos & Chaves, 1970). However, in our previous work (Laidlaw et al., 1994), we could find no evidence of systematic changes in skin reactivity due to repeated allergic skin testing.

Further, during the baseline session in the current study, subjects were not aware of what would be required of them in the subsequent intervention session, and the term "hypnosis" was never used in the study. It seems unlikely, therefore, that expectations of hypnosis could explain the results obtained. The sessions were ordered in this way to avoid the use of relaxation and/or imagery during the baseline session.

These data would suggest that the mood of the subject at the time of the testing was a mitigating factor in his or her ability to use imaginal suggestions to reduce histamine- and allegen-induced weals. Further research is clearly required to determine the extent of the interaction between mood and suggestibilty.

## REFERENCES

Aronoff, G. M., Aronoff, S., & Peck, L. W. (1975). Hypnotherapy in the treatment of bronchial asthma. *Annals of Allergy, 34,* 356–362.

Black, S. (1963a). Shift in dose response curve of Prausnitz-Kustner reaction by direct suggestion under hypnosis. *British Medical Journal, 6,* 990–992.

Black, S. (1963b). Inhibition of intermediate-type hypersensitivity response by direct suggestion under hypnosis. *British Medical Journal, 6,* 925–929.

Black, S. (1969). *Mind and body.* London: William Kimber.

Black, S., & Friedman, M. (1965). Adrenal function and the inhibition of allergic responses under hypnosis. *British Medical Journal. 1,* 562–567.

Black, S., Humphrey, J. H., & Niven, J. S. (1963). Inhibition of Mantoux reaction by direct suggestion under hypnosis. *British Medical Journal. 6,* 1649–1652.

Bowers, P. (1978). Hypnotizability, creativity and the role of effortless experiencing. *International Journal of Clinical and Experimental Hypnosis. 26,* 184–202.

Collison, D. R. (1975). Which asthmatic patients should be treated by hypnotherapy? *Medical Journal of Australia. 1,* 776–781.

Erickson, M. (1965). Editorial. *The American Journal of Clinical Hypnosis, 8,* 1–2.

Ewer, T. C., & Stewart, D. E. (1986). Improvement in bronchial hyper-responsiveness in patients with moderate asthma after treatment with a hypnotic technique: A randomised controlled trial. *British Medical Journal. 293,* 1129–1132.

Kershaw, C. J. (1987). Therapeutic metaphor in the treatment of childhood asthma: A systemic approach. In S.R. Lankton (Ed.), *Central themes and principles of Ericksonian therapy. Ericksonian Monographs, 2,* 83–96.

Kirsch, I., Mobayed, C. P., Council, J. R., & Kenny, D. A. (1992). Expert judgments of hypnosis from subjective state reports. *Journal of Abnormal Psychology, 101,* 657–662.

Laidlaw, T. M., Booth, R. J., & Large, R. G. (1994). The variability of type 1 hypersensitivity reactions: The importance of mood. *Journal of Psychosomatic Research, 38*(1), 51–61.

Laidlaw, T. M., Booth, R. J. & Large, R. G. (1996). Reduction in skin reactions to histamine following a hypnotic procedure. *Psychosomatic Medicine, 58,* 242–248.

Laidlaw, T. M., Richardson, D. H., Booth, R. J., & Large, R. G. (1994). Immediate-type hypersensitivity reactions and hypnosis: Problems in methodology. *Journal of Psychosomatic Research, 38*(6), 569–580.

McNair, D. M., Lorr, M., & Droppleman, L. F. (1971). *Profile of mood states manual.* San Diego, CA: Educational and Industrial Testing Service.

Naliboff, B. D., Benton, D., Solomon, G. F., Morley, J. E., Fahey, J. L., Bloom, E. T., Makinodan, T., & Gilmore, S. L. (1991). Immunological changes in young and old adults during brief laboratory stress. *Psychosomatic Medicine, 53,* 121–132.

Spanos, N. P., & Chaves, J. F. (1970). Hypnosis research: A methodological critique of experiments generated by two alternative paradigms. *American Journal of Clinical Hypnosis, 13,* 108–127.

Wilkinson, J. (1981). Hypnotherapy in the psychosomatic approach to illness: A review. *Journal of the Royal Society of Medicine, 74*(7), 525–530.

Zachariae, R., & Bjerring, P. (1993). Increase and decrease of delayed cutaneous reactions obtained by hypnotic diphenylcyclopropenone. *Allergy, 48*(1), 6–11.

Zachariae, R., Bjerring, P., & Arendt-Nielsen, L. (1989). Modulation of type I and type IV delayed immunoreactivity using direct suggestion and guided imagery during hypnosis. *Allergy, 44,* 537–542.

# Applications and Research

# 11

# Application of Ericksonian Principles to Larger Systems

*Stephen R. Lankton and Carol H. Lankton*

## THE STORY OF THE CORPORATE DIRECTION

This true story begins with an example of a corporation context in need of knowledge engineering and interface management. (Company names and products are disguised under hypothetical names.) One of the country's five largest companies makes a device used by

We wish to acknowledge the interactive development of some of the tools and methods of the approach illustrated here by crediting the team efforts of several of our closest consulting colleagues: George Williams and Melinda Williams of Strategic Solutions, Inc., electronic publishing company; Louie Kramer of Xerox, Inc., document consulting group; and Estal Fain of Enterprise Management Systems, Inc., a consulting and financial modeling group. Via mutual collaboration over the last few years, each of these persons has brought a great deal of background and methodology to our training and theories. Together, we have found a synchronous compatibility and synthesis of ideas. Our choice of terms and methods for Knowledge Exchange meetings and Enterprise Financial Modeling reflects these contributions.

thousands of employees in other large companies. Specifically, Acme Manufacturing Company produces copiers for General Motown Corporation. Acme's unique printers take documents from the work station PCs of every worker who pushes the right buttons and copies, reproduces, and collates them into an expected output. But the Acme product will potentially perform 10 other automatic functions, including automatically e-mailing or faxing the copies, archiving copies on optical storage media, and retrieving and attaching up to 10 of the most recent documents also related to any key word in the document. That is, upon printing, the Acme product can search out any other optically stored data about the content in the document and print and attach this material for immediate convenience and reference. Of course, this, too, can be faxed easily, and all that is required is just a few keystrokes by the user at the time the print command is issued. Acme really believes that this product will revolutionize the way business is done. And the managers of this part of the corporation are enthusiastic visionaries, who also predict that the product will revolutionize businesses, not to mention making money for Acme, furthering personal careers, and assuring customer satisfaction. And the product might actually do all that. So what is the problem?

The problem lies in the discrepancy between the potential and actual use of the features by the employees at General Motown and the companies that buy it. General Motown is not getting the most out of the expensive product and not realizing the business advantage this can have. Similarly, Acme is unhappy that its product has not been used to full potential. The company fears that the dream will not be fulfilled.

The need to realize and apply needed resources in larger systems is parallel to such needs in individual and family systems. Erickson described psychological problems as existing because people are somehow constrained and do not know how to get the available and desired resources into the situations in which they are needed. What is needed in both therapy and corporate settings is a means to retrieve and organize the already available resources, and associate them with relevant contexts. In therapy, this might mean applying experiential resources to pain management or family reorganization. What these situations have in common is the fact that the information and knowledge (resources) needed for optimal functioning are not flowing properly (are not in the context in which they are needed). Some difficulty exists in stimulating the correct reaction, or, as Erickson said, in making association to needed resources.

Knowledge Engineering and Interface Management are labels we have used to describe our consultation services for several large, primarily *Fortune* 1000, corporations, in which we help them build needed connections to resources and information flow, which maximizes their potential. The problem-solving and change work with corporations essentially follows the same principles we use in change work with the unconscious, with individuals, and with couples and families. Consider the well-known influence that Erickson's work has had on both family therapy (Lankton, Lankton, & Matthews, 1994) and on hypnosis (Matthews, Lankton, & Lankton, 1994). These seemingly diverse areas of psychological work are actually very similar when an epistemological shift is made to view the client system according to the principles of an Ericksonian approach (Lankton, 1985). And we can view corporate systems from that same epistemological perspective. The same principles apply whether helping a person interface memories and experiences to overcome back pain or helping the Acme Corporation successfully interface with the employees of General Motown to realize the full potential of the printers. And it is the same principles used in working with couples when one spouse learns to communicate with the other to help build the cooperation and love that they can potentially experience. None of these are examples of simple communication skills training, but rather reflect a network of complex principles in an arrangement to facilitate complex associations in experience.

People typically expect that a clinician doing corporate work is doing something akin to stress management; communication skills training; creativity workshops; motivational, positive-thinking coaching; or corporate therapy. Just what any of these translate to in actual practice is subject to wide interpretation. There are mixed reviews, especially of corporate therapy, and these seem to be based primarily on the same stereotypical reactions to "seeking therapy" that the psychological profession has experienced for years. The term "therapy" carries a lot of baggage, ranging from fears that the corporation will be placing or receiving blame, that the activity will dig into past matters and not stay with current goals and projects, to the fear that it will just be money wasted on mere talking. While any set of tactics and interventions that brings an improvement in the corporate climate, increases profit, or reduces a product or service's "time to market" could be referred to as corporate therapy, that is not the best description for the activities and services of Knowledge Engineering and Interface Management. Performing only those tasks underutilizes the clinician's skills in the corporate workplace. It is similar to the way that traditional approaches to therapy also under-utilize the clinician's skills, as well as minimize the potential and power and inherent health of the client. The epistemological change that Erickson's work represents also broadens the influence that the clinician can bring to a corporate context.

## WHAT IS KNOWLEDGE ENGINEERING?

In the corporate context, Knowledge Engineering means making all the changes necessary throughout the corporation to facilitate the making of creative and efficient business decisions. As such, it is a broad field that spans psychology, mechanics, computer science, and business economics. Corporate leaders see it from a high-level analysis that spans the four symbiotic areas of processing, human decision making, commerce, and information exchange or transfer. The most tangible and broad implementation of Knowledge Engineering is Interface Management, which is the method of managing how people approach any interface—within the self, between the self and others, between the self and machines, or between machines. We are using the term "interface" as a noun, but it is not necessarily an easily found object in the world. An interface is the point at which data or information is exchanged between any two "things." The interface can be a "thing" itself, but neither the interface nor two "things" exchanging information are necessarily tangible. They can be tangible, for example, in the case of a keyboard, computer screen, modem, printer, homeowner, or insurance policy, but there is also information exchange, for example, between the conscious and unconscious parts of a person, and this interface is obviously not a thing—it is an invention of the observer for the sake of convenience. It is the contact boundary of Fritz Perls' (1947) Gestalt therapy.

Tangibility aside, questions of how users of any interface come together are investigated in Interface Management. The needs and desires of the people who use all interfaces are studied and identified, whether they are talking to each other face to face or through some other method of communication. For example, in the Acme situation, representatives from General Motown's data processing, printing, customer satisfaction, legal, and marketing departments attended. The division head who manages the use of printers and several employees, both those who use the printers and those who make little use of them were also included. Then, questions were posed to these representatives to determine what they needed in the interface, how they needed to have their information, what the budget department had in mind when it thought it would save money, and so on. Essentially, what will make the interfaces work in an ideal fashion where the sender sends what is needed?

We want to facilitate the creation of the most conducive interface filter by first determining the requirements of that interface. We want to reengineer that interface, whether it is a computer screen, paper document, or verbal communication, so that needed information is quickly found where, when, and how it is needed, and sequenced, framed, and packaged so as to facilitate decision making and taking the desired action in the least amount of time, in the fewest number of steps, and with the greatest degree of accuracy. This is parallel to what we do with individuals and families when we help them find a way to examine and use personal experiences and family resources to maximize their joy.

The terms "Knowledge Engineering" and "Interface Management" can essentially be used synonymously, in much the same way that "applied psychology" and "psychotherapy" are often used synonymously even though they are actually overlapping subsets of psychology. Interface Management is a subset of Knowledge Engineering, although we are using both terms somewhat interchangeably here. Knowledge Engineering is actually the process and Interface Management is the practice. We are interested in the highly specific and practical implementation of Interface Management in corporate contexts in the same way we are when looking at therapy in the practical way Erickson did: How can we help people associate the resources to the context in which they need to have them?

## SELF-IMAGE THINKING, KNOWLEDGE EXCHANGE MEETINGS, AND RAPID PROTOTYPING

We have long appreciated the paradigm shift represented by Erickson's clinical wisdom. Outstanding among his ideas was that "cure" results with psychotherapy clients when we are able to facilitate a "reassociation and reorganization of ... experiential life" (Rossi, & Erickson, 1980, p. 38). That is, clients have no problem when they discover that needed experiences are available in contexts in which they are wanted and needed. Erickson's approach is characterized by being goal/future oriented. The same goal-directed premise is to be found pervasively in all aspects of the strategic psychotherapy described as Ericksonian. Therapy helps people use the resources they have to accomplish their desired goals. In addition, it values a practical style of approaching a workable solution. Erickson's work discouraged the "expert" stance of a professional, "giving" answers, cures, or changes. Therapists do not change anybody; they simply help create a context in which it is possible for people spontaneously to change themselves.

We have implemented these principles and guidelines in our role as therapists and similarly as corporate consultants. We can facilitate the evolution of this change-facilitating context by articulating the process, that is, by detailing a common goal or mission statement and identifying and retrieving or developing and linking all of the resources needed to achieve the goal. One of the ways in which we have implemented these guidelines in therapy is with a process we have referred to as Self-Image Thinking. We suggest that this was a central theme of Erickson's work, and it is most certainly central in our therapy work. One of its most tangible aspects is seen when we ask clients to visualize how they will appear when they are feeling and using their desired resources in interactions with others. It serves as an organizing principle that frames therapy as a partnership to cocreate "desired state maps" and provides a way to approximate that desired state rapidly, through imagining potential prototypes. The method relies on feedback at each stage to modify either the goal or the specific resources applied to reaching that goal most satisfactorily. Those portions of Self-Image Thinking in which clients rapidly design prototypes, or approximations to the desired state, are called scenarios. People visualize and experience practical self-image scenarios as quickly as they can imagine them, which is usually almost instantly. In this way, they associate needed resources with the anticipated context and try it on for size or "goodness of fit" to determine through feedback what needs to be adjusted so that it is compatible with both the real world and their desired state. At the same time, they are mentally rehearsing scenarios; they are strengthening the psychobiological associations they actually need to achieve those outcomes.

Knowledge Exchange refers to an activity that is the corporate equivalent of the Self-Image Thinking work in therapy. This activity takes place in meetings or in workshops. In Knowledge Exchange workshops, representatives are gathered from every part of the corporation that is concerned with either the goal we are trying to reach or the way in which the company is trying to reach it. This might include representatives from legal, marketing, customer service, executive management, sales, information services, and so on. The goal of the group is to examine specific details and to share aspects of the common vision that will satisfactorily reach the targeted goal. This goal is the same as the desired state map in Self-Image Thinking. Just as parts of the individual contribute to the individual's self image, representatives from each part of the corporation contribute to the desired goal or corporate image. These activities of Knowledge Exchange and Self-Image Thinking are parallel. And just as Self-Image Thinking is explained by and built upon Ericksonian principles in therapy, Knowledge Engineering and Exchange represents one application of Ericksonian principles in larger systems. A corporate Communication Interface Strategy (CIS) provides heuristics and algorithms that guide all corporate communications in accordance with the mission statements. The CIS takes into account when to use an interface, what to use it for, and how to formulate communications at any given moment and even over time. The corporate CIS parallels the Self-Image Thinking strategy.

What do they really want, exactly? Through process articulation, we as group leaders must identify exactly what the representatives need in order to accomplish what they want, what they need, and what they must have. Group members discover, in the process, an appreciation for the needs of other parts of the corporation that must be met in the final solution. They identify a deeper understanding of the unified contributions and resources of others in the company. They will also suggest numerous possible wishes and solutions before reaching agreement or making policy changes. Knowledge Exchange meetings provide a means for collective, corrective modeling, which represents a welcome departure from a usual corporate method of "trying" to do it "right" the first time with little information from employees, often at the price of numerous, costly, and lengthy meetings. The Knowledge Exchange alternative considers all input on the way to the eventual solution to be "right." The consultant helps articulate the developing process, capturing and summarizing suggestions and offering approximations and, finally, designing and delivering the product or solution and any necessary training to use it.

As a result of the Knowledge Exchange workshop at Acme, enough information was taken regarding the needs of all people who contact the complex printer, as well as an assessment of the needs and possible motivations of the low-end users, to design possible solutions. The possible solutions are called rapid prototypes. Those are like interventions in family therapy. They may bring matters to a resolution, or they may need to be modified immediately based on feedback from the client. Within three iterations of this presentation and feedback cycle, a final model of the changes was presented and implemented for Acme and General Motown. This is the usual process for all corporate clients.

In the case of Acme, the meetings resulted in a wealth of information that made it possible to reach the desired goals by redesigning two important interfaces. The first was the existing interface between the end users of the printers and the printers themselves. This did not involve remanufacturing the printers but, instead, applying an add-on color-coded guide to the existing proprietary control panel for people actually standing at the printer. The second interface had not existed prior to the Interface Management project. In order to ensure that the end users of General Motown's product would get the most efficient help they needed when they needed it, an interactive "help" program was designed and placed in the General Motown computer network. It worked because frequent users could continue to do what they already knew how to do by habit, but low-end users could click on the help agent at any time in the process when they got confused or stuck. It was an icon on their computer screen that, when called upon, was ready to carry out the next steps and illustrate what it was doing with vivid and simple lights and arrows on the screen as it continued. This was possible because the help agent continually monitored the employee's activity with regard to the printer and knew at what step the employee was at all times. It would even suggest the logical additions to the work the employee had initiated. That is, if the employee was printing a stockholder's report to be e-mailed to executive management, the help agent might suggest that it would be possible at one stage to attach background financial reports that had been optically stored in its database. The help agent might also suggest that the employee archive the current report with suggested key words. These features, which had previously been used very little, became instantly available to anyone with a computer monitor, and there was almost no chance for the user to make an error.

It is important to note that the help screens on the monitors were designed according to the determined needs of the employees and not from the ideas of engineers. The location, colors, size, and other variables were designed with behavioral-science logic and input from employee end users. The monitor essentially illustrated every choice with easy-to-interpret icons. It instantly educated users about the amazing choices available from the complex printer. What is more, for even the most complicated task, all the employee needed to do in most cases was merely to click single keys or icons representing the desired tasks (on graphical operating systems) and the computer would take the next steps to reach the goal.

Each step was clearly illustrated, and so it trained as it assisted. Essentially, the new interface helped the Acme Corporation coretrieve the resources and associations to facilitate decision making with the employees of General Motown. Acme saw this new interface as an information exchange between the company and the employees of General Motown. Acme downloaded information about usage from these computer help agents weekly and used it both to improve the use of the printers in the existing help screens and future design and to accumulate reliable information about which features were used and how often. Not only did Acme then know that the features were being put to use, it also knew whether employees had any difficulty using them. General Motown found productivity and accountability increased because of a reduction in the time needed for filing and archiving information, as well as a reduction in telephone calls from *its customer* asking for additional supporting documentation for material received by fax or e-mail. In other words, several areas and groups benefited: Acme's customer satisfaction increased, which translated into more sales. General Motown, as well as all other Acme customers, benefited. General Motown's employees found that they could do more work in less time more comfortably. And the customers of General Motown received supporting documentation in less time with fewer follow-up calls.

Returning to how this process parallels Ericksonian approaches to therapy, this example is a bit like helping grandparents make changes in the family by communicating better with their grandchildren. We have helped the grandparents institute a method to share directly with the grandchildren. And no matter what size system we work with, whether private, interpersonal, couple, familial, or corporate, we work:

1. to be goal directed;
2. to assess the meaning, needs, motivation, and contributions of each participating component (or person);
3. to design temporary models (as in the self-image thinking process, for experiencing associations for pain control and role playing encounters in families);
4. to view hesitation, resistance, lack of fit, and so on, as feedback to help aid correction of the model or the operator; and all
5. within a developmental framework (including the developmental evolution of the corporation itself, or the division we are working with, as well as the stage of development and related needs of key individuals who work for the corporation).

## INTERFACE MANAGEMENT

Interface Management is guided by information that is accumulated in Knowledge Exchange workshops and other activities. We track the flow of information, decision making, and knowledge leading to the desired goal within the corporation. Careful and thorough attempts are made to assess the most salient features of each interface relevant to the goal according to the representatives in the room. But common goals are reached not only by the people in the room. Shared visions may also have to be modified and compromised according to this needs of far more people than those present at the meeting. Input and assessment must also address the interfaces with others throughout the corporation and all departments, such as new product development, and other management divisions outside the company. This includes interfaces between the corporation and the external world, such as marketing, current news media concerns, availability of money, and what the competition is doing.

The environment in which the corporation operates is assessed, as is a means for interacting with it. Popular opinion, awareness, or historical trend with regard to a related service or product is a factor we must consider, as well as the corporate self-image and its interface with the outside world. How consistent is the corporate image with a change in its product or a new service? It must be consistent with those influences outside of corporate control but to which the corporation must conform to stay in business (the commerce interface). Like parts of a person, all parts must be consulted or considered and involved with the end product (or the individual or family goal). While it is theoretically possible for a person to maintain an attitude of confidence in an even terrible environment, it is easier when the environment complements the desirable attitude and behavior. Similarly, the influence of the larger environment in corporate work must be considered to achieve the best possible fit that does not detract from implementing and using the resources that best satisfy the common goal. So, an attempt is made to include every possible interface in the process, articulating how information might best be perceived, stored, exchanged, absorbed, regulated, and used, and what impact will result.

Interface Management concentrates on the behavior of interfaces because it is only by means of interfaces that we have information and knowledge. In Knowledge Exchange sessions, just as in family therapy, the therapist or consultant attends first to interfaces among the people present and is also sensitive to those persons and things not present with whom the participants interact. This includes interactions with the external world, with people and their machines, with machines and other machines, and, of course, also within themselves and how they most efficiently use themselves. Usually, interventions directed to the intrapsychic level receive the least attention in corporate consultational, though, interestingly, it is the level that most people would expect a therapist in corporate context to primarily provide.

## COEFFICIENT OF CONFIDENCE

The consultant, through the entire process of Knowledge Engineering, using Knowledge Exchange for Interface Management, assumes, much like a strategic therapist does in working with an individual or a family system, that needed resources lie within the system and that some manner for associating and linking them can be established to facilitate their occurring in desired contexts more predictably. In either case, all we need is to be instructed by ongoing feedback as we strategically facilitate movement closer to common goals. What has been mentioned so far suggests that business decision making becomes more efficient as the corporations are reengineered from the perspective of Knowledge Engineering and Interface Management Science. While this is potentially true, the reality is that an entire corporation does not often undertake such a change. In our experience, so far, only smaller companies have been prepared for such a comprehensive undertaking. Larger corporations, instead, implement Knowledge Engineering and Interface Management for only a single division or sometimes for a large project within a department.

This is similar to the mental health situation in which a family decides to enter therapy to accomplish a very important but limited improvement, such as a child's performance or a spouse's anxiety, and does not intend to, or contract to, achieve the comprehensive changes that might be possible. The extent of change sought is determined by the availability of time and money as well as by such factors as need and motivation. We may inform a family that therapy is most likely to succeed if the entire family attends the sessions. Family members can use the information to decide what their involvement will be. The corporate parallel to informing clients about the best prognosis requires that we realistically acknowledge that it may not be relevant to seek change in all areas of the corporation.

In corporate contexts, we respond to the initial assessment of goals and resources with a coefficient-of-confidence rating—that is, a percent of confidence that a win–win situation will be brought about by the Interface Management systems, with Knowledge Exchange and other programs. This is an actual rating calculated from the most comprehensive assessment we can make of the various factors contributing to desired goals. In the event of a low coefficient-of-confidence rating, the company or division is not seen as having a goodness-of-fit condition between the existing practices or resources and the programs desired. It is possible to engage problem-solving consultation at that point to improve any areas that are thought by the company or division to be problematic and contributing to the lack of fit.

The coefficient of confidence is developed only after assessment at both the suprastructure and infrastructure levels. The suprastructure assessment includes an understanding of the corporate culture, technical resources, financial support of the project, time factors related to goals, current assessment, and desired state. Infrastructure ingredients also involve current assessment and desired state, but, in addition look at management practices and resources, personnel resources, document trails, decision points, and reputation for change. This is influenced by such features as adaptability, plasticity, fault tolerance, and self-organization. Each corporate context is unique, just as individual and family systems are, and these unique features must be taken into account in designing and tailor fitting any implementation plan.

In some companies, where there is a strong, charismatic CEO, it is absolutely imperative that he or she be involved. In other, more egalitarian companies, it may be more important that representatives of executive and upper management be involved in the Knowledge Engineering projects. In all companies, such factors as financing, order of products released, and activities of competitors contribute to the equation. We rank and rate all important factors and calculate the final coefficiency rating. After this is discussed with the client, an informed decision is made to proceed with the project or do some remedial reworking of the important factors that lead to a low rating of confidence. In other words, we might find that our confidence factor was calculated at 72%, which means that we have 72% confidence (due to these factors) that the project will have the desired outcome. The decision to proceed with the project is left to the client, who will be given options as to how to improve the low areas if desired. Just as we might urge a spouse to seek drug detoxification before returning for therapy, we might insist that executive management become involved before we can give the project a high confidence rating. Even with a low rating of confidence, companies may choose to continue the project due to their own fervor or they may choose to walk away from the opportunity. In either case, everyone proceeds with a high degree of openness and accountability regarding the expectations.

## PRIMARY INTERFACE LAYER PRINCIPLES AND VARIABLES

Desired outcomes for corporate clients are diverse. In projects such as the Acme example, the buyer's use of printer–fax–optical archives resulted in the design of a new seller-to-user interface. Simple reengineering of paper document families is sometimes all that is requested. Procedures for the resolution of credit card disputes have resulted in revising the interface of customer service letters to credit card users. Billing statements for telephone companies have been improved at the interface of accounting department to customer. Focus groups and surveys are used to accomplish customer polling and assessment. While different in scope, these desired outcomes are parallel to goals that therapy clients might bring in terms of accomplishing more efficient use of resources in relevant contexts. In all the varied cases, there are information and data to be exchanged across interfaces.

Organizing the data from these different domains is influenced by certain principles. That is, if we examine how information moves and becomes experience and decisions, it does not matter whether we are looking at computers and networks, people and answering machines, managers and salespeople, customers and billing statements, or families and presenting problems. The organizing principles of information science are the same across any interface. We can facilitate information flow and experience retrieval, knowledge exchange, and decision making by manipulating interface variables. These factors are the same whether we are dealing with a person interfacing with personal memories, urges, ideas, and experience to overcome pain; with family members interfacing with one another to build a strong problem-solving family; or with any of the corporate examples above. Operating from a posture where we view clients, problems, and goals through these "patterns that unite" (Bateson, 1972) is perhaps the most compelling reason to credit Erickson's problem-solving approach as foundational to this work in larger systems.

Any time there is data exchange (whether that leads to knowledge or noise), there are two aspects operating: an interface delivery system (IDS) and an interface contact layer (ICL). Several specifically delineated interface elements and dynamics are shown in Figure 11.1. Ideally, an interface captures attention, directs it to critical decision-making information, and facilitates the use of information, including learning. Data, when organized into a meaningful context, become information. The point at which data are organized into meaningful information is an interface or an ICL. For instance, a piece of notebook paper can serve as an ICL for the marks penciled on it. A computer screen is the final ICL for the bits and bytes of data in the computer's storage areas that have been processed by software into potential information. Data from a human body may be organized by the conscious mind ICL into feelings of well-being, joy, sadness, or pain.

While the information on a computer screen interface is ever changing, so, too is the information in the conscious mind interface. But sometimes the information is not useful or relevant. At other times, the information is only useful after it has been given much attention, changed, massaged, reworked, and made into the desired format. For instance, a checking account statement (a paper interface) does not typically arrive in the most usable form possible. Information is there but it contains "noise" or useless data as far as the recipient is concerned. It has to be reworked into another form to become most useful. This process may leave a trail of numbers written in margins or on paper scraps that have been crossed out and checked off and the customer is surrounded with several supporting documents, including the check register, which eventually contains bank information in its most usable form. An ideal bank statement interface would begin with this usable form. The same is true for the conscious mind interface with the body. If data are not immediately useful, the person has to add to the data, talk to others, alter the data, stretch, take medication, add information from an expert, and so on, until relative satisfaction is achieved. This is, in fact, one operational definition for what therapy means: helping people change the way they interface with themselves, each other, and the world, in order optimally to meet their needs. Similarly, Interface Management works to make information valuable by helping people use it correctly, that is, in such a way as to achieve desired outcomes. We want to help reverse the unfortunate and inefficient situation where many people seem to be "working for their interfaces" instead of having their interfaces optimally designed so that they work for the people.

We want to reduce the margin of error typically present in exchanges of complicated information. Knowledge depends on processes of storage, retrieval, and association of information, which are influenced by certain rules. Failing to take those rules into account results in lost or unspecified misinformation. Distorted information results in poor decisions and crisis management. By contrast, feedback exchanged in small, frequent bits ensures smooth calibration, negotiation, and decision making.

A complex system will reiterate the interface complexities at each level of the structure. Intelligent participation between the people and the interfaces throughout the work culture guides change, but the structure of the work process must teach employees how to create changes throughout the overall process and not merely provide content. In that way, the organization becomes a growing, changing organization.

Figure 11.1 clarifies that between any two entities there is an interface layer that filters information according to certain variables. These major variables are feedback, information chunk size, multichannel noise and data, framing cues, communication protocol, information syntax, contextual punctuation, and focal information. To the right and left of this layer are identical entities, which represent any two "things" exchanging information. Those two things can be person to person, person to private experience, person to computer, person to document, computer to printer, and so on. In any event, the two entities will have certain needs for perception, processing, storage, retrieval, decision making, and action. This represents an interface

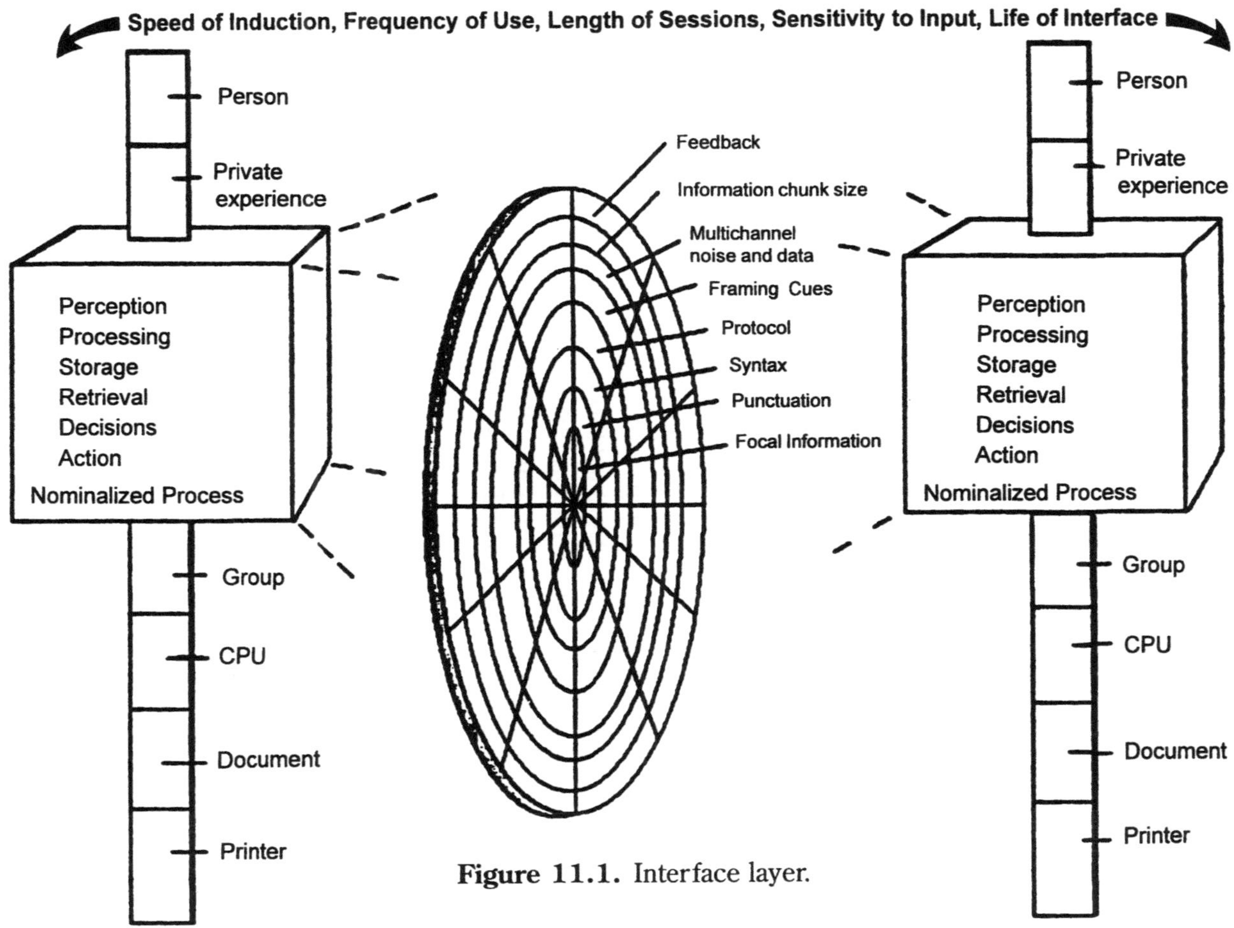


**Figure 11.1.** Interface layer.

in which one part does not exist without the others. There are some overall characteristics of this interface, such as the speed of induction (time involved to orient to and invite movement to a different state), frequency of use, length of sessions, sensitivity to input, and duration of the interface. Although vastly different, all interfaces are affected by these same rules of information science that determine how data are acquired, whether in corporate or private systems. We turn now to a brief description of the eight variables we have found most relevant in almost all of our work.

*Feedback* provides a means of calibrating associations and depends on the ability of the user of the interface to query and ask for the repackaging of data and information. The way in which feedback is obtained, if at all, in certain interfaces is absolutely vital to growth, creativity, understanding, and action.

*Information chunk size* determines whether a small amount or a great deal of information is shared in a transaction. Large bursts of data offer the introduction of more error, but also offer the possibility of greater efficiency. For instance, written or spoken communication is often difficult to understand if it contains long paragraphs with many ideas, long sentences or nominalizations, or simply continues on without an intermission. Information "size" affects the ease of acquiring information, sorting it, storing it, and recombining it. In addition to human communication, consider the problem that plagues many computer users who have large files that exceed the capacity of data storage on a floppy disk. The chunk of that information makes exchange more problematic.

*Multiple channels* refer to concurrent threads of association. The signal/noise ratio in communication is an example of multichannel information. In human interfaces and multimedia, there is a true multichannel experience. In the interface layer, this refers to the actual analysis of how the signal noises are regulated or used, whether they are congruent, and the extent to which they increase information integrity and retention.

*Frame cues* refer to the markers that signal shifts in context, such as the shift from the introduction to the body of a paper, or from a theoretical notion to an example or an aside. They inform as to the beginning and ending of sets of associations and into which frame of information data belong, and tell us when to use or ignore any of the other multi-channeled information at a given time. Framing or reframing allows for the planned deviation from the original cues of logic governing a presentation. In a theatrical or drama interface, for instance, a dream sequence does not further the plot but rather invites the audience to consider a political or existential applicability to the plot. A television commercial in which the character becomes part of a fantasy, memory, or painting is an example of this sort of interface alteration.

*Protocol* refers to themes of association or presentation of data or ideas in a certain order. The protocol in most communication is not prescribed intentionally or expressly. In human systems, it is often taken for granted that information will be presented within a domain of expression customary to the norm of the group. There are clearly defined, well-established, and agreed-upon rules of protocol, as well as highly idiosyncratic and little-known expectations. Failure to follow protocol may render the entire message useless or make it totally misunderstood, whether we are dealing with modems, newsletters, video standards, or family reunions. Each sensory system has its own needs for appropriate protocol, as well as its own logical syntax.

*Syntax,* as it concerns people, refers to the arrangement and interrelationship of parts of a communication. It is like the language in which data are shared. In nonhuman exchange systems, this refers to the order and format of the data. For instance, the syntax will tell a receiver that the first transaction is a request to continue, that the next transaction will include the length to follow, that the next is the decryption method to apply, and so on. This is somewhat similar to human speech by telephone: "Hello, Harry. I wanted to talk to you about the shipment. Do you have a few minutes?" Special syntax applies to every type of interface, from those within a computer operating system to file formats for each program, to font instructions, to the required movement of fingers on a keyboard. For the syntax element of an interface, the major opportunity is in training the interface to recognize conversation between people, hardware, software, and so on.

*Punctuation* rules which associations must be followed in order to create an agreed-upon rhythm in communication. Any ongoing stream of information must be divided for various outcomes to be achieved.

In human speech, elements of pausing, inflecting, and interrogating are handled with punctuation changes that native speakers produce unconsciously. In written communication, this is accomplished with familiar grammatical punctuation marks. In graphical expression and in visual media, however, this becomes less standardized. In these cases, punctuation can be handled with color, shape, location, size, and style. In all cases, even those where unconscious punctuation is typical (such as human speech), there is the option willfully to decide how, when, and what to punctuate with attention to the end goal. It is especially important for therapists to recognize their strategic opportunity in this regard, as we have explained elsewhere (Lankton, et al., 1991).

*Focal information* refers to stimulus-response pairings that are association dependent. Most human understanding happens due to our network of associations and much of each interface contact layer is concerned with shaping understanding and, therefore, with making associations in an efficient manner. The information that any communication is "about" *is* the focal information. Bits of data are intended to bring a deliberate association regardless of how they are organized in the information. They comprise conditioned experiential associations. For instance, a silver cross worn on a necklace (part of the multichannel communication) of a school teacher will be certain to associate thought in some religious manner. If it is the focal information of the interaction, that set of associations will carry more meaning than when the cross's only a marginal bit of data on the necklace.

Interface Management applies behavioral science and information science rules and research to the reengineering of interface contact layers so as to improve the use of these eight elements in any interface that is involved in reaching the contracted goal. The movement between interface layers requires that a shift take place in all of the parameters to accommodate the information exchange requirements of the new context, as in the transition from interpersonal to written interface. If the center wheel in the illustration rotated, each of these eight elements would change according to the needs of the new senders or receivers. In interpersonal situations, a certain set of standards for each of these eight elements is required in order for people to understand one another. People must speak the same language, allow certain feedback, modify information "size" when asked, frame the activity as a similar event, and so on. Adhering to these requirements makes it possible for internal processing by the brain to input, store, associate, and respond. When the speaker examines his or her thoughts and memories or when the former speaker turns to a written document, the interface variables must change. The eight variables still exist but their arrangement takes on an entirely different complexity, in much the same way that a completely new design is created from the same elements when a kaleidoscope wheel turns. In written documents, each of these eight elements has to be changed to best fit the new interface requirements (color, font, location on the page, side boxes, and the like). The same sort of changes are true when speakers turn to internal memory and the interface it provides. In this situation, requirements for optimal information transfer suggest that feedback needs to be more rapid, information size needs to be smaller, framing cues need to recede quickly, and focal information needs to have greater integrity.

The transition between states represents a kind of induction stage, parallel to hypnotic induction, which invites a transition from a "waking" state to an altered state of internally focused concentration. Any time we communicate to orient a listener to a new task or state of attention, we engage in an induction. The transition between talking to another person or reading a book and then switching to the interface for certain *internal experience* is also an induction. Problems may be created when the induction fails to account for internal, erroneous interpretation. When a mother says, "Please do your homework," and the child interprets it as, "My mother is always pushing me around," miscommunication has occurred. When an insurance company mails a customer a written policy and the customer only feels confused upon studying it, there is a problem. Even the translation from paper to paper can lose much of the immediate original impact and depth of meaning unless it is correctly engineered into the proper interface required by the readership.

In the business world, all types of communications take place without a thought as to the proper and efficient use of the interface. When misunderstanding or failed communication occurs, solutions are usually attempted by the marketing or graphic design staff. This may not be the best choice considering what information science and behavior science can offer. That is where the application of this material becomes exciting and important.

## MEASUREMENT OF SUCCESS

Profit is a relatively easy item to measure, and the application of these principles in a business environment must increase profit, either directly or by reducing the time to market for a product, or by reducing other expenditures. Businesses often calculate profits from one year to the next and find it difficult to appropriate personnel resources to study a global financial perspective. Changes in business decision making might seem to be an elusive target to measure in terms of immediate dollar-and-cents savings, but this is not the case. The profit and other financial success can often be measured by simple reductions in the cost of customer support phone calls, by an increase in responses to core document communications, by customers' paying statement balances more quickly, or in the case of Acme Company, by increased customer satisfaction ratings and subsequent sales. However, these are not the only measurable profits.

A more accurate accounting of profits from our consulting activities involves a sophisticated measurement based on what we call Enterprise Financial Modeling. This procedure will allow a corporation to know exactly how much time, how many people, and how many other resources each activity and each decision-making step in all work processes cost, both before and after changes brought on by Knowledge Engineering and Interface Management.

## CONCLUSION

This chapter has drawn on a problem-solving approach used for changing family systems and extended those principles into larger systems, such as large companies, corporate subgroup practices, corporate divisions, intercorporation business exchanges, and even entire corporate reorganization. It has illustrated a way of viewing problems and solutions in larger systems by focusing on Knowledge Engineering and Interface Management.

When tackling business problems in this manner, it is not necessary that a consultant understand all aspects of the particular business. The consultant's expertise lies in creating a context in which the existing knowledge resources of the company can work in a goal-directed manner and by making changes to achieve a more productive decision-making process. This paradigm shift away from a linear model of problem solving finds the concept of improving interface design to be the pivotal dimension in systems of any size. Interface Management Science is concerned with examining and building or improving information exchange, retrieval, storage, and processing; decision making; and the resulting actions (including human and nonhuman involvement in each of these areas).

Just as in clinical therapy, there are never singular causes or singular contributions to a solution, but rather a cocreated group effort. As any portion tends to improve, all other portions find it possible to improve as well. This is also true in corporate change management. It appears that as one small part of a company changes, a generative change begins to overtake greater parts of the company. That is, there is a snowball or domino effect for the type of paradigm shift that consulting sets in motion. It is exciting to speculate how much impact this growth will have over the years on the corporations with which we contract. It appears that lasting and, in fact, increasing change is the result of the approach.

Interface Management, again like therapy, is a cocreation of the intervention teams and the corporation. It does not impose rules that will elicit resistance due to poorness of fit or authoritarian manner. It changes and measures the ability to make decisions and works to ensure the vision of the corporate leaders by improving the skills of both the people and the system working as a unit. While this is, in many ways, a large departure from Dr. Erickson's work (I [Stephen] recall one time when he said to me, "I wouldn't know what to say to a business executive"), it also represents a perfect fit with his underlying epistemology and approach to problem solving as we see it.

Corporations may initially oppose using ideas from psychotherapy due to the traditionally negative perception that it creates more questions than answers, more history than future, more talk than action, and more manipulation than cocreation. However, the emerging paradigm shift in therapy, epitomized by Erickson's contributions, is resulting in an entirely new approach to change, in both clinical and corporate cultures. The connections and parallels are significant and relevant to creating optimal influence on client systems of any size.

## REFERENCES

Bateson, G. (1972). *Steps to an ecology of mind.* New York: Ballantine.

Bateson, G. (1979). *Mind and nature.* New York: Dutton.

Perls, F. (1947). *Ego hunger and aggression.* New York: Vintage Books.

Lankton, C. (1985). Elements of an Ericksonian approach, In S. Lankton (Ed.), *Ericksonian monographs, number 1,* New York: Brunner/Mazel. pp. 61–75.

Matthews, W., Lankton, S., Lankton, C. (1992). An Ericksonian model of hypnotherapy, In E. Kirsch, S. Lynn, & J. Rhue (Eds.), *The handbook of clinical hypnosis.* Washington, DC: American Psychological Association.

Lankton, S., Lankton, C., & Matthews, W. (1991). Ericksonian family therapy. In A. Gurman & D. Kniskern (Eds.), *The handbook of family therapy, vol. 2.* New York: Brunner/Mazel.

Rossi, E. L. (Ed.). (1980). *The collected papers of Milton H. Erickson on hypnosis: Vol. 4. Innovative hypnotherapy.* New York: Irvington.

# 12

# Eye Movement Desensitization and Reprocessing: Research and Clinical Significance

*Francine Shapiro*

Eye Movement Desensitization and Reprocessing (EMDR) is a complex, eight-phase methodology and approach to the treatment of psychological trauma that integrates the salient aspects of most of the major therapeutic modalities. When integrated into a comprehensive treatment plan, EMDR appears to accelerate the treatment of pathologies that are based on disturbing life experiences. Successful EMDR treatment is defined not as a mere desensitization, such as no longer feeling anxious about a traumatic event, but rather as a complete processing of the target traumata. Among treatment outcomes are a more adaptive emotional state, a new cognitive perspective that includes the integration of insights and recognition of life patterns that can guide a person's future actions, the adoption of useful behaviors, and the enhancement of a generalized sense of self-efficacy.

In this chapter, we review the Accelerated Information Processing model that guides EMDR's therapeutic use, the research that has revealed EMDR's place among the various posttraumatic stress disorder (PTSD), treatments, recommended criteria for the investigation of the procedure, the eight-phase clinical methodology, and professional implications.

## ACCELERATED INFORMATION PROCESSING MODEL

The Accelerated Information Processing model (Shapiro, 1994b, 1995) posits that all pathologies, except those organic/chemical in origin, are the result of early life experiences that have been dysfunctionally stored in a state-dependent form in the nervous system. That is, the perceptions that occurred at the time of the event continue to be stored as they were then, rather than being adequately processed over time. Observations of thousands of EMDR sessions indicate that there is an innate physiological information-processing system that is geared to take disturbing information to a level of mental health. This physiological system provides a functional parallel to other mechanisms of the body that lead to an optimum level of physical health, such as recovering after surgery. However, when a trauma occurs, the information-processing system appears to become imbalanced and the perceptions are held in biochemical stasis in an isolated neurophysiological network. The conjecture that a physiological imbalance prevents adequate processing is consistent with contemporary studies on the effects of neurotransmitters (van der Kolk, 1994; Watson, Hoffman, & Wilson, 1988; Zager & Black, 1985). Therefore, part of the pathology is the inability of this network to link up with any more adaptive information so that appropriate processing can take place. The triggering of these locked perceptions by a variety of internal and external stimuli is the basis of PTSD symptomatology, including nightmares, flashbacks, and intrusive thoughts, as well as the underlying cause of a variety of other disorders (see Shapiro, 1995).

The procedural elements of EMDR, combined with the successive sets of sensory or motor activities (e.g., eye movements, hand taps, tones), appear to catalyze the information-processing system by holding it in a dynamic state that allows the dysfunctionally stored target material to proceed to an adaptive resolution. Accelerated information processing can essentially be equated with accelerated learning, in that useful information is incorporated, is stored with appropriate affect, and becomes available to guide the individual in the future. Additionally, that which is useless (e.g., the negative affect, physical sensations, self-denigrating thoughts) is discarded. This transmutation of the target information is able to occur rapidly because of an apparent direct stimulation of the physiological system. While rapid treatment results have also been documented with hypnosis, direct comparisons using electroencephalograms (EEGs) (Nicosia, 1995) indicate that EMDR is characterized by a brain wave pattern unlike that of hypnosis, and well within the parameters of a normal waking state.

A number of neurophysiological theories have been advanced regarding the underlying basis for the effects of the sets of stimulation (e.g., eye movements, hand taps, audio tones) used in EMDR. These include the beneficial effects of rapid eye movement (REM) sleep, bihemispheric activation, dual attention, and counterconditioning (see Shapiro, 1995). However, the proposed physiological mechanisms alone are not sufficient to account for the magnitude of treatment effects. Therefore, as with any method, clinicians must be guided according to certain principles of practice in order to allow maximum use of the varied procedural elements. The Accelerated Information Processing model (Shapiro, 1994b, 1995) assists clinicians in adopting an integrated treatment approach.

In many ways, the model appears to be extremely compatible with Ericksonian thought, in that it underscores the uniqueness of the client by its emphasis on the individual person rather than utilizing a global diagnosis. During the EMDR session, the client takes the lead in a rapid “treasure hunt” through the personal experiences that are associated with the pathology, which may previously have been below the conscious threshold. As the information-processing system is catalyzed, clients arrive, by means of their own creativity, to insights and conclusions that allow past perceptions to be dramatically altered. Like Ericksonian hypnosis, EMDR is a pragmatic, reality-based approach that demands of the clinician a flexibility and an awareness of nonverbal signals that essentially dovetail with his or her clinical skill. It is not a simple technique that can function with a “cookie-cutter” clinical stance.

## CASE STUDIES AND CONTROLLED RESEARCH

Originally introduced by a controlled study of its efficacy for treating PTSD (Shapiro, 1989), EMDR has been utilized by clinicians with a variety of populations, including victims of sexual assault (Puk, 1991; Wolpe & Abrams, 1991; Spector & Huthwaite, 1993), of combat (Carlson, Chemtob, Rusnak, & Hedlund, 1996; Lipke & Botkin, 1992; Daniels, Lipke, Richardson, & Silver, 1992; Thomas & Gafner, 1993; Young, 1995), of accidents (McCann, 1993; Puk, 1992; Solomon & Kaufman, 1992), of crime (Cocco & Sharpe, 1993; Kleinknecht & Horgan, 1992; Page & Crino, 1993; Shapiro & Solomon, 1995), and of excessive grief as a result of witnessing traumatic deaths (Puk, 1991; Solomon & Shapiro, in press). Additional reports have indicated EMDR's efficacy with a wide range of problems (Marquis, 1991; Spates & Burnette, 1995; Vaughan, Wiese, Gold, & Tarrier, 1994), among which are panic disorder (Goldstein, 1992; Goldstein & Feske, 1994), sexual dysfunction (Levin, 1993; Wernik, 1993), phobias (Kleinknecht, 1993), substance abuse (Shapiro, Vogelmann-Sine, & Sine, 1994), and dissociative disorders (Paulsen, 1995; Paulsen, Vogelmann-Sine, Lazrove, & Young, 1993; Young, 1994).

It may come as a surprise to some that there are already more controlled studies supporting the use of EMDR in the area of PTSD than of any other type of treatment for trauma (Shapiro, 1995). Although PTSD was categorized in the third edition of the *Diagnostic and Statistical Manual* in 1980, a review of the literature published 13 years later (Solomon, Gerrity, & Muff, 1992) indicated that, excluding drug trials, there were only six controlled treatment outcome studies in the published literature. One study compared 45 sessions of desensitization with a no-treatment control group (Peniston, 1986). Three flooding studies confined the evaluation of subjects to traumatized, compensated combat veterans (Boudewyns & Hyer, 1990; Cooper & Clum, 1989; Keane, Fairbank, Cadell, & Zimering, 1989). One study compared flooding with stress inoculation therapy and supportive counseling (Foa, Rothbaum, Riggs, & Murdock, 1991) with rape victims while another compared desensitization, hypnosis, and psychodynamic therapy as treatments for a variety of traumata (Brom, Kleber, & Defaresk, 1989). The paucity of controlled research in PTSD while millions suffer yearly from this malady is a source of great concern (Shapiro, 1995).

According to a report disseminated by the APA Task Force on Promotion and Dissemination of Psychological Procedures (Chambless et al., 1995), exposure techniques, such as flooding, are the only methods currently validated for use in PTSD. This designation appears to be based on the clinical results of only one study (Foa et al., 1991). However, in addition, flooding for participants suffering from PTSD was the subject of four prior controlled studies (Boudewyns & Hyer, 1990; Cooper & Clum, 1989; Keane et al., 1989). Evaluation of these studies indicates that EMDR meets or exceeds equivalent standards of verification and has demonstrated clinical significance that is far superior to that typically obtained in studies of flooding.

According to the standards outlined in the task force report (Chambless et al., 1995), EMDR appears to have met the criteria for empirically validated, well-established treatments. The initial controlled study (Shapiro, 1989) showed significant treatment results with 22 victims of trauma, which have been replicated in four other controlled studies, all showing EMDR's superiority to another treatment (Boudewyns, Hyer, Peralme, Touze, & Kiel., 1995; Carlson, Chemtob, Rusnak, & Hedlund, 1996; Levin, Grainger, Allen-Byrd, & Fulcher, 1994; Vaughan et al., 1994). In addition, EMDR has proved superior to wait-list controls in two controlled studies (Rothbaum, 1995; S. A. Wilson, Becker, & Tinker, 1995a). Substantial alleviation of PTSD symptoms has also been documented in two controlled component analyses (Renfrey & Spates, 1994; D. Wilson, Silver, Covi, & Foster, 1996), as well as in the case studies listed above.

In order to draw distinct parallels, it may be noted that the Keane et al. (1989) study of exposure compared 11 flooding participants with a wait-list control and found statistically significant, although small, clinical effects. A wait-list control was used in one EMDR study (Rothbaum, 1995) and delayed treatment controls were used in three other studies (Shapiro, 1989; D. Wilson et al., 1996; S. A. Wilson et al., 1995a). All four studies revealed substantial clinical effects for EMDR that were reliably greater than those of the control groups. All four studies also reported clinical significance with one to three EMDR sessions—an outcome greatly surpassing that found for the 14 to 15 sessions used in the Keane et al. study.

Additionally, the Cooper and Clum (1989) and the Boudewyns and Hyer (1990) studies compared flooding with standard Veterans Administration (VA) treatment controls. Boudewyns, Stwertka, Hyer, Albrecht, and Sperr (1993) and Boudewyns et al. (1995) likewise compared EMDR with standard VA counseling. Boudewyns et al. (1993) found EMDR to be superior in terms of subject and therapist evaluations and Boudewyns et al. (1995) found it superior on standard PTSD and physiological measures, in addition to subject reports. Treatment effects of all of these studies, whether of flooding or of EMDR, are hampered by the reliance on subjects who are receiving compensation and so have a tendency to overreport negative effects (see Boudewyns et al., 1993). Additionally, while physiological measures have not been reported to change with multiply traumatized combat veterans (Boudewyns & Hyer, 1990), some physiological changes were noted in the Boudewyns et al. (1995) study of EMDR. Nonetheless, the specific problems that characterize PTSD studies with combat veterans will be reviewed in the following section.

As previously mentioned, the Foa et al. (1991) study of rape victims compared flooding with stress inoculation training and supportive counseling. Only small clinical differences were reported among the three controls at follow-up. Likewise, a comparative design was used by Vaughan et al. (1994), and showed EMDR to be equal or superior to exposure and relaxation controls, although 60 and 40 minutes of additional daily homework over a two- to three-week period was given for the two control groups, respectively, but none for the EMDR group. EMDR was found to be superior to supportive counseling in a study of Hurricane Andrew victims (Levin et al., 1994). A comparative design was also used by Carlson et al. (1995), who found EMDR superior to a biofeedback relaxation control group and a group receiving routine VA clinical care. Unfortunately, although clinical differences were well documented, all of the studies, including the one by Foa et al., were hampered by small sample sizes, which precluded large statistical effects.

However, whereas the Foa et al. (1991) study collected data on 27 participants (nine per cell), the EMDR comparative studies by Boudewyns et al. (1993, 1995) reviewed data on 81 participants, and the remaining three comparative studies (Carlson et al., 1995; Levin et al., 1994; Vaughan et al., 1994) evaluated a total of 116 participants.

In addition to using a larger subject pool in its comparative studies, EMDR appears to result in a much lower attrition rate than do other methods tested. For instance, while the Foa et al. study began with 66 participants, data were collected on only 27 of them, which, the investigators argue, is standard for a clinical course of treatment. In contrast, the studies by Rothbaum (1995) and S. A. Wilson et al. (1995a) experienced only a 10% attrition rate, together with a much greater treatment effect, which was obtained in less than half the time necessary, in the Foa et al. study.

Of all the controlled studies of flooding listed above, only two showed improvement rates that exceeded 30%. The Brom et al. (1989) study reported clinical improvements in 60% of the subjects. There were no significant differences in outcomes among desensitization, hypnosis, and psychodynamic procedures, and treatment effects were derived after 15 treatment sessions. Foa et al. (1991) reported for both stress inoculation training and flooding that at the follow-up of a previous set of seven treatment sessions, 55% of participants no longer met PTSD criteria, compared with supportive counseling, in which 45% no longer met PTSD criteria. In contrast, a recent EMDR study completed by the second author of the Foa et al. study (Rothbaum, 1995) found that after EMDR treatment sessions, 90% of the participants no longer met the criteria for PTSD. The follow-up of the S. A. Wilson et al., (1995b) study found that 15 months after EMDR treatment 84% of the participants no longer met PTSD criteria. In addition, an open trial of seven participants (Lazrove et al., 1995), including mothers who had lost their children to drunken drivers, indicated that, after EMDR, 100% of participants no longer met PTSD criteria at follow-up. All three studies used only three EMDR treatment sessions, standardized PTSD measures, and independent assessors.

In sum, while we have reached a stage where large-scale comparisons of treatment methods would be desirable in the area of PTSD research as a whole, there appears to be sufficient evidence accumulated over the studies described to establish EMDR as an empirically validated treatment for PTSD. Those studies that found only small effects were hampered by a subject pool of chronic, multiply traumatized veterans, largely receiving disability compensation (i.e., evincing secondary gains), lack of adequate treatment fidelity, and/or insufficient treatment time (Boudewyns et al., 1993, 1995; Jensen, 1994;

Pitman et al., 1993; Shapiro, 1995a). Even so, the results of three of these studies compare favorably with those three studies that used flooding with comparable populations. The remaining nine EMDR studies have documented large and long-lasting treatment effects that compare favorably in magnitude and rapidity to the best results reported in controlled studies of all the other researched treatments of PTSD.

## REVIEW OF RESEARCH CRITERIA

Evaluation of the controlled research reviewed above indicates that the field of trauma studies is plagued by substandard practices. Four criteria must be met for the development of a substantial base of well-conducted research that can best serve the field of psychology.

**1.** Researchers should be trained in the entire treatment methodology and should implement the protocols actually used in clinical practice. Fidelity checks should be performed by competent instructors or clinicians to assess the validity of the researcher's use of the method. For instance, a fidelity check reported in one study (Jensen, 1994) indicated that the researcher was applying the method inadequately. Nevertheless, this study was published, even though the negative outcomes that were obtained could not be attributed to a deficiency in the method itself.

**2.** When the effects of procedures on memory are being tested with multiply traumatized subjects, researchers should use measurement tools that are capable of assessing change when a single memory is successfully processed. Global measurements do not serve this purpose. For instance, such global measures as the CAPS, SI-PTSD, and Mississippi Scale for Combat-Related PTSD were used in studies with combat veterans (Boudewyns et al., 1993, 1995; Jensen, 1994; Pitman et al., 1993) in which EMDR treatment was applied to only one or two out of many problematic memories. Clearly, assessments of global functioning will not change without addressing the majority of the presenting complaints. When global measures are used on multiply traumatized subjects, treatment time should be sufficient (e.g., more than one to three sessions) to target the relevant issues appropriately. This was done in the Carlson et al. (1995) study, which achieved a measurable change in the global measures.

**3.** Research subjects should meet reasonable criteria for the actual possibility of clinical change. For example, chronically impaired combat veterans currently receiving disability compensation should not be the primary subject pool to test new methods of treatment, because they are likely to be very resistant to change. It should be clear to practicing clinicians that secondary gains must be addressed before large treatment effects can be expected. Larger magnitude changes have been achieved in those EMDR studies that used only single-trauma victims (Lazrove et al., 1995; Levin et al., 1994; Renfrey & Spates, 1994; Rothbaum, 1995; Shapiro, 1989; Vaughan et al., 1994; D. Wilson et al., 1995; S. A. Wilson et al., 1995a). Likewise, the only known flooding study of single-trauma victims (Foa et al., 1991) achieved greater magnitude of effect than did the previous three studies of combat victims (Boudewyns & Hyer, 1990; Cooper & Clum, 1989; Keane et al., 1989).

**4.** In order to maximize treatment effects, component analyses should be done with subjects who are the victims of only a single trauma and who are not receiving compensation. Obviously, a sufficient number of subjects should be used to obtain statistical power. For instance, the Renfrey and Spates (1994) component analysis study, comparing EMDR with eye movement with EMDR analogues, eliminated PTSD diagnoses for all but one of the patients in the eye-movement condition and all but three in the eye-fixation condition. Subjects in the eye-movement condition received 3.9 sessions while those in the fixated condition received 5.4 sessions. However, although substantial effects were achieved, the small sample size (e.g., approximately seven subjects per cell) precluded the achievement of statistical significance. Likewise, the Pitman et al. (1993) study obtained a decrease in PTSD symptomatology, which, according to the principal investigator, compared favorably (e.g., fewer complications and dropouts than with flooding) to the data reported in the Keane et al. 1989 study. However, the use of a small number of multiply traumatized combat veterans precluded effect sizes that were large enough to allow the drawing of any conclusions. The problem of significant interpretation was also compounded by the use of an EMDR analogue as a control condition that included eye fixation, hand taps, and the waving of the therapist's hand across the subject's line of vision. The complexity of this control precludes any meaningful interpretation of the results, especially since hand taps have been used clinically as a standard part of the EMDR protocol for years (Shapiro, 1994a, 1995) and should not be included in a procedure that is supposed to serve as a placebo control. The only component analysis with PTSD subjects that has been able to draw definitive conclusions is the D. Wilson et al. (1996) study, which identified a signature physiological effect in the eye-movement condition, but none in the controls.

Although component analyses of EMDR undoubtedly will serve to improve the methodology, evaluations should be done on a sufficient number of single-trauma subjects, using the standard clinical protocols applied by well-trained researchers with appropriate checks of procedural fidelity.

The EMDR research in PTSD has been evaluated by these criteria (see Shapiro, 1995) with a primary exclusion criterion for studies in which the investigators had received no training in EMDR (e.g., those by Montgomery & Ayllon, 1994)—even though the results were generally supportive. Studies were included even when the researcher had begun training, but not completed it, and even when the results were generally negative. Unfortunately, studies for which the desired fidelity checks were negative have nevertheless been published (Jensen, 1994). It seems clear that, as a field, it behooves us to address questions regarding scientific rigor and the value of research as it applies to actual clinical practice. For instance, the original EMDR research article (Shapiro, 1989) applied the method only to PTSD and did not even mention a possible applicability to phobias. Subsequent clinical work by trained clinicians has proved efficacious with this population when specific EMDR protocols were followed (see Shapiro, 1995). However, a review of the published studies on EMDR and phobias, once again, reveals a pervasive substandard practice in the area of research.

**1.** Sanderson and Carpenter (1992) received no training in EMDR, eliminated most of the standard protocol described in the original research article (Shapiro, 1989), failed to use the EMDR phobia protocols, and provided only seven sets of restricted eye movements, which they compared with image exposure. They found no differences, as there was a drop of 20 (out of 100) Subjective Units of Disturbance (SUD) (Wolpe, 1990) in both conditions. They considered this to be a highly successful treatment, even though no well-trained

EMDR clinician would view the drop of only 20 SUD as a meaningful change in more than two sets. In addition, all the subjects were told to use image confrontation on themselves at home for a month. It seems clear that these "comparison" results cannot validly guide the practicing clinician.

**2.** Acierno, Tremont, Last, and Montgomery (1994) received no EMDR training (although, interestingly, they report that the person who administered the psychometrics was trained in that role). They then misinterpreted the procedure described in the original research article (Shapiro, 1989) and had the client relax completely after each set, which is entirely contrary to the standard protocol. In addition, they did not use any of the protocols for the treatment of phobias. Thus, although published in a peer-reviewed journal, their null results do not appear to be empirically valid and, therefore, cannot enhance the scientific knowledge base.

**3.** Muris and Merckelback (1995) participated in only half of the standard training course, yet they proceeded with their research, and they failed to provide treatment tapes for fidelity checks as they had originally planned. The standard EMDR protocol was discarded "because only 1 hr was available" (p. 442). Even with faulty application, all measures (SUD, fear inventory, and BAT) showed substantial improvement in the two spider phobics. The Spider Phobics Questionnaire was almost completely flat for both subjects. One subject went up one step (on an eight-step avoidance scale) to being able to let a spider out of the jar, and the other, who had not been able to achieve step 1, went to step 4. Then, the researchers gave both subjects two and one-half hours of in vivo exposure (i.e., two and a half hours, compared with the one hour of EMDR) and because both clients improved, they concluded that they had failed to substantiate the efficacy of EMDR. It appears that there should be higher standards of scientific rigor in the peer-review process.

**4.** Lohr, Tolin, and Kleinknecht (1995) took only half of the standard EMDR training and truncated the EMDR phobia protocol to concentrate on a component analysis. Changes were documented in SUD, three fear inventories, and behavioral reports. However, the fact that one subject was found to have relapsed when contacted six months later, and now feels "disappointment and consternation that the treatment had worn off [and] declined additional psychological treatment" (p. 146), poses new research questions. For example, should researchers who do not use the clinical protocol in their research so inform their participants? EMDR clients are also instructed to watch for any fear triggers and, if they arise, to return for subsequent processing. Should research subjects be informed of these limitations in the study's protocol? Have subjects been offered the opportunity for informed consent if they believe they have been clinically treated by a research protocol that was incomplete? Are journal readers misled if the lack of fidelity to clinical protocols is not explicitly stated in the article?

It seems clear that although the field of psychology endeavors to serve the public by basing clinical practices on research validation, standards of publication and research are sadly lacking. As a profession, we must strive to upgrade standards of scientific scrutiny. However, as the cursory examination of the published EMDR phobia research shows, we have a long way to go. The only other published phobia research by trained researchers indicated a rapid desensitization of a blood phobia (Kleinknecht, 1992), and a component analysis, using students with test anxiety, indicated a larger drop in subjective anxiety in the eye-movement condition with no effect for subject expectancy (Gosselin & Matthews, 1996).

As previously mentioned, clinical research, if it is to be truly useful, must conform to adequate standards of clinical practice. Therefore, any evaluation of EMDR's effects must take into account the many procedural elements that make up its complex methodology.

## THE EIGHT PHASES OF EMDR TREATMENT

An EMDR treatment consists of eight essential phases. It should always be used within a comprehensive treatment plan and should never be attempted without appropriate training, preparation, and the opportunity for reevaluation. The following is a brief delineation of the critical phases of EMDR clinical application.

### *Phase One: Client History and Treatment Planning*

Effective treatment with EMDR demands an understanding of both how and when to use it. Therefore, the first phase of EMDR treatment includes an evaluation of the client safety factors that will determine client selection, including the client's ability to withstand the potentially high levels of disturbance engendered by the reprocessing. For clients selected for EMDR treatment, the clinician takes the information needed to design a treatment plan. This part of the history taking evaluates the entire clinical picture, including the dysfunctional behaviors, symptoms, and characteristics that need to be addressed. The clinician will then determine the specific targets that must be reprocessed and the order in which that will be attempted.

The reprocessing of past events, however, does not guarantee that the therapeutic goals will be met. Therefore, with EMDR, equal attention is placed on present situational disturbance and the provision of the education needed by the client to make functional decisions, and to behave accordingly, in the future. The use of EMDR as a comprehensive treatment approach, combined with the principles of learning theory, indicates that the appropriate targets for reprocessing include the past memories and present stimuli that are causing stress. Physical and psychological symptoms, as well as interpersonal difficulties that may be inhibiting, present adaptive functioning, are identified for targeting. In addition, EMDR is used to incorporate self-empowering beliefs, new skills, and healthier behavior patterns (Shapiro, 1995).

### *Phase Two: Preparation*

The preparation phase includes establishing the appropriate therapeutic relationship, briefing the client on the theory of EMDR and its procedures, offering some helpful metaphors to encourage successful processing, and training the client in a variety of self-control techniques, possibly utilizing self-hypnosis, in order to deal with the disturbing information that may arise during and between sessions. EMDR is an interactive model that strives to invest the client with a sense of empowerment and control. Since avoidance behavior is clearly a part of the PTSD configuration, it is mandatory to prepare the client to maintain the dual awareness of present safety and dysfunctional material from the past that is arising internally.

### *Phase Three: Assessment*

Assessment is the third phase of EMDR treatment, during which the clinician identifies the components of the target. Once the memory is identified, the client selects the image that best represents the event. Then she or he chooses a negative cognition that expresses a dysfunctional, maladaptive self-assessment related to her or his participation in the event. These negative beliefs are actually considered verbalizations of the disturbing affect and include such statements as, "I am useless/worthless/unlovable/dirty/bad." The client then identifies a positive cognition that will be used as a replacement for the negative cognition during the installation phase of processing (phase five). Such statements should incorporate an internal locus of control, when possible, such as, "I am worthwhile/lovable/a good person/in control" or "I can succeed." Then the client assesses how valid the positive cognition seems using the one-to-seven Validity of Cognition (VOC) scale (Shapiro, 1989a), where one signifies "completely false" and seven signifies "completely true." The negative emotion that accompanies the target is delineated and measured on the 0- to-10 Subjective Units of Disturbance scale (Wolpe, 1990). A rating of 10 means the greatest level of disturbance the client can imagine and 0 means calm or emotionally neutral. Next, the client identifies the location of the physical sensations that are stimulated when she or he concentrates on the event. The assessment stage provides a response baseline for the target memory, as well as the specific components necessary to complete processing. The alignment of the individual components of memory is compatible with the independently derived BASK (Behavior, Affect, Sensation, and Knowledge) model (Braun, 1988) and appears to facilitate the processing of the target information.

### *Phase Four: Desensitization*

The fourth phase is called desensitization because it focuses on the client's negative affect as reflected in the SUD rating. This phase of treatment encompasses all responses, regardless of whether the client's distress is increasing, decreasing, or "stuck."

During the desensitization phase, the clinician repeats the sets, with appropriate variations and changes of focus until the client's SUD levels are reduced to a 0 or 1 (when ecologically valid). This indicates that the primary dysfunction involving the targeted event has been cleared. However, the reprocessing is still incomplete and the information will need to be further addressed in the crucial remaining phases.

### *Phase Five: Installation*

The fifth phase of the treatment is called installation because the focus is on incorporating and strengthening the positive cognition that the client has identified as the replacement for the original negative cognition. For example, the client might begin with an image of her or his molestation and the negative cognition, "I am powerless." During this fifth phase of treatment, a positive cognition, "I am now in control," might be installed. The caliber of the treatment effects (that is, how strongly the client believes the positive cognition) is then measured using the VOC scale.

### *Phase Six: Body Scan*

After the positive cognition has been fully installed, the client is asked to hold the target event in mind and identify any residual tension in the form of body sensations. These somatic feelings are then targeted for reprocessing. Congruent with principles of mind/body psychology, evaluations of thousands of EMDR sessions indicate that there is a "physical resonance" to the cognitive process that allows dysfunctional material to be effectively targeted. Positive treatment effects are evaluated, in part, on the basis of physical responses, a strategy that is compatible with conjectures by van der Kolk (1994) that functional memory storage resides in the declarative memory system while state-specific physical sensations are made manifest in nondeclarative memory.

### *Phase Seven: Closure*

The client must be returned to a state of equilibrium at the end of each session, regardless of whether or not reprocessing is complete. A variety of self-controlled, guided visualizations or hypnosis techniques may be used to close the session. In addition, the client is briefed on what to expect between sessions, and how to use a journal to report on the experience.

### *Phase Eight: Reevaluation*

The eighth phase of treatment includes the additional targeting, reaccessing, and review necessary to ensure optimal treatment effects. After any reprocessing session, effects should be reevaluated at the beginning of the following session. The reevaluation phase guides the clinician through the various EMDR protocols and the full treatment plan. Comprehensive treatment includes the processing of the earlier memories that set the groundwork for the dysfunction, the present conditions that stimulate the disturbance, and the incorporation of positive templates for appropriate future actions. Successful treatment can only be determined after sufficient reevaluation of reprocessing and behavioral effects over time.

Space considerations do not permit a complete description of the procedure or of the variety of patterns and responses that demand specific choices on the part of the therapist (Shapiro, 1995). An appropriate response to these choice points, however, is crucial for effective therapeutic results and client safety. Appropriate supervised training and practice are necessary because EMDR entails a great deal more than simply guided eye movements (Shapiro, 1991a, 1991b, 1993, 1994, 1995).

## PROFESSIONAL IMPLICATIONS

The introduction of any effective brief method into the field of psychotherapy can be of great benefit to clients in the present era of managed care and cost consciousness. However, as the advent of EMDR (as well as of MRI brief therapy before it) has indicated, the adoption of new methods involves a paradigm shift that may be difficult for many long-term practitioners to accommodate. Nonetheless, it may be argued that brief therapies catalyze a change that allows the client's mind to heal at the same rate as the rest of the body. That is, after a rape, for example, with appropriate medical care, the body is expected to heal in days or weeks. Brief therapy merely allows an equally paced recovery to take place in the mind of the victim.

But regardless of how tempting such new paradigms might be, it is of great importance that proposed treatments be objectively tested with scientific rigor. Unfortunately, as can be seen by the earlier review of EMDR research, valid scrutiny is often sorely lacking. It is, therefore, incumbent on the psychology profession as a whole to upgrade research standards in order to test appropriately those treatments that can be of potential benefit. In addition, we should attempt to standardize and strengthen dissemination practices so that the best of the validated, available treatments are not unduly withheld from the public because of excessive skepticism or outmoded paradigms.

## REFERENCES


Acierno, R., Tremont, G., Last, C., & Montgomery, D. (1994). Tripartite assessment of the efficacy of eye-movement desensitization in a multi-phobic patient. *Journal of Anxiety Disorders, 8,* 259–276.

Boudewyns, P. A., & Hyer, L. A. (1990). Physiological response to combat memories and preliminary treatment outcome in Vietnam veteran PTSD patients treated with direct therapeutic exposure. *Behavior Therapy, 21,* 63–87.

Boudewyns, P. A., Hyer, L. A., Peralme, L., Touze, J., & Kiel, A. (1995, August). *Eye movement desensitization and reprocessing and exposure therapy in the treatment of combat related PTSD: An early look.* Paper presented at the annual meeting of the American Psychological Association, Los Angeles.

Boudewyns, P. A., Stwertka, S. A., Hyer, L. A., Albrecht, J. W. & Sperr, E. V. (1993). Eye movement desensitization and reprocessing: A pilot study. *Behavior Therapy, 16,* 30–33.

Braun, B. G. (1988). The BASK model of dissociation. *Dissociation, 1,* 4–23.

Brom, D., Kleber, R. J., & Defaresk, P. B. (1989). Brief psychotherapy for posttraumatic stress disorder. *Journal of Consulting and Clinical Psychology, 57,* 607–612.

Carlson, J. G., Chemtob, C. M., Rusnak, K., & Hedlund, N. L. (1996). Eye movement desensitization and reprocessing treatment for combat PTSD. *Psychotherapy, 33,* 104–113.

Carlson, J. G., Chemtob, C. M., Rusnak, K., & Hedlund, N. L. (1995, June) *A controlled study of EMDR and biofeedback assisted relaxation for the treatment of PTSD.* Paper presented at the Fourth European Conference on Traumatic Stress, Paris.

Chambless, D. L., Babich, K., Crits-Christoph, P., Frank, E., Gilson, M., Montgomery, R., Rich, R., Steinberger, J., & Steinberg, J. (1995). Training in and dissemination of empirically-validated psychological treatments: Report and recommendations. *The Clinical Psychologist, 48,* 3–23.

Cocco, N., & Sharpe, L. (1993). An auditory variant of eye movement desensitization in a case of childhood posttraumatic stress disorder. *Journal of Behavior Therapy and Experimental Psychiatry, 24*(4), 373–377.

Cooper, N. A., & Clum, G. A. (1989). Imaginal flooding as supplementary treatment for PTSD in combat veterans: A controlled study. *Behavior Therapy, 20,* 381–391.

Daniels, N., Lipke, H., Richardson, R., & Silver, S. M. (1992, October). *Vietnam veterans' treatment programs using eye movement desensitization and reprocessing.* Paper presented at the annual convention of the International Society for Traumatic Stress Studies, Los Angeles.

Foa, E. B., Olasov Rothbaum, B., Riggs, D. S., & Murdock, T. B. (1991). Treatment of posttraumatic stress disorder in rape victims: A comparison between cognitive behavioral procedures and counseling. *Journal of Consulting and Clinical Psychology, 59,* 715–723.

Goldstein, A. (1992, August). *Treatment of panic and agoraphobia with EMDR: Preliminary data of the Agoraphobia and Anxiety Treatment Center, Temple University.* Paper presented at the Fourth World Congress on Behavior Therapy, Queensland, Australia.

Goldstein, A., & Feske, U. (1994). EMDR treatment of panic disorder. *Journal of Anxiety Disorders, 8,* 351–362.

Gosselin, P., & Matthews, W. J. (1996). Eye movement desensitization and reprocessing (EMDR) in the treatment of test anxiety: A study of the effects of expectancy and eye movement. *Journal of Behavior Therapy and Experimental Psychiatry, 26,* 331–337.

Jensen, J. A. (1994). An investigation of eye movement desensitization and reprocessing (EMD/R) as a treatment for posttraumatic stress disorder (PTSD) symptoms of Vietnam combat veterans. *Behavior Therapy, 25*(2), 311–326.

Keane, T. M., Fairbank, J. A., Cadell, J. M., & Zimering, R. T. (1989). Implosive (flooding) therapy reduces symptoms of PTSD in Vietnam combat veterans. *Behavior Therapy, 20,* 245–260.

Kleinknecht, R. A. (1993). Rapid treatment of blood and injection phobias with eye movement desensitization. *Journal of Behavior Therapy and Experimental Psychiatry, 24*(3), 25–31.

Kleinknecht, R. & Morgan, M. P. (1992). Treatment of post-traumatic stress disorder with eye movement desensitization and reprocessing. *Journal of Behavior Therapy and Experimental Psychiatry, 23,* 43–50.

Lang, P. J. (1977). Imagery in therapy: An information processing analysis of fear. *Behavior Therapy, 8,* 862–886.

Lazrove, S., Kite, L., Triffleman, E., McGlashan, T., & Rounsaville, B. (1995, November) *An open trial of EMDR in patients with chronic PTSD.* Paper presented at the 11th annual conference of the International Society for Traumatic Stress Studies, Boston.

Levin, C. (1993, July). The enigma of EMDR. *Family Therapy Networker,* 75–83.

Levin, C., Grainger, R. K., Allen-Byrd, L., & Fulcher, G. (1994, August). *Efficacy of eye movement desensitization and reprocessing for survivors of Hurricane Andrew: A comparative study.* Paper presented at the annual conference of the American Psychological Association, Los Angeles.

Lipke, H., & Botkin, A. (1992). Brief case studies of eye movement desensitization and reprocessing with chronic post-traumatic stress disorder. *Psychotherapy, 29,* 591–595.

Lohr, J. M., Tolin, D. F., & Kleinknecht, R. A. (1995). Eye movement desensitization of medical phobias: Two case studies. *Journal of Behavior Therapy and Experimental Psychiatry, 26,* 141–151.

Marquis, J. (1991). A report on seventy-eight cases treated by eye movement desensitization. *Journal of Behavior Therapy and Experimental Psychiatry, 22,* 187–192.

McCann, D. L. (1992). Post-traumatic stress disorder due to devastating burns overcome by a single session of eye movement desensitization. *Journal of Behavior Therapy and Experimental Psychiatry, 23,* 319–323.

Montgomery, R. W., & Ayllon, T. (1994). Eye movement desensitization across images: A single case design. *Journal of Behavior Therapy and Experimental Psychiatry, 25,* 23–28.

Muris, P., & Merckelback, H. (1995). Treating spider phobia with eye movement desensitization and reprocessing: Two case reports. *Journal of Anxiety Disorders, 9,* 439–449.

Nicosia, G. (1995) Brief note: Eye movement desensitization and reprocessing is not hypnosis. *Dissociation, 8,* 65.

Page, A. C., & Crino, R. D. (1993). Eye-movement desensitisation: A simple treatment for post-traumatic stress disorder? *Australian and New Zealand Journal of Psychiatry, 27,* 288–293.

Paulsen, S. (1995). Eye movement desensitization and reprocessing: Its cautious use in the dissociative disorders. *Dissociation, 8,* 32–44.

Paulsen, S., Vogelmann-Sine, S., Lazrove, S., & Young, W. (1993, October). *Eye movement desensitization and reprocessing: Its role in the treatment of dissociative disorders.* Paper presented of the 10th annual conference of international Society for the Study of Multiple Personality Disorders, Chicago.

Peniston, E. G. (1986). EMG biofeedback-assisted desensitization treatment for Vietnam combat veterans' post-traumatic stress disorder. *Clinical Biofeedback and Health, 9,* 35–41.

Pitman, R. K., Orr, S. P., Altman, B., Longpre, R. E., Macklin, M. L., Poire, R. E., & Lasko, N. B. (1993, May). *A controlled study of EMDR treatment for posttraumatic stress disorder.* Paper presented at the 146th annual meeting of the American Psychiatric Association, Washington, DC.

Puk, G. (1991). Treating traumatic memories: A case report on the eye movement desensitization procedure. *Journal of Behavior Therapy and Experimental Psychiatry, 22,* 149–151.

Puk, G. (1992, May). *The use of eye movement desensitization and reprocessing in motor vehicle accident trauma.* Paper presented at the eighth annual symposium of the American College of Forensic Psychology, San Francisco.

Renfrey, G., & Spates, C. R. (1994). Eye movement desensitization and reprocessing: A partial dismantling procedure. *Journal of Behavior Therapy and Experimental Psychiatry, 25,* 231–239.

Rothbaum, B. O. (1995, November). *A controlled study of EMDR for PTSD.* Paper presented at the 29th annual convention of the Association for the Advancement of Behavior Therapy, Washington, DC.

Sanderson, A., & Carpenter, R. (1992). Eye movement desensitization versus image confrontation: A single-session crossover study of 58 phobic subjects. *Journal of Behavior Therapy and Experimental Psychiatry, 23,* 269–275.

Shapiro, F. (1989). Efficacy of the eye movement desensitization procedure in the treatment of traumatic memories. *Journal of Traumatic Stress Studies, 2,* 199–223.

Shapiro, F. (1991a). Eye movement desensitization and reprocessing procedure: From EMD to EMDR—a new treatment model for anxiety and related traumata. *The Behavior Therapist, 14,* 133–135.

Shapiro, F. (1991b). Eye movement desensitization and reprocessing: A cautionary note. *The Behavior Therapist, 14,* 188.

Shapiro, F. (1993). The status of EMDR in 1992. *Journal of Traumatic Stress, 6,* 413–421.

Shapiro, F. (1994a). Alternative stimuli in the use of EMD(R). *Journal of Behavior Therapy and Experimental Psychiatry, 25,* 89.

Shapiro, F. (1994b). EMDR: In the eye of a paradigm shift. *The Behavior Therapist, 17,* 153–157.

Shapiro, F. (1995). *Eye movement desensitization and reprocessing: Basic principles, protocols and procedures.* New York: Guilford.

Shapiro, F., & Solomon, R. (1995). Eye movement desensitization and reprocessing: Neurocognitive information processing. In G. Everley & J. Mitchell (Eds.), *Critical incident stress management.* Elliot City, MD: Chevron.

Shapiro, F., Vogelmann-Sine, S., & Sine, L. (1994). Eye movement desensitization and reprocessing: Treating trauma and substance abuse. *Journal of Psychoactive Drugs, 26,* 379–391.

Silver, S. M., Brooks, A., & Obenchain, J. (1995). Eye movement desensitization and reprocessing treatment of Vietnam war veterans with PTSD:

Comparative effects with biofeedback and relaxation training. *Journal of Traumatic Stress, 8,* 337–342.

Solomon, R., & Kaufman, T. (1992, October). *Eye movement desensitization and reprocessing: An effective addition to critical incident treatment protocols.* Preliminary results presented at the annual conference of the International Society for Traumatic Stress Studies, Los Angeles. (Submitted for publication.)

Solomon, R., & Shapiro, F. (in press). Eye movement desensitization and reprocessing: An effective therapeutic tool for trauma and grief. In C. Figley, B. Bride, & N. Mazza (Eds.). *Death and trauma.* London: Taylor & Francis.

Solomon, S. D., Gerrity, E. T., & Muff, A. M. (1992). Efficacy of treatments for posttraumatic stress disorder. *Journal of the American Medical Association, 268,* 633–638.

Spates, R. C., & Burnette, M. A. (1995). Eye movement desensitization and reprocessing: Three complex cases. *Journal of Behavior Therapy and Experimental Psychiatry, 26,* 51–55.

Spector, J., & Huthwaite, M. (1993). Eye-movement desensitisation to overcome post-traumatic stress disorder. *British Journal of Psychiatry,* 106–108.

Thomas, R., & Gafner, G. (1993). PTSD in an elderly male: Treatment with eye movement desensitization and reprocessing (EMDR). *British Journal of Psychiatry,* 106–108.

van der Kolk, B. A. (1994). The body keeps the score: Memory and the evolving psychobiology of posttraumatic stress. *Harvard Review of Psychiatry,* 253–265.

Vaughan, K., Armstrong, M. S., Rold, R., O'Connor, N., Jenneke, W., & Tarrier, N. (1994). A trial of eye movement desensitization compared to image habituation training and applied muscle relaxation in posttraumatic stress disorder. *Journal of Behavior Therapy and Experimental Psychiatry, 25,* 283–291.

Vaughan, K., Wiese, M., Gold, R., & Tarrier, N. (1994). Eye-movement desensitisation: Symptom change in post-traumatic stress disorder. *British Journal of Psychiatry, 164,* 533–541.

Watson, J. P., Hoffman, L., & Wilson, G. V. (1988). The neuropsychiatry of post-traumatic stress disorder. *British Journal of Psychiatry, 152,* 164–173.

Wernik, U. (1993). The role of the traumatic component in the etiology of sexual dysfunctions and its treatment with eye movement desensitization procedure. *Journal of Sex Education and Therapy, 19*(3), 212–222.

Wilson, D., Silver, S. M., Covi, W., Foster, S. (1996). Eye movement desensitization and reprocessing: Effectiveness and autonomic correlates. *Journal of Behavior Therapy and Experimental Psychiatry, 27,* 219–229.

Wilson, S. A., Becker, L. A., & Tinker, R. H. (1995a). Eye movement desensitization and reprocessing (EMDR) treatment for psychologically traumatized individuals, *Journal of Consulting and Clinical Psychology, 63,* 928–937.

Wilson, S. A., Becker, L. A., & Tinker, R. H. (1995b, May). *EMDR: 15 month follow-up of a controlled study.* Paper presented at the annual conference of the American Psychiatric Association, Miami, FL.

Wolpe, J. (1990) *The practice of behavior therapy* (4th ed.). New York: Pergamon.

Wolpe, J., & Abrams, J. (1991). Post-traumatic stress disorder overcome by eye movement desensitization: A case report. *Journal of Behavior Therapy and Experimental Psychiatry, 22,* 39–43.

Young, W. (1994). EMDR treatment of phobic symptoms in multiple personality. *Dissociation, 7,* 129–133.

Young, W. (1995). EMDR: Its use in resolving the trauma caused by the loss of a war buddy. *American Journal of Psychotherapy, 49,* 282–291.

Zager, E. L., & Black, P. (1985). Neuropeptides in human memory and learning processes. *Neurosurgery, 17,* 355–369.

# Name Index

# Subject Index

For Product Safety Concerns and Information please contact our EU
representative GPSR@taylorandfrancis.com
Taylor & Francis Verlag GmbH, Kaufingerstraße 24, 80331 München, Germany

www.ingramcontent.com/pod-product-compliance
Ingram Content Group UK Ltd.
Pitfield, Milton Keynes, MK11 3LW, UK
UKHW021300190926
475701UK00009B/164
* 9 7 8 1 1 3 8 8 8 3 7 6 5 *